18.50

GV 811 J36
California Maritime Academy Library (CSU)

3 0060 00020268 7

20268

CALIFORNIA
P. C
VALL

D0713034

WITHDRAWN

GV
811   20268
J36   Jarman
           Coastal cruising

Library
California Maritime Academy
Vallejo, CA 94590

COASTAL CRUISING

20268

COLIN JARMAN

Coastal Cruising

WITHDRAWN

LIBRARY
CALIFORNIA MARITIME ACADEMY
P. O. BOX 1392
VALLEJO, CA 94590

ADAM & CHARLES BLACK · LONDON

First published 1975
by A & C Black Ltd.
4, 5 & 6 Soho Square London W1V 6AD

© Colin Jarman 1975

ISBN 0 7136 1569 9

All Rights Reserved. No part of this publication may be
reproduced, stored in a retrieval system, or transmitted, in
any form or by any means, electronic, mechanical, photo-
copying, recording or otherwise, without the prior permission
of A & C Black Ltd.

576 V 35

Filmset and printed in Great Britain by
BAS Printers Limited, Wallop, Hampshire

CONTENTS

LIST OF DIAGRAMS

List of illustrations

List of illustrations

LIST OF PHOTOGRAPHS

ACKNOWLEDGEMENTS

A surprising number of people become involved during the writing and production of a book – most of them unwittingly. A chance remark during a general conversation triggers off an idea or reminds you that you should have mentioned something in a particular section. Then again you may be sailing with someone and a situation arises to which he has an answer different from your own, thus producing another view of things. I am afraid I can't possibly remember all of these people, but I am grateful to them.

More specifically I would like to say thank you to Anthea Helps, Art Editor of Motor Boat and Yachting, for her work on the diagrams and illustrations, and to A & C Black for their help and encouragement. I would also like to express my thanks to the Editors of both Yachting Monthly and Motor Boat and Yachting for permission to use photographs and material already published in their magazines.

INTRODUCTION

In this book we are interested in the arts of coastal cruising, that is to say in making modest passages from one port to another along a coastline, rather than being at sea for many days and crossing whole seas or even oceans. That all comes later, first we learn to walk. Cruising is very much a family affair in which each member can play a full and significant part, gaining much pleasure from doing so. It is no longer the preserve of 'fit young men' and the occasional Mum – which is all to the good, but being a family hobby brings its own tensions and problems, mainly of parents having considera-tion for the opinions and desires of their children, and children expressing themselves yet obeying their parents *instantly*. It's all good fun, in retrospect at least, and the sea really does act as a great leveller.

It is almost impossible and certainly very dangerous to be dogmatic when talking about the sea and consequently much of what I have put down in this book is personal opinion. The advice I have given is what I have found most often to be true. You may find that something else works on a particular occasion. We are both right, but another time we could both be wrong. This is where seamanship comes in, a feeling and sense for the sea that grows over the years and must be cared for and nurtured.

A reasonable knowledge of sailing has been assumed in the reader of this book and so I have left out much traditional material of the 'this is the bow, this is the stern, this is how you tie a reef knot' type. I have laid emphasis on safety and prudence and have concentrated as far as possible on *practical* cruising rather than theoretical in the firm belief that what you *do* at sea is infinitely more important than what the theorist tells you should happen in an ideal situation. Still, reading about an essentially practical subject is a poor substitute for 'getting up and doing it'. I can only hope that this book will whet your appetite for doing just that.

Some subjects such as pure navigation and meteorology have been covered only briefly since they require volumes to themselves and should be studied more thoroughly outside this book. I have only really tried to introduce such subjects. A broadside could also be levelled at the appropriately numbered Chapter 13 for laying it on a bit thick, but don't despair, life at sea is rarely that bad though the possibility of severe weather must be considered. Remember when reading it that the sun does shine sometimes.

There are great times and bad times at sea. The great far outweigh the bad, though it is the bad we talk most about. Don't, however, talk to me about 'beating the sea' as if telling of some wrestling match. Though the sea is beautiful, she is a low lady not averse to a sneaky attack upon the unwary. If you come through a rough patch safely it is because she has taken a lady's prerogative to change her mind and let you pass. Be thankful and prepare for the next time.

CHAPTER 1

Cruiser Choosing

One of the first things a prospective owner has to consider is the question of where he wants to base his cruiser, as this can have a strong influence on the type of boat he buys. For instance, anyone hoping to cruise in shoal waters is going to deny himself a great deal of pleasure if he rushes out and buys a boat with a 6ft draught. Instead, by buying a cruiser with shallow draught, say a bilge keel design, he will open up a whole host of delightful and secluded anchorages tucked away at the heads of narrow creeks where the deep-draught boys can't go. On the other hand, if you are going to keep your boat on a rugged and exposed coast, a little estuary cruiser with a drop keel and most of her ballast inside the hull is the last thing you should be looking for. In these waters a sturdy, fin keeled boat able to stand up to a blow and claw her way round a rocky headland is much more the order of the day.

When you have made up your mind about the general area you want to be in, a visit to a few of the anchorages in the vicinity will show what boats other people have chosen. You may not find any one *class* in overwhelming numbers, but you are sure to discover that the majority of boats conform to a type. A chat with members of the local sailing club can often be of help as well; they can not only tell you about the boats they own, but can also give you a good idea of the kind of sailing to be found in the area.

Crew Numbers

A very basic thing to think about is how many people you expect to have on board at the same time. After all, it would be very embarrassing to set off for your first weekend and find you have one more crew member than there are berths.

Underway and outward bound at the start of a cruise.

1

On the other hand there is not much point in buying a six berth boat if the crew is going to consist of just yourself and one or two others. The question of crew-to-berths ratio will reappear in Chapter 3 when we look at the problems faced by a group of people living together in a rather confined space for any length of time.

Moorings

While carrying out a grand tour of inspection of possible home ports, you would be well advised to make preliminary enquiries about the availability of suitable moorings. It's no longer possible to paddle out from the bank of some little creek and drop a sinker in the mud, attach a buoy with your boat's name on it and pay a nominal fee to the local water bailiff. The laying and positioning of moorings is now subject to very tight controls, with most of them belonging either to sailing clubs, boatyards, or the local council.

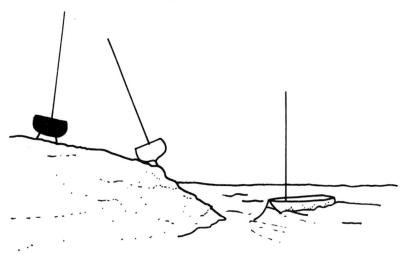

1   On a drying mooring life aboard the black hulled bilge-keeler remains *reasonably comfortable, while for the crew of the single keeled boat it will be most unpleasant.*

Moorings follow two types: those that dry out and those that do not, with marinas coming into the latter category. Many moorings are only accessible for a few hours either side of high water and dry out completely at low water, a situation often quite alien to a yachtsman based in an area where moorings are mostly deepwater ones. Drying moorings are yet another good reason for choosing a bilge-keeler – she stands duck-like waiting for the tide, while her deep draught sister heels over at a painfully rakish angle.

Deepwater moorings are of course nice to have, as you are then independent of tide and if they are single moorings round which the boat is free to swing, you are also saved the worry of another boat chafing alongside. This is one of the big drawbacks to 'trot' or 'pile' moorings, where each boat is moored fore and aft, and often alongside another yacht. The wash of a passing craft, or the chop kicked up by a strong blow will set adjacent boats rubbing and bumping together, to the detriment of fenders, warps, paint and owners' peace of mind.

Vast numbers of boatowners are now keeping their craft in marinas, where they moor alongside a pontoon or staging and can step ashore (or aboard) without recourse to the dinghy. The arguments rage on about the merits and demerits of marinas, but the basic fact remains that boats have to have moorings, and this seems to be the most practical way of coping with the problem.

Trailer Sailing

Having just stated that boats have to have moorings, let me now contradict myself and talk about a phenomenon that is fairly new in the UK but has become very popular in America: trailer sailing. You can forget all visions of ketch rigged trailers running down the trade wind routes of the world, as this is, in fact, the name given to the practice of keeping a boat on her trailer in the backyard and towing her to the coast each time you want a sail. Although it allows the owner to skip paying mooring dues, and offers unlimited changes of cruising ground, it does mean that he is involved with launching and recovering his boat before and after each sail. With modern trailers and winches this need not be an over-arduous task, but it further involves finding a suitable launching ramp or hard, and asking permission to use the site before paying for the privilege. Still, it is cheaper than having a permanent mooring, and you are likely to take a small boat further

3

afield in the course of a few seasons than you would from a fixed base.

New ? Secondhand ? DIY ?

When you start to think seriously about buying a cruiser, the age old question of whether to buy a new or secondhand one heaves its bulk over the horizon and fetches up right across your track. Almost everyone you ask will give you a different answer, so let us look at the pros and cons.

Taking new boats first, I would suggest that there are three main points in their favour:

1 The boat is new, therefore it is not likely that much will go wrong with either the structure or the fittings – always assuming that she has been well built.

2 It may be possible to incorporate some of your own ideas at the building stage, for instance, variations in the interior layout.

3 You can choose the gear and equipment to suit your own requirements.

Set against these points are four disadvantages:

1 The other side of the last 'plus' point, ie the extra cost involved in equipping the boat, and the knowledge required to do so adequately.

2 A new boat is more expensive (when fully equipped) than a comparable secondhand one.

3 It takes several seasons to adapt and adjust a new boat to your own tastes – fitting lockers, moving cleats, making a stowage place for charts, and so on.

4 There may be anything up to a year to wait between ordering and actually taking delivery of a new boat.

Turning to secondhand boats, I think there are five points in their favour and three against them. The good are:

1 You can often get more boat for your money than you would be able to if buying new.

2 The boat is already equipped and fitted out.

3 Everything has been tried and tested, and more than likely altered if found wanting.

4 The novice has the benefit of someone else's experience in terms of gear, equipment and gadgetry.

5 She is immediately available.

The three points against secondhand boats are:

1 You have only the owner's account of how he has handled the boat, where he's been and what sands the boat has been bounced on.

2 You will need to pay for a condition survey of the boat.

3 On an old boat there may well be quite a lot of repair work and replacing of old gear to be done to bring her up to a good sea-going standard.

Trying to draw any sort of conclusion about this matter is an entirely personal thing, so I will refrain from commenting further. Of course there is an alternative to buying either new or secondhand, and that is to build, though here again you have a choice to make – build from a kit, or from scratch.

Except in the case of plywood boats where a kit consists of the plans and the rough-cut wood, building from a kit generally means buying the plans and a bare glassfibre hull and putting in the interior woodwork and trim, then fitting the whole boat out. Building from scratch really does mean starting from square one. All you get is a set of plans. After that you are on your own. Not surprisingly it is a bit cheaper than a kit, but is likely to take longer. In any case, building yourself a boat is cheaper than buying her complete, but the real economies stop once you have completed the hull, since masts, spars, sails, rigging and fittings are all the same price no matter who builds the hull.

Chartering and Crewing

As a newcomer to cruising you may feel (very sensibly) that you would like to get some experience before jumping in with both feet and buying a cruiser. Two courses are open to you, namely chartering and/or crewing. Both are excellent ways of putting in some sea-time, and may also provide the opportunity of trying out one of the boats you are thinking of buying.

A lot of yacht clubs keep a list of people who want to be put in touch with skippers and of skippers who want to find a crew. Don't be put off by the fact that you don't know too much. Sailing people are a pretty friendly bunch and most are only too pleased to help others to learn.

With regard to chartering, you can either look for a firm

whose boats have a permanent skipper aboard to instruct charterers, which is probably your safest bet if you have little or no cruising experience, or else take a bare boat charter and look after yourself. In the latter case you will probably be required by the charter firm to supply some evidence of experience.

Possibly the ideal combination of crewing or chartering comes in the form of the Island Cruising Club of The Island, Salcombe, South Devon, which owns several boats, and whose members form the crews under permanent club skippers. Their boats range from the schooner *Hoshi* and the beautiful old Brixham trawler *Provident* down to various classes of dinghies.

Woman Appeal

This may seem a slightly odd heading, but yacht designers in recent years have realised that sailing is no longer a sport reserved solely for men, and consequently have begun to pay some attention to woman appeal in their boats. The most obvious example is in galleys, which have been drastically altered, many being fitted with multi-burner stoves, grills, ovens and even refrigerators. A sink of some sort is more or less obligatory, and most have freshwater pumps fed by built-in tanks, rather than having to pour water out of jerry cans. Even very small boats are now expected to have standing headroom somewhere in the cabin, and only the most spartan do not have a separate toilet compartment – gone are the days of the bucket-and-chuck-it thunder boxes. Very much larger engines are being fitted than ever used to be the case, not only to ensure one's ability to be in the office on Monday morning if the wind drops, but also to make motor sailing feasible when the going gets a bit rough. The other phenomenon is the double berth/dinette arrangement where the cabin table folds down to form part of the bunk.

The only two of these that I can justify an objection to are the double berths, on the grounds that it is extraordinarily difficult to stay in them in a seaway, and the standing headroom if it means that the cabin top has to be very high. This increases windage and makes keeping your footing while working on deck difficult in a rough sea.

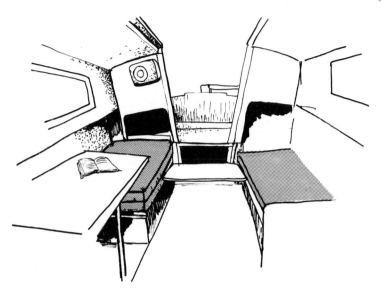

2   The dinette on a cruiser can be used in the raised position as a table, or can be lowered to form a berth.

The Search Begins

I have tried already to point out the relative merits of buying a new or secondhand boat, leaving the final decision up to you. Once that choice has been made you can get down to the real business of sorting out what is available. All boats start life as new ones so let's begin there, and I suggest that the first thing to do is look through the advertisements in yachting magazines and pick out a handful of possibles. The next move is to write to the builders or distributors for a full specification and price list of each boat.

When you receive all the relevant literature, study it carefully and you will quite likely find that half the boats immediately cross themselves off your list for one reason or another. Having thus reduced the list to say three or four boats, list exactly what 'optional extras' you will in fact need for each. The prices may then look quite different.

The list you started off with should now be down to a couple of real possibles, and for these you should get in touch with the builders (or distributors) and try to arrange a trial sail. It is most important to try to have a sail in a boat before you buy her, for no matter how glossy the brochure and how attractive the boat looks in some showroom, it is a boat in commission that you are interested in. Boats represent a large investment of capital for most of us and as such it would be foolish to sign a cheque, take delivery of the boat, and then discover that she doesn't suit you after all.

Going back to secondhand boats, the process is similar in its stages, but somewhat wider ranging. Starting in the same way as for a new boat, a look at the advertisements in magazines may well send you off in search of a particular class of boat. Whether it does or not, the next stage is in fact three stages in one. Assuming that you only sail (or hunt for boats) at weekends, you can spend a weekday evening browsing through the classified advertisements in the backs of one or two yachting magazines to see if there is anything there that sounds at all possible. If so, then write off to (or call) the owner and ask him for a full specification and inventory of the boat. The other thing to look for in the magazines is any advertisement for yacht brokers handling craft of the type you want. Either send a letter to them stating *as precisely as you can* the kind of boat you are after, the approximate price you have in mind and so on, or if they are in the area you hope to base your boat in, call in and leave them the same details.

The danger with searching the boatyards is not so much being taken for a ride by an unscrupulous salesman, as becoming so addicted to poking around under dusty covers and peering into dark corners that you may well lose sight of your objective – to *buy* a boat. It's been done, so look out.

The great day for a proud new owner when he sees his boat take to the water for the first time.

Lloyd's Certificates

Many small cruisers are being built under conditions and of materials that conform to the stringent requirements of Lloyd's Register of Shipping for their Series Production Certificates. If the boat you are thinking of buying has a Series Production Certificate, you may be reasonably sure that she was at least constructed to a high standard even if she has not been looked after too well since.

At the very top end of the small cruiser range, you may find a yacht that has been individually supervised by Lloyd's surveyors and classed with the internationally recognised ✠ 100A1. The Maltese Cross signifies that the boat has been

9

built under Lloyd's supervision throughout, while the 100A means that the materials used and the workmanship involved conform to good practice. The final digit 1 shows that the boat carries anchors, cables and warps adequate for her size.

All of Lloyd's certificates apply first to the building of the boat, though many large yachts are also maintained to the ✠ 100A1 standard. Just because the boat was built to a high standard it unfortunately does not necessarily follow that she will still be in good condition when she is put on the second-hand market, so it is wise to get an up-to-date condition survey report.

Surveys

Though the seller of a secondhand boat may tell you in all good faith that she is sweet and sound, he may be in complete ignorance of, say, rot in the stern post or some such defect. The usual practice is for the potential buyer to make an offer for the boat 'subject to survey', and if this is accepted, then he agrees to pay the cost of having the boat slipped, opened up, surveyed, and returned to her original condition in the event of his deciding not to buy. On receipt of the surveyor's report, the buyer can present a list of defects to the owner who can either make a cash adjustment to the price or agree to make good these faults.

A lot of surveyors advertise for business in the small ads. section of the yachting press, but it is possible to obtain a complete list from the Yacht Brokers, Designers and Surveyors Association, Orchard Hill, Farnham Lane, Haslemere, Surrey. As you will have to pay his travelling expenses it is as well to find a surveyor who lives locally.

Finance

With the cost of boats, both new and secondhand, rising fast it is not at all uncommon for a prospective owner to seek some sort of financial aid for his purchase. Several finance houses have plans that cover boats, and it is worth consulting more than one of these firms to find the most suitable for you. Basically marine finance falls into three categories, namely hire purchase, credit sale or marine mortgage.

The difference between the first two of these is that with hire purchase you, the purchaser, do not become the owner of the boat until you have made the last payment to the finance house, while credit sale makes you a proud owner as soon as you make the first payment and the financial wizards agree the transaction. The two main requirements for a marine mortgage are that the purchaser is over 18 and that the boat is registered with the Department of Trade.

A finance company will insist on seeing a recent survey before agreeing to back you, and also that the boat is comprehensively insured to her full value and has third party cover. After that, deposit scales and repayment rates vary from company to company.

Bills of Sale

A final point to insist on when buying a boat is that you exchange Bills of Sale with the seller. If the boat is registered you *must* do this, but even if she is not, it is still advisable in case you go abroad or ever seek to register her. In either case you could need it for proof of ownership. Bills of Sale are obtainable from HM Customs and Excise, Forms Office, Kings Beam House, Mark Lane, London EC3.

If the boat you are buying is registered, you will have to re-register her in your own name. To do this, you have to get a Bill of Sale from the registered owner, who also completes a declaration of ownership for the Registrar of Ships of his home port. On receipt of the boat's British registry papers, the Bill of Sale and the declaration of ownership, the Registrar will re-register the boat in your name.

CHAPTER 2

Types of Cruiser

Sailing cruisers can be split by design intention into six separate categories, namely estuary cruisers (the smallest), coastal cruisers, multihulls, motor sailers, cruiser/racers, and offshore cruisers. Each of these types is planned with particular conditions for use in mind, and provided that the owner limits his ambitions to those conditions, then his boat should be able to cope with all but the most severe wind and water situations.

Estuary Cruisers

These boats are intended for pottering round the relatively sheltered waters of river estuaries. Their shallow draught, normally provided by a centreplate or small bilge keels, make them ideal for working right up to the head of a creek and lying there in comfortable seclusion, while their accommodation is somewhat spartan and suitable only for overnighting. Being relatively small and cheap they are the starting point for many people: they form a transition from dinghy to cruiser.

To call estuary cruisers overgrown dinghies, or dinghies with lids on, is in no way derogatory for this *is* more or less what they are. In many cases much of the ballast is internal and the crew has to sit to windward when the boat is close-hauled or hard pressed. Unlike a dinghy however, they are self-righting (or certainly should be) though a knockdown in an estuary is very rare.

The small size and light displacement of an estuary cruiser makes her ideal for trailer sailing. They are easy to load onto a trailer, they require only a small family car to tow them, and launching is no great physical problem, in fact with

3

practice a fit man should be able to manage singlehanded.

While an estuary cruiser is better equipped to sail in choppy conditions than a dinghy, she is still in no way suitable for long open water passages. True, such craft have made spectacular long distance voyages, but these have been made after much preparation by highly experienced sailors. They definitely should not be emulated by less skilled people.

Coastal Cruisers

Coastal cruisers are a bit larger than estuary cruisers and are designed to give the crew a little more space and comfort. The cabin is big enough to include a proper galley and sink, and the toilet may even be separated in its own compartment, though more usually it is just curtained off from the main cabin area. In fact the extra couple of feet or so in overall length makes a surprising difference to the amount of accommodation space available, and whereas a 16-footer can really only be used overnight, an 18-footer is fine for a week or more.

4

Deeper draught with more ballast in the keel means that a greater sail area can be carried. The keel may be fin, centre-plate housed in a ballast stub, or twin bilge keels, but in any case it (or they) forms the major part of the boat's ballast. This higher displacement coupled with the greater sail area means that a coastal cruiser can be kept driving to windward against seas that would stop a lighter boat dead. It does not mean that on many occasions you won't lop up and down in the same hole, but in general the boat will drive on more powerfully.

Small Multihulls

Perhaps the greatest attraction of a multihull is her speed off the wind, followed a close second by the palatial accommodation provided in even the smallest of these boats. Although the cruising multihull is considerably heavier than a racing catamaran or trimaran, she does still have this ability to bear

5

away and go tearing off downwind.

In comparison to a monohull she also heels very little, making her attractive for sailing with youngsters. It's a strange sensation for anyone used to monohull sailing, because as the wind gusts, instead of laying over to it, the boat just accelerates.

While speed and accommodation are two of the attractive aspects of cats and tris, one of the less happy points is the possibility of a capsize. The first time I was let loose in a dinghy I was told quite simply, if firmly, 'don't capsize', and the same applies here. If you realise the danger and take care you will be all right.

Designers' understanding of the stresses and strains in multihulls has improved greatly in the last few years and many of the early troubles have been ironed out. One does still hear of them breaking up, but these are boats that have been caught in very severe conditions. Provided that the basic rules of seamanship are adhered to there is no reason at all why multihulls should not be used quite happily as cruising boats.

What may irk people is that many harbour and port authorities charge a higher rate for multihulls than they do for monohulls, on the grounds that they take up twice as much room.

Motor Sailers

6

As their name implies, motor sailers are boats with performance under either sail or power, and indeed sail and power together. They are fast gaining favour with two completely different groups of people. The first is the couple whose children have grown up and left home and who feel that they want to be able to start the motor knowing that it has the power to take them into both wind and tide without too much effort on their part. At the other end of the scale there are the young couples whose children are too small to be of much help in working the boat, and who take up rather a lot of their mother's time, leaving father on his own.

Motor sailers have frequently been referred to as 50/50s

when describing their motoring and sailing rôles, but it is not really a description of what is wanted from them. It would be better to call them (and design them to be) 100/100s, that is, with full capabilities under sail and the same under power. Too often in the past they have been either motor cruisers with a little steadying sail, or else sailing cruisers with a big engine.

Cruiser/Racers

In much the same way as motor sailers are a compilation of the conflicting requirements of a sailing cruiser and a motor boat, so the boats described by their builders as cruiser/racers are a balance between racing needs and cruising needs. Strictly speaking a racing boat is designed to be sailed as fast and hard as her crew can possibly drive her, so to this end she has very basic accommodation and is designed with maximum sail area. On the other hand, a cruiser is intended to take her crew from port to port without overtiring or

7

straining them and at the same time provide them with comfortable living quarters. Her sail area is also reduced for ease of handling by one watch, without having to call out the rest of the crew. Thus a cruiser/racer has to carry more sail than a cruiser, but less than a racing boat, and have more comfortable accommodation than a racing boat, but perhaps less than a cruiser. A fine balance.

Offshore Cruisers

8

Distinguishing between a coastal cruiser and an offshore cruiser presents very similar problems to those encountered when trying to define estuary and coastal cruisers. The majority of the larger coastal cruisers are suitable for offshore work provided that they have beefed up rigging and all gear and equipment is up to scratch. These boats need to be capable of staying at sea in bad weather, and even of clawing their way to windward against a rising gale in order to put some sea-room between themselves and the land. It takes courage to bash *away* from a harbour knowing that you are in for a real buster, and any boat intended for cruising in deep waters has to inspire great confidence in her crew.

CHAPTER 3

Cruiser Design

The design of a small cruiser is like a three dimensional jigsaw puzzle where all the pieces have variable shapes. Do you have four berths and a tiny galley, or three berths and room to swing a cat, or even three berths, a galley and a toilet compartment? The mathematics of yacht design are fortunately none of our concern as we are only interested in the end product, but the main features should be studied with an eye to how they affect our choice of boat.

Livability

Since we sail for fun, it is only reasonable to expect a comfortable standard of living on board our boats. I don't mean that every 18-footer should have reclining armchairs and deep pile carpets throughout, but there should be a full length bunk for each member of the crew and adequate cooking and toilet facilities.

In fact bunks are a facility to which designers appear to pay far too little attention. The first requirement for a berth to be usable in a seaway is for it to be narrow enough to hold the occupant against the motion of the vessel. At the head the bunk need not be more than the width of a man's shoulders, and at the foot it can be half that width. The other requirement is that each berth should be fitted with some form of leeboard or cloth to hold the sleeper in place if his is an 'uphill' bunk. Opinions vary as to whether boards or cloths are better, and it is really a matter of personal preference. Both stow out of the way under the berth cushions when not in use.

Generally speaking bunks have either grp (glass reinforced polyester) or plywood bases and 2–4in thick foam rubber

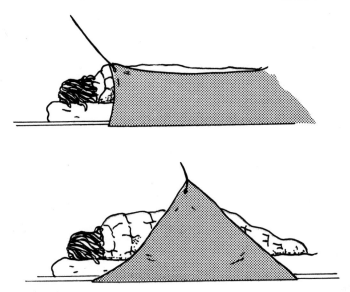

9 *Quadrilateral and triangular leecloths – either type make sleeping at sea much easier.*

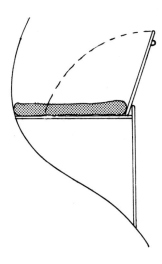

10 *An alternative to leecloths is the leeboard shown here. Like the cloths it stows under the mattress.*

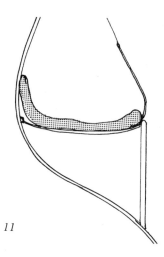

11

mattresses. Because this is the general pattern of things, it does not necessarily mean that it is the best idea. Much greater comfort can be achieved by having a canvas or rubber webbing base with a very thin mattress that is about $1\frac{1}{2}$ times the width of the bunk. This wide mattress can then be laid either up the ship's side (if that is to leeward) or up against the leecloth if that is on the downhill side. Such an arrangement allows you to sleep, whatever the boat's antics, without having to lash yourself to the bookshelf or brace yourself against each lurch.

Another 'happy sleeping' idea is that of reducing the crew-to-berths ratio. For a week's cruise on say a four berth boat take only three people. This leaves more room for everyone and there is a choice of bunks for the man coming off watch. This crew-to-berths ratio is applicable on any boat in our size range and for anything over a weekend it makes a big difference to comfort and tempers.

On a very small cruiser cooking at sea is seldom more than heating up the odd can of soup or boiling a kettle, but for larger boats there are many excellent little stoves with a couple of burners and even a grill and oven on the bigger ones, making 'proper' cooking quite feasible. But in many cases life can be made easier for the cook by fitting the stove with gimbals and providing it with fiddles. The gimbals are a kind of swinging bracket, so that the stove is always upright even if the boat is heeled well over. Fiddle rails are run round and across the stove to make sure that pots and pans don't slide off. These fiddles are more important still if gimbals are not fitted.

Although most boats are fitted with Calor gas stoves there are many people who prefer to cook on paraffin or alcohol stoves with their reduced risk of explosion. Calor or Gaz users will of course argue that a paraffin stove can flare up, but (as with gas explosions) this can be avoided by proper handling.

These days it's unusual to find even the smallest cruiser with a simple bucket-and-chuck-it toilet arrangement, most having either a full blown sea toilet or else a natty little chemical affair. People are rather touchy about the subject of toilets, and in the confines of a small family cruiser they are a problem difficult to ignore. A number of river and harbour

 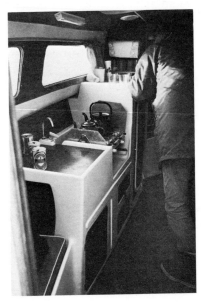

Although it may not look like it, the kettle on the gimballed stove on the left is upright and the boat is heeled. Beneath the stove can be seen two gas bottles, one in use and the other a spare. Many people prefer to have bottles stowed out in a cockpit locker that drains overboard, but placing them right under the cooker reduces piping to a minimum and it soon becomes a habit to turn the gas off at the bottle every time it is used, not just on fine nights and when going ashore. The galley on the right is on a smaller boat where space is at a premium and the gas cylinders are perforce stowed outside the cabin. The stove is gimballed, and under the working surface which has the beer cans on it is a small sink with the freshwater pump standing just beside it. Beneath the cooker and sink are several lockers for food storage.

authorities are already opposed to the use of sea toilets in their areas and I don't suppose that it will be many years before all boats have to have holding tanks – though goodness knows where you find room for them. These tanks will have to be emptied at specified points ashore, the effluent then being pumped into the domestic main drainage and so disposed of.

Keeping clothes and other gear dry and free of damp and condensation on a small boat is no mean feat. Many people use very big plastic bags of the kind found on sale in launderettes. These will take all the clothes you want and can be pushed down into a locker where they serve the dual purpose of keeping it all together and stopping it getting wet. These bags are also very useful for hanging up in the companionway as splash flaps for the quarter berths, whose occupants otherwise suffer from rain and spray each time the hatch is opened. Of course, on a small boat the old adage of a place for everything and everything in its place is totally applicable. Just one point though; it's as well, psychologically speaking, for each crewman to have one locker where he can dump his gear in any sort of a jumble he likes – a small area he can call his own, and which no one else will touch. This used to be a man's bunk, where he could leave things and know they wouldn't be disturbed, but on modern boats with bunks doubling as settees this isn't always possible.

Workability

Although there are several people on board, the family man is very often sailing his boat virtually singlehanded. At times when a crew is most useful, such as getting underway or picking up a mooring, his wife may be looking after the children trying to keep them out of harm's way. Consequently the skipper needs to have a carefully worked out plan of campaign for these situations and, to help himself, he also needs to ensure that the boat is laid out most conveniently for single-handed use.

The deck and its associated hardware is a prime example of an area on a boat where thought can make working so much easier. In the first place the deck is put on to provide protection for the watch below – otherwise they wouldn't be below – and it also in many cases forms a stepping point

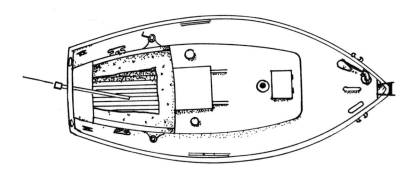

12 Deck layout needs to be simple, keeping working spaces uncluttered. The scheme here shows stemhead roller (for anchor chain), fairleads on the toerails with cleats close by, a mooring cleat, anchor and navel pipe by port toerail, forehatch, ventilators, tracks on either side deck to take jib sheet fairleads, sheet winches mounted on pads outside the cockpit coamings which, with the cleats also on the outside, reduces the likelihood of tearing clothing on them, and finally quarter fairleads and cleats. All the basics are there and yet nothing is badly cluttered. The diagram below shows a good way of stowing a CQR anchor using deck chocks to lash it down.

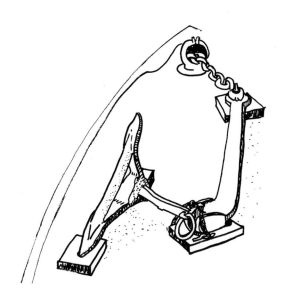

for the mast. Beyond that it is simply a platform for working the boat from. Certain fittings have to clutter it up: the fore-hatch is desirable if only as a second means of escaping from the cabin, and a certain number of cleats and fairleads are needed, though these can be placed near the toerails. A samson post – a strong post passing through the deck and down to the keel – used to be stuck in the centre as a mooring point, but this has generally been superseded by a big cleat through-bolted to a heavy back-up plate. An anchor stowed in the middle of the foredeck is ideal for stubbing toes on, as is a navel pipe (a tube carrying the chain down to its locker).

All of these fittings can be kept out of the way with a little thought, leaving you what is wanted: a deck area where you can stand, sit or kneel depending on the conditions. I don't know why it is rarely seen these days, but once it was common practice to lead all halyards aft to the cockpit, enabling the sails to be hoisted from an area far more pro-tected than a bucking foredeck. Equally it is only sensible on a small boat that all the sheets be lead to cleats within reach of the helmsman, so that when he is on watch alone he does not have to leave the tiller to trim them.

Sometimes he will need to leave the helm, whether to look at the chart, make a check on the lashings of some item up forward, or just to call the next watch, and for these occa-sions an easy way of fixing the helm is useful. If the tiller passes over an after deck, then a row of holes into which pegs can be dropped on either side of the tiller is very simple. Otherwise a lashing to a cleat will steady her, in which case I would advise using shock cord to absorb the snatching of the rudder.

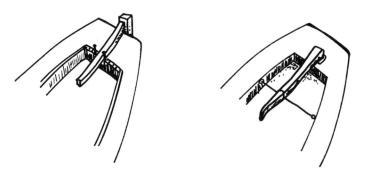

13   *On the left a pin rail to fix the helm, and on the right a lashing.*

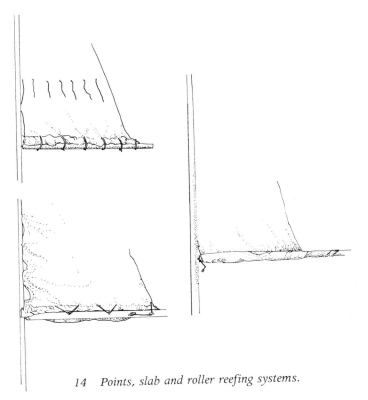

14   *Points, slab and roller reefing systems.*

A simple reefing method is most desirable when you are short handed. The points method is rather slow and cumbersome, though there is no denying that it does produce a very good and neat reef. Its more modern counterpart is the 'slab reefing' system shown in the diagrams. Here, instead of tying individual reef points, a continuous line is rove through eyelets in the sail and is hauled down over hooks on the boom. As yet it is still a system found mainly on racing boats, but it will probably grow in popularity for cruising as well. Most boats have what is called roller reefing. In this case the mainsail is rolled round the boom by means of a reefing handle operating a worm gear which in turn revolves the boom. One man can slacken off the halyard and turn the boom at the same time, but a much better reef is obtained if a second person can be on hand to pull the slack of the sail out towards the outboard end of the boom to stop it folding and puckering. Once the required amount of sail has been rolled up, the halyard is retensioned. The drawback is that the more you

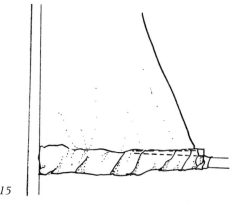

15

roll round the boom the more the sail bunches up at the inboard end, and the outboard end droops until it bashes you over the head each time you tack. The way to avoid this is to fit tapered battens to increase the diameter of the boom end.

Sail Plan

Modern cruising boats are virtually always bermudan rigged and gaff rig has become the rare exception. Admittedly a bermudan mainsail with its single halyard is easier to set than a gaff sail, but it is still a shame to see gaff rig fading slowly, especially as it has some advantages over a bermudan sail. What we are left with is a miniaturisation of the rig developed for offshore racing with miniscule mainsails and a range of headsails from the pocket handkerchief to the 'my bankroll's bigger than your bankroll'.

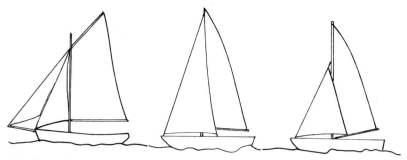

16   A gaff cutter, masthead rigged bermudan sloop, threequarter rigged bermudan sloop.

When working on deck in a seaway one is always far safer sitting or kneeling to a job. Where the going is rough, a life-jacket or life-harness should be worn and the latter clipped on to a strong point. The girl having to stand to reach the head of the mainsail is sensibly wearing an inflated life-jacket plus a life-harness clipped on to a jackstay along the deck, which allows free movement between cockpit and foredeck. The harness does not interfere with the life-jacket — and the girl has wisely braced a foot behind her in case a sudden lurch should throw her backwards.

The real trouble with these small mainsail/large headsail rigs, from the point of view of the family cruising man, is that his wife may very well not have the muscle power to sweat in a big genoa without the aid of costly winches or complicated tackles. Let's face it, the man himself will have his hands more than full trying to get one of these monsters off in a squall. The big headsails mean frequent changes of sail in order always to have set the one best suited to the prevailing conditions, and working on the foredeck is no joke when the going gets rough. It is precisely the time when you want a snug rig needing little attention so that father can stay at the helm and be seen to be in charge of the boat, while mother attends to the children. If she points into the cockpit and says, 'Look we're quite safe, Daddy's there', and finds that in fact Daddy is once again dancing on the foredeck, then a certain amount of confidence is going to be lost. What has to be done is to snug down *early* and perhaps be under-canvassed for a while.

For shorthanded sailing a most useful device is the Wyke-ham-Martin furling gear for jibs. This consists of a swivel at the head of the jib and another at the tack, the latter having a drum on which is wound a thin line. By easing the sheets and pulling on this line the sail can be rolled around its own luff – roller blind fashion. The mistake is to think that it can be rolled part way in order to reef the sail. If this is done it will quickly distort and damage the sail. A solid luff spar is required for roller reefing a jib and they are on the expensive side.

The Auxiliary

Since they are fitted as auxiliaries, boat engines are of fairly low horsepower (though increasingly large ones are being installed) and consequently must not be expected to do the impossible. For instance, it would be both foolish and unfair to ask an auxiliary to pull you off a lee shore into the teeth of a gale. It is only when you get up to the motor sailer class that the engine gives the boat equal sailing and motoring performance.

Where you have any say in the matter, choice for an auxiliary lies between outboard engines and inboard petrol or diesel. The outboard is generally mounted on a lifting bracket

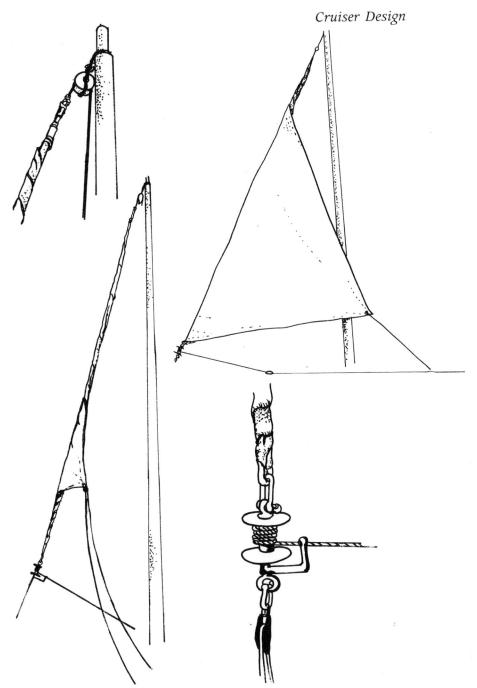

17   *The Wykeham-Martin gear with jib furled, partly unfurled, and details of head and tack arrangements.*

on the transom where it takes up no space in the boat. Unfortunately, being right aft the propeller will often lift out of the water on a wave and so lose thrust. To get round this problem some designers put in an outboard well, that is a moulded trunk through the bottom of the boat somewhere at the after end of the cockpit. By mounting it in such a well, the outboard is protected from being swamped by a following sea, and its propeller is placed deeper in the water, making it less likely to jump out and giving it a much greater bite on the water. The power-to-weight ratio of an outboard is very good and many have a built-in battery charger, making electric lighting and even electric starting feasible.

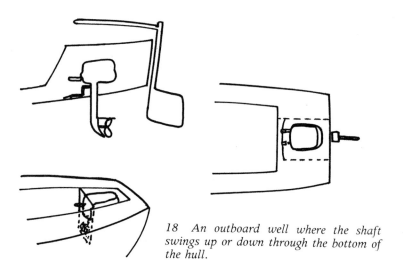

18 *An outboard well where the shaft swings up or down through the bottom of the hull.*

For inboard engines the choice between having a petrol or a diesel engine is difficult as there are numerous pros and cons for each. Taking petrol first, you have a motor that is comparatively cheap, but a fuel that needs lead-coated cheques to stop them bouncing! Petrol engines are fairly light but you have to carry a large quantity of highly inflammable fuel. Looking at diesels, on the other hand, the initial cost of buying the motor is high, but the fuel bills are much lower. Where petrol engines need electrics, which are affected by the salt atmosphere at sea, a diesel needs none. In fact its correct description is a 'compression ignition' engine. However, because the fuel is ignited by compressing it, the cast-

The worst possible (I hope) situation with an engine installation – the cabin steps have been removed and the 'access' panel opened to reveal the flywheel and practically nothing else. Even with the remaining panels unscrewed and removed, it would still be very awkward indeed to work on this engine at sea. It is important to be able to make space simply and quickly for running repairs and routine maintenance.

ings for the engine need to be very heavy to withstand the high pressures.

The governing factor in choice of auxiliary may well turn out to be space under the cockpit sole, for that is inevitably where the motor will have to be installed. It may not be an ideal place as the boat's stern will be weighed down and access for maintenance will be strictly limited, but who wants to have an engine sited in the middle of the cabin?

Keels

There are three types of keel arrangement in general use on small sailing cruisers: twin bilge keels, a single fin keel, and a centreplate.

The bilge keels can in fact be sub-divided into two kinds – twin ballasted keels attached to the hull below the turn of the bilge, or a central ballast stub with twin bilge plates on either side. These plates are just sheet steel, whereas the bilge keels proper are either bolted-on lumps of cast iron, or else glassfibre encased weights.

Fin keels are single, centrally placed, deep ballast keels

with the majority of their weight concentrated in the lower part. It is generally accepted that a well designed fin keeler will have a better windward performance than a twin keeler, but downwind there will be nothing in it. At the lower end of the cruiser size range there is frankly little difference in performance between fin and bilge keeled boats on any point of sailing, and other factors should guide one's choice of keel arrangement.

19   *Left to right: fin keel, bilge keels (twin keels), centreboard – which swings up into the ballast stub keel.*

The centreboard is really an attempt to achieve a combination of the advantages of a fin keel with the shallow draught of a twin keel boat. Again there are two forms of centreboard, or more accurately centre*plate,* as metal is used in cruising boats. In one case the ballast is put in a shallow keel outside the bottom of the boat, and the centreplate retracts almost wholly into this. In the other case, the ballast is concentrated in the centreplate itself with some extra ballast inside the boat, and the plate retracts into a box that inevitably protrudes into the accommodation. And here you have one of the least liked facets of centreboarders.

When talking about keels we are interested really in three things; their righting power, their ability to stop a boat making leeway, and the draught they add onto the hull. The keel(s) of any boat being considered for safe cruising *must* have sufficient righting power to bring the boat up from a 90 degree knockdown. That is to say, if for the purposes of a test the boat was hauled down so that her mast lay flat on the water – smooth water – and was then released, the boat should return to the upright position. This was a test first introduced by the Junior Offshore Group (JOG) who have done much to promote the designing of safe small cruisers.

What about the advantages and disadvantages of each of these keel types? Fin keels require plenty of depth of water, but make the boat close winded. Bilge keels may not provide quite the same windward ability, but stop the boat rolling so much downwind, and they make shoal water cruising possible, with the bonus of letting the boat take the ground without recourse to legs (props fitted to the gunwales to stop her falling over). The centreplate also provides good windward performance and allows the boat to enter shallow waters safely, but centreboard boxes have a tendency to leak, and if there is an external ballast stub the boat will heel over when dried out.

Hull Shape

Hull shape is to some extent determined by what the designer wants to put inside. For instance if he wants to cram in an extra berth, then somehow he is going to have to give the boat enough beam to take it. However, for a hull to have a good windward ability, it generally has a fine entry allowing the boat to slice through waves losing as little way as possible, but this reduces the space inside the boat up forward. To overcome this loss of space the designer may spread the bow sections a bit, but if he goes too far and the hull becomes bluff bowed, then she will be stopped by waves and will tend to gripe when hard pressed. Just to complicate things, a boat wants to have some fullness in her bow and stern sections to provide buoyancy. She also wants to have some beam to provide a degree of stability, but not too much coupled with slack bilges, or else she will roll in a seaway. Going to the stern of the boat, the transom should never be allowed to drag in the water, but should be trimmed just clear to allow a clean flow past it.

Depth of freeboard is also a difficult one. Too much and the boat will be blown downwind, but she needs to have enough to provide at least sitting headroom in the cabin and to help make the hull buoyant when heeled. When you choose a boat, obviously you can't say, 'I want six inches chopped off the topsides,' but it is a point worth sizing up when you first look the boat over.

Cockpits

Since the majority of one's sea time is spent in the cockpit it has to be carefully planned. Most boats have a self-draining well with pipes running out through the hull – usually the bottom, though sometimes the transom – to take the water away. With the modern idea of enormous cockpits extending right aft to the transom so that the crew can lounge about on moorings, self-draining is essential. Taking the cockpit right aft like this creates a serious problem with reserve buoyancy in the stern sections, and in my opinion they are not always a very bright idea. I would rather see a good area of after deck, a small foot well, and *large* drain holes of at least 1½in internal diameter. Too many of the drains fitted are just about big enough to empty a tea cup, and then only if they are not blocked up.

To make a cockpit self-draining the sole has to be at some height above the waterline, which in a small boat means that the well is somewhat shallow, making it less safe for the crew. The minimum depth for comfortable leg room is about 15in.

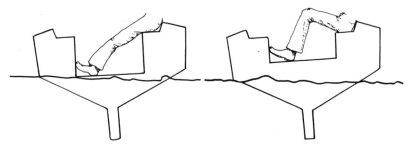

20   *The cockpit on the left is too deep to be self-draining, but it is comfortable to sail in, while the one on the right is shallow enough for draining, but it is uncomfortable and poorly protected.*

For comfort the crew should be able to sit to windward and brace their feet against the opposite bench, and when they lean back the coamings should be high enough to support them, but should slope slightly outboard to stop them digging into anyone's back. Another thing to be avoided is having cleats or winch handles that dig into you or catch and tear oilskins or trouser pockets.

Two quick points about self-draining outlets: where they are below the waterline, they should be fitted with a sea-cock which can be reached easily, and also they must not have any bends round which you cannot easily push a piece of wire to clear a blockage.

Building Materials

If you buy a new boat the odds are very heavily in favour of her being built of grp – glass reinforced polyester – glassfibre. Certainly for small cruisers, this material has predominated in recent years doing a rapid takeover from plywood, which was the material that put pocket cruisers on the market. The advantage of grp from the builders' point of view is that it is ideally suited to mass production techniques, the same mould being used over and over again to turn out identical hulls. For the consumer, grp means little or no say in interior layout, but great benefits in terms of reduced maintenance and a leak free boat.

Plywood is still an excellent material for small boats, particularly for home boatbuilders, since it is very easy to work with and is strong and light. What must be watched very carefully indeed is the quality of the plywood used. The minimum standard for marine use is BS 1088. This is a minimum and there are better quality plywoods about, but such materials as 'exterior' grade should never be used, no matter how well they are painted or varnished. If you are looking at a secondhand plywood boat careful note should be made of any rippling of the outer laminates or any opening up of the ends – called delamination – as this will lead to trouble.

'Conventional' carvel or clinker planking construction is rare now in small new cruisers, as it is a very expensive way of building. Many secondhand boats are carvel or clinker, and if a surveyor's report declares them sound, then there is no earthly reason for passing them over just because they are slightly outmoded. The thing to remember is that they need a lot of maintenance, and as they get older this will increase.

Strip planking has been hovering on the fringe of things for many years. The method involves building the boat upside down (normally) over a frame by laying very narrow strips of wood in a carvel form and gluing and nailing them. It's not a terribly easy method for the amateur compared to plywood, and I think that is probably the reason it has never really caught on.

Steel, aluminium and ferro cement are three other building materials, but none of them is much used in the size of boat we are interested in. Why steel and aluminium have not been used more is something of a mystery, because with care to use compatible materials and avoid electrolytic action, they are immensely strong and durable. Ferro cement is growing in popularity, but is not economical for a hull less than about 30ft.

Spars and Rigging

Virtually all new boats today are equipped with alloy spars and stainless steel rigging. This does not mean that wooden spars and galvanised rigging are no good, it is simply that they require more maintenance. Wooden spars are also heavier than alloy ones and extra weight aloft should be avoided if possible. The drawback to stainless steel rigging is that it gives little or no warning before breaking, while galvanised wire shows signs of strain and wear some time before parting.

CHAPTER 4

Gear and Equipment

The range of gear and equipment available to boat owners is quite staggering. Chandlers' catalogues are crammed with bits and pieces ranging from the highly practical such as anchors and fenders, to the highly sophisticated electronic gadgetry beloved of offshore racing types, but frankly out of place on a small cruiser. The trouble is to sort out what is really needed, for most owners of small boats are in the market at the 'highly practical' end of things rather than the gold plated taps and monogrammed tea towels.

When you study the brochure on a particular class of boat you find tucked away amongst the glossy bikinis and yo ho hearties two lists of gear and equipment, one usually headed 'standard inventory' and the other 'optional extras'. Exactly what is included in the standard inventory, and therefore in the basic price of the boat, and what has to be added from the extras list, can make a very big difference to the boat's total price. Take two 20-footers with the exciting names Boat A and Boat B. They are near enough the same, and you are trying to decide which to buy. Boat A costs £2500 and Boat B costs £2000. Which would you go for?

If we look at the standard inventory list for Boat A, which happens to be just under a distracting picture, we find that the basic price includes mainsail, jib, storm jib, engine, cooker, anchor and cable, fenders, warps and guardrails, thus needing only a few extras to make her seaworthy. But Boat B, the apparent bargain, only offers mainsail, jib, engine and pulpit, leaving a lot to be added. In fact it's not impossible that Boat B will turn out in the end to be more expensive than Boat A. The thing is to check very carefully what you are getting for your (or your bank manager's) money.

Basic Essentials

Having warned that there are pitfalls when considering gear and equipment we can now look at what is essential to make a boat seaworthy, what is desirable to make seagoing more comfortable, what is needed on top of all this to make the boat cruiseworthy, and finally some of the more practical luxuries. By seaworthy in this context I mean a boat suitably equipped to be taken to sea in safety, and which is capable of withstanding bad weather commensurate with her design limitations. A cruiseworthy boat is a seaworthy one with the additional bits and pieces for living aboard, such as a cooker, crockery, bedding and so on – described as 'well found'. Most standard inventories take a midway position, but I hope you will see that we must first look at the basic items needed to make the boat *seaworthy*. These are:

Mast and spars
Standing rigging
Running rigging
Mainsail
Working jib
Steering compass
Bower anchor
Cable
Kedge and 3 fathoms chain
Suitable (kedge) warp
Leadline/echo sounder
Heaving line
Odd spare lines, shackles, tape, seizing wire, hanks, slides, bulldog clips.
2 springs $1\frac{1}{2}$ times length of boat
2 head ropes twice length of boat
Navigation lights
Lamp oil, if navigation lights oil-fired
Charts
Radio capable of picking up shipping forecasts (1500m) and spare batteries

Watch or clock (with second hand) of known error
Pencils
Sharpener
Rubber
Parallel rulers/Douglas protractor/Hurst plotter
Dividers
Reed's Nautical Almanac
Local pilots
Distance log
Log book
Note books
Engine and stern gear (or outboard and bracket) and fuel tanks
Fuel and spare can
Grease and lubrication oil
Fuel funnel (where needed, eg to fill outboard tank)
Engine spares and manual – plugs, leads, filters, points
Tool kit – spanners, screwdrivers, hacksaw, screws, nails, hammer, pliers
Tender

Painter
Oars and rowlocks
Dinghy bailer/sponge
Fire extinguishers
Pyrotechnics
First aid kit
Fog horn
Life-jackets (one per crew-
man)
Life-buoy
Grp repair kit
Odd bits of plywood and
timber
Spare reefing handle
Spare winch handles (if win-
ches fitted)
Bilge pump with extension
hose, spare washers,
gaskets, diaphragm

Sail mending kit – needles,
palm, thread, scissors,
sail cloth
Knife
Marlin spike
Torch and spare batteries
Matches
Water tanks
Stemhead roller
Fairleads
Bitts or samson post
Fenders
Door lock
Black ball and cone (anchor
and motorsailing) – large
as possible though 2ft
regulation diameter
impractical on 18-footer
Bucket on line

Highly Desirable

If you equip your boat with the 'essential' gear listed above,
and assuming she is sound in wind and limb, she will be
capable of withstanding normal seagoing conditions, but the
crew's existence will be pretty spartan. There is only a very
fine line drawn between what is essential and what is desirable, still here goes.

Sheet winches
Halyard winches – larger
boats
Oilskins
Life-harnesses (one per crew-
man)
Sea boots
Dodgers/pram hood for com-
panionway
Spare battens
Emergency tiller
Burgee/wind indicator
Barometer

Chart table – larger boats
Handbearing compass
Tidal stream atlases
Binoculars
Pulpit, pushpit and lifelines
Life-raft (bigger boats)
Genoa, storm jib (and trysail
for bigger boats)
Shroud rollers/sail protectors
on crosstree ends
Flag halyards
Ensign and staff
Code flags U, G, H, Q, N, C

Radar reflector
Interior lights and battery
Lifebuoy lights

Tapered wooden plugs for
skin fittings
Collision mat in extreme case
of hull being punctured –
pessimists

Cruising Gear

Now that we have fitted the boat out for sea, what about putting her in a 'cruiseworthy' state? The list below contains several items that won't be found amongst the extras offered with the boat, but they are nonetheless necessary. Some you may already have available amongst your household goods.

Cooker and gas bottle or
paraffin or methylated
spirits
Gimbals and fiddles
Pots and pans
Washing up bowl – washing
up, washing clothes,
washing crew, washing
filters
Cutlery
Crockery
Thermos flask
Matches

Tea towels
Towels
Sleeping bags
Berth cushions
Bunk leeboards/leecloths
Riding light
Boat hook
Heads
Toilet paper
Ventilators
Deck mop/brush
Boarding ladder – dependent
upon size of boat

Luxuries

These are the kind of things that can be added if and when wanted, and if and when money allows.

Gas detector
Radio direction finder
Cabin heater
Sextant
Self steering gear

Department of Trade registra-
tion – useful if going
foreign
Spreader lights
Outboard for dinghy

I do not doubt for one moment that some people will disagree with the way I have categorised gear and equipment, but at least these lists will act as a guide. Exactly what gear you choose, and it will probably be an amalgam of all the lists, will depend to a very high degree on what size and type of boat you have. For instance, sheet winches are a tremendous help on a 25-footer, but are not really needed on an 18-footer, where either simple man power can be employed or else a two-part tackle can be rigged up.

The Three Year Plan

What has to be kept in mind when choosing your boat is the fact that you are going to buy quite a lot of expensive gear over and above the initial purchase price. In other words, if you have say £2500 to spend, you would do well to stick to a boat costing about £2000 so that you can then spend the £500 on equipping her, insuring her and finding a mooring. Once you have fitted your boat out with the basic equipment needed, you can use the boat as she stands for a season and then see what gear you need and how much of it you can afford. Thus the next season she will be a little better equipped and if you do the same the following season, you will steadily build up a very good cruising inventory over a three year period.

Most of the items you don't buy immediately will be in the 'highly desirable' category, but economies can be made even in the essentials, for instance by using a hand leadline rather than lashing out on an echo sounder. The luxuries, of course, come much later.

Considering Cordage

Very few people now use natural fibre ropes, everyone having been won over by the greater durability and strength of synthetic fibre ropes. There are in fact many occasions on a boat when natural fibres would do just as well, if only because one can afford to replace such a rope a couple of times before reaching the cost of a synthetic rope suitable for the same purpose. However, we are mainly interested in the synthetics, so let us look at the characteristics of the main types.

Nylon is the strongest of the synthetics with tremendous 'give' or elasticity. It is resistant to attack by alkalis but not acids. Because of its elasticity it is ideal for mooring and kedge warps, where it will absorb much of the snatching and snubbing as the boat moves and surges. For the same reason, nylon should not be used for halyards, since you will spend your whole time retensioning them as they stretch under load.

Polyester, which most of us know under the trade name Terylene, is nearly as strong as nylon, but has very much lower stretch characteristics, especially in a form appropriately called 'pre-stretched'. Polyester is resistant to attack by alkalis and to a lesser extent by acids.

Polypropylene and polythene (often called Courlene) are somewhat weaker than either nylon or polyester and are susceptible to abrasion, but have the advantage of being light and buoyant. Care should be taken when purchasing ropes made from these materials to ensure that they incorporate inhibitors against deterioration by ultra-violet radiation. British standards insist on this, but some foreign makes are available which do not include any such inhibitor. Polypropylene is resistant to attacks by most acids and alkalis. It should be noted that while synthetics are generally resistant in some degree to attack by acids and alkalis, they all suffer under attack by solvents in paint.

21   *Right and left-hand laid ropes. Right-hand lay spirals clockwise away from you, and left-hand anti-clockwise.*

When we think of the general term 'rope', not worrying about what material it is made from or anything else, we tend to think of a three-strand hawser laid line, and this is in fact still the most common type. Sometimes you come across a three-strand rope with a left hand lay, but it is only occasionally. The other variable with the lay of a three-strand rope is the length of jaw – the distance travelled along a rope by following one strand through one complete twist – but these

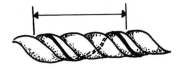

22   Jaw length.

days we have to accept whatever is on offer. Three strand ropes are good general purpose ropes for such jobs as mooring warps or halyards, but are not so good for (say) anchor warps, since the direction of twist imparted under load is critical. Pre-stretched Polyester should be used for halyards in preference to nylon which is far too stretchy, while the reverse should be operated for mooring warps.

Plaited ropes which mostly have a much lower stretch characteristic than an equivalent laid rope, take two basic forms: the normal multiplait and the plaited core and sheath, the latter being sold under the trade name Braidline. Where a plaited rope is made up from staple (non-continuous) filaments, it is virtually indistinguishable from plaited cotton and is very kind to the hands, making it excellent for use as sheets. Braidline is an immensely strong rope and is highly suited to use as halyards and sheets. One of the main points about plaited rope is that it does not matter in which direction twist is imparted, so that it is the only rope to use for the line of, say, a towing log.

It is a bit difficult to be dogmatic about how much of what kind of warp a small cruiser should carry, but apart from

23   Cable laid rope, very good for anchor warps, and the core-and-sheath Braidline.

halyards, sheets and anchor cable, the following should act as a rough guide.

1 kedge warp of 20 fathoms by 8–10mm diam nylon or plaited (Braidline).
2 springs 1½ times length of boat by 12mm diam nylon.
2 head ropes twice length of boat by 12mm diam polypropylene.
2–3 lengths of odd stuff about 5 fathoms each.
1 heaving line 4–5 fathoms plaited 8–10mm diam.
1 hank codline, hambro or similar.

After a few seasons you will have had to replace perhaps a halyard and a pair of sheets, and these can be put in the rope locker to see out their days in other employ.

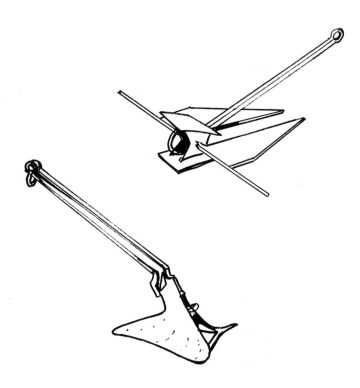

24 *Types of anchor – top: Danforth; lower: CQR.*

While on the subject of choosing suitable gear, let me just say a word about anchors and cables. Assuming that you plump for either a CQR or Danforth type of bower anchor, then you should get one whose weight corresponds roughly to 1 lb for 1ft of boat, with a tendency towards a heavier anchor than this formula gives. For boats under 20ft the cable should be $\frac{1}{4}$in short link chain and at least 15 fathoms should be carried. Over 20ft and up to 30ft, 5/16in chain is more suitable with 20–25 fathoms being carried. If you choose to carry an anchor warp rather than cable, there must be at least 3 fathoms of chain between the anchor and the warp, or else you will have trouble with dragging anchors. Hanging a heavy weight some distance down the warp from the boat's bow also helps to reduce the surging and snatching. In the case of catamarans the boat should ride to a bridle from each bow rather than from a central fairlead.

CHAPTER 5

Trial Sailing

Right from the start I should make it quite clear that you cannot *test* a boat when you take her out for a few hours. No matter what the weather and no matter how experienced you are, to test a boat you would need to live aboard for a time, take her out in fair weather and foul, sail her day and night and generally see how she goes in rough as well as smooth water. All of which takes a long time, and in the end you would either love or hate the boat, but either way be quite unable to make an objective criticism of her. This of course is exactly the predicament that the yachting journals find themselves in when they try to review a boat.

Most of the magazines carry these reports, but the people who write them would, I am sure, be the first to admit that they can only express a personal opinion based on a few hours sailing the boat and mentally comparing her with all the other boats they have been on of a similar type. Hence these reports are in no way a substitute for sailing the boat yourself, but can only act as a guide and comparison with your own findings.

When you have reduced your list of possible boats to just two or three, then is the time to get in touch with the builders or agents and ask for a demonstration sail. Most firms have a demonstration boat available and will be pleased to take you out, but don't waste their time if you are not very seriously interested. If the firm does not have a boat available, or if you are buying secondhand and the boat you are after cannot be got into the water conveniently, then you are reduced to relying on any magazine reports you can find, or if she is a class boat, trying to get in touch with the Owners' Association (where there is one) and seeing if another owner will either give you an off-the-cuff opinion of the boat, or better, take you out in one.

Having got out on the boat there are certain simple manoeuvres and exercises that you can carry out to gain an idea of how she handles and whether or not she is going to suit you. Before you even set sail you will look at the boat and that first impression is likely to be a lasting one. It can tell you a lot about the boat. There's an old maxim that if a boat looks good she probably is good, though occasionally an ugly boat can be found that sails well.

A boat with a fine entry, not much freeboard and perhaps a deep keel will probably go well to windward, but the crew will be soaked. One with high topsides and a big cabin top has a lot of windage and will probably make a lot of leeway in consequence. If a boat has a hard turn to the bilge, a shallow hull and some beam ending in a wide transom, she will prefer downwind sailing. If again she has a lot of beam, but rather slack bilges, then she will probably roll in a seaway. A nice clean run aft, where the water will obviously flow easily away from the stern, points to a boat that will keep going even in the lightest of winds.

So much for first appearances, now let us get down to sailing the boat. There is no point in going out literally for a demonstration sail, you must be at the helm yourself, and there is also no point in simply sailing straight out and back; you won't learn much that way. The various manoeuvres described here are in no particular order, but each tells us something about the boat.

Under Mainsail Only

When entering an anchorage under sail, many people like to get the jib off and leave the foredeck clear for handling the anchor, but to do this safely the boat must remain totally controllable, being able to beat, run, reach, tack and gybe. The same applies when getting underway. If the boat is lying head to wind, it is often easier to drop the mooring or get the anchor and sail away under main alone.

Until the last few years a sloop with all her working sail set had the majority of the area in her mainsail, but recent trends have led to a reduction in the size of mainsails and a great increase in headsail areas. This has meant that whereas a boat was once a lot handier under main alone than jib alone, the reverse is now often the case.

When you have sailed out into clear water, drop the jib and try making the boat run, reach, gybe and tack just to see how she goes. Don't expect her to be quite as responsive as with a jib set, or to point as high or particularly to tack as smoothly, but she should still be able to make up to windward, and most important, you should still feel in control.

Foresail Only

On many occasions it is not only easy, but extremely pleasant to get underway under jib alone. For instance if the wind is aft you can hoist the jib, let it flap while you clear the moorings, then sheet in and sail quietly off downriver. A boat designed with a big mainsail/small headsail rig cannot be expected to do much more than run, reach or possibly close reach, but if the headsail is larger than the mainsail you should be able to sail closehauled and make up to windward.

Once again, work out into clear water, then drop the main and see what she will do under jib alone. Don't expect a sparkling performance, but look warily upon a boat that gets into irons every time you try to tack. See how close to the wind she will sail, and whether the sheeting arrangement makes handling the jib fairly simple.

Heaving To

People tend to associate heaving to with extreme weather conditions when progress is halted and the only thing to do is ride it out, but fortunately it is unusual for the weekend yachtsman to find himself in this predicament. Why he should be interested in how his boat heaves to is rather for stopping her while he has lunch, does some navigation or pulls down a reef. All quite legitimate uses of heaving to but much less hairy and frightening.

The basic process for heaving to is to sail the boat closehauled then tack her, but instead of letting fly the jib and sheeting it home on the other side, you leave it alone so that as the ship's head comes through the wind, the jib is left aback. The mainsail tacks across normally and the helm is put right down. To summarise, the jib is held aback, the mainsail is partially drawing, and the helm is trying to turn the bows up into the wind. In this position the sails can be trimmed and the helm altered until the boat stops in the water and just makes a little leeway. Or that's how it should be. Try it and see, but if you have a full mainsail and big genoa set, don't be surprised if she still forereaches quite fast. Preferably change down the headsail and try again.

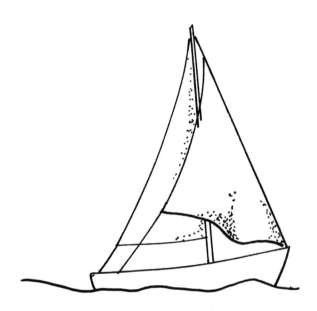

25   *Hove to with jib aback and mainsail partially drawing.*

Lying Athwart the Wind

If you are sailing shorthanded and want to change the jib, often the easiest way to do it is to free the sheets right off and let the boat lie athwart the wind just idling along but not really making any way. When she is in that position, and usually the helm doesn't even need lashing, you can go forward and drop the jib then hank on and hoist the new

51

26 *Boats lying athwart the wind with sheets slack and sails shaking.*

one. The same can be done if you want to reef without having a mainsail full of wind to contend with. Not all cruisers will sit quietly like this as they are often too delicately balanced, but if the one you are trying out is happy, then you will find shorthanded or singlehanded sailing that much easier.

Light Air Manoeuvres

Obviously all the manoeuvres we are discussing can be per-
formed in light airs, but most of them want a bit of a breeze
to show the boat's real worth (or otherwise). When you do
happen to go out in really light conditions, it is possible to
get a feeling of how the boat will react in a stronger breeze
by bringing her up onto the wind and trimming the sails so
that she is sailing nicely, then when she has some way on,
put the helm hard down and sit back. She should tack round
and with the jib aback, continue round until she gybes and
comes up on the wind again, all without the sheets or helm
having been touched.

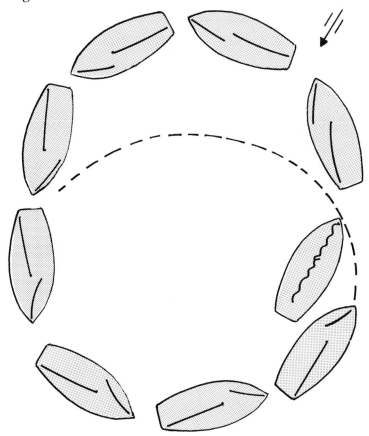

27 *The circuit of luffing, tacking and gybing with sheets fixed and helm
held down.*

While this operation does not mean a great deal in terms of normal boat handling, it does give an idea of her responsiveness. In a moderate breeze she should in fact tack and gybe round and round, more or less continuously, but in really light weather she can only be expected to do it once or maybe twice.

It is interesting to pick a fixed object and sail up to it then shoot up into the wind and see how far the boat carries her way. This is an essential piece of information when trying to come into an anchorage or trying to pick up a mooring where you want to stop the boat in exactly the right place. A very light displacement boat with a lot of tophamper will bring up quickly, whereas a heavier displacement boat will carry on for some distance, but in either case it is quite surprising how far the boat travels before stopping. It is lack of knowledge of this aspect of their boat that makes so many owners overshoot their moorings or leave some poor crewman stretched between buoy and boat.

Reefing

When you are trying a boat out it is a good idea to take down a deep reef, say 5–6 rolls, and see how well the sail sets. If the boom end droops excessively you may have to tack battens on to fatten it and take up the belly of the sail. The other point to make note of while trying to reef is how the gear is arranged and whether it is possible for one man to work it easily. Tied in with that is the need for good working space around the foot of the mast, space that has a good non-slip surface on it.

Setting and Changing Sails

When setting out on a trial sail, it is probably best to keep clear and let the chap from the builder hoist sail and work her out of her berth (unless he asks for help), but once in clear water you should drop the sails and start from scratch yourself. By doing it all yourself you will find out whether the cleats and any winches on the mast are laid out for easy use, and if there is a bit of a lop on the water, then you will soon find out if her foredeck is an easy platform to work on, or if she needs to have some more non-slip put on in way of the mast step. This last is a common fault with grp boats, especially on hatches, which are frequently left smooth and glossy, making them lethal when wet.

Headsail halyards should be long enough so that they can be shackled or clipped onto the head of the sail while it is still on the deck. The big thing is to try to imagine yourself changing headsails or reefing the main on a dark night, and see if the halyards would come readily to hand, and if you can turn them up on their cleats without taking the skin off your knuckles on some sharp projection.

Weather Helm

When a boat is said to carry weather helm it means that the tiller has to be held up towards the windward side (a-weather) to stop her luffing up into the wind. It is good for a boat to carry a little weather helm as it not only gives a bit of 'feel' to the helm, but it also acts as a safety device, in that should the helmsman let go of the helm (perhaps he is unfortunate enough to fall overboard) then the boat will luff up head to wind. But for easy shorthanded sailing she should only do this slowly, otherwise handling sheets and so on will become a frantic dash between tiller and cleat.

With a rather tubby family pocket cruiser it is occasionally found that when she heels in a gust she will gripe up to windward. What you must watch for is that this does not require a heavy pull on the helm to correct it, or else sailing through an anchorage will turn you grey before your time.

Handling Under Power

Much has been written (and even more argued) about an effect called paddlewheeling. Let me now stick my oar in. The idea is that a righthanded propeller (one which revolves clockwise when looked at from astern) will tend to move the stern to starboard, and a left handed prop will tend to move it to port. If a propeller of some 20in or so diameter were fitted this effect would be quite pronounced, but when a prop of half that diameter or even less is fitted it can more or less be ignored. In my experience there will be virtually no

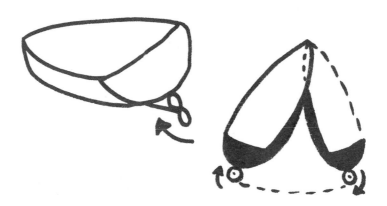

28   *Paddlewheeling can best be imagined by mentally replacing the propeller with a wheel and turning it so that the boat pivots on her stem.*

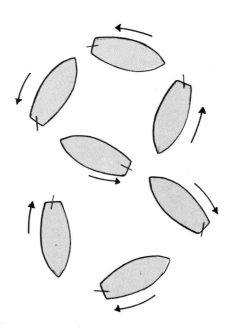

29   *If a boat can describe a figure of eight going astern she becomes a joy to handle, but with many it is hard enough trying to keep in a straight line.*

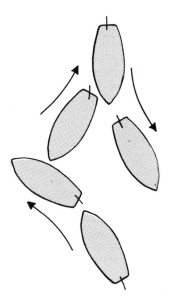

30 Backing and filling to make a '3-point turn' using short, sharp bursts of power.

paddlewheeling effect on a small family cruiser, but it is only sensible to check when you are out on trials. To do this, put her up to moderate revs then put the helm hard over and when she crosses her own wake, judge how many boat lengths the diameter of the described circle is. Then straighten up and make a turn in the opposite direction noting the diameter of the second described circle. A significant difference would indicate paddlewheeling, and if it is found you must remember it and allow for it when manoeuvring the boat – it can be either a help or a hindrance depending upon the circumstances.

Once you have got the feel of the boat going ahead under power, stop her and try moving in a straight line astern. After that try describing a figure of eight still in astern gear. Please note that whatever type of gearbox is installed, it will last longer if you pause in neutral before going into astern, ditto from astern to ahead.

Going back to turning the boat, in the light of what you have discovered about her handling in ahead and astern, see how she will come round by backing and filling in a kind of 3-point turn. By using judicious bursts of ahead and astern like this she should pivot almost on her own axis.

Engine Access

I'm afraid that most sailing people overhaul their boat's engine when fitting out in the Spring and then completely ignore it until something goes wrong, usually at a very awkward moment. But assuming that you promise yourself you are going to be the exception to prove the rule, you will have to have easy access to the engine to carry out the routine maintenance.

Regrettably, many marine engines are installed in such a way that it is either impossible to get at them without taking half the boat apart, or else you need to be a 'bendy man'. On small boats it is difficult to put the motor anywhere but under the cockpit sole – assuming an inboard engine – simply because no one wants it stuck in the middle of the cabin. Even so it should be possible to get at the main parts without major upheaval. Anyway, check and see. Main things to be got at are the sparking plugs, fuel lines and filters, carburettor, oil filters and fillers, magneto if there is one, or fuel pump and injectors on a diesel.

Outboards are a bit easier, but if the one you are looking at is transom mounted, make sure that it is possible to bring it inboard. Leaving it trailing when sailing is not ideal and trying to work on it when leaning out over the transom is just asking for trouble – plugs can't swim.

Fuel tanks must have fillers arranged so that they can be topped up from on deck and without pouring fuel all over the decks. Dirt and water traps must also be accessible. Make a note also whether the tanks are fitted with a fuel gauge or a dipstick – the latter is often more accurate.

One last point, if the engine is fitted for electric starting, I would strongly advise that a hand starting mechanism is also provided. Though you may have suffered a flat battery on your car and managed to bump start it, you can't do the same for a boat.

Further Points

Not a lot here, but study the interior layout and try to imagine living on board when the boat is heeled over. Will locker doors fly open? Indeed, are there sufficient lockers? Are there fiddles on the cooker? Is it gimballed? Are leeboards provided for the bunks or will you have to add them later? Can the toilet be used without chucking everyone out of the cabin? Is there any sail stowage or will the bags have to be moved from empty bunk to empty bunk? Is there somewhere you can do chartwork? Does your wife think there is suffi-cient working area round the galley? Are there plenty of grabrails?

Are the decks adequately covered with an effective non-slip material? Is the working area on deck – especially in way of the mast – reasonable and is it fairly clear of toe stubbers? Are the chain plates, grabrails, cleats and so on through-bolted to large back-up plates?

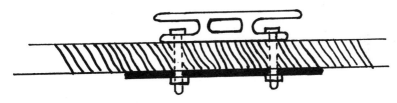

31   *A cleat through-bolted to a large back-up plate which spreads the load over a good area.*

CHAPTER 6

Tenderising

No matter where you keep your boat, whether it is in a marina, on a deepwater mooring or on a drying one, you must have a dinghy for use as a tender. Dinghies come in all shapes and sizes but are indispensable. Not only do they transport you and your crew besides all the dunnage to and from the boat, but in dire emergency they also act as life-rafts. With such a complicated rôle to play a dinghy has to be carefully designed and equipped.

Choosing a Tender – Rigid or Inflatable

When choosing what dinghy to use as a tender your first decision must be whether to have a rigid dinghy or an inflatable. Both have their merits and it is impossible to give a straightforward 'you should have' type of answer. By asking yourself which you want you provoke a second question: are you going to have one or two tenders? Most of us answer that we can't possibly afford two, which is reasonable, but if you have two you can use a rigid, large capacity dinghy to take all your junk out to the boat in one go and have an inflatable stowed away on board. Luxury indeed.

Assuming you plump for just one tender you must weigh up the pros and cons. First, a rigid dinghy is robust and size for size has a greater volume for carrying people and gear than does an inflatable. Unfortunately though, a rigid dinghy towed astern of a small cruiser will knock her speed down drastically. An inflatable on the other hand may not have the same volume of space, but it can carry a great weight. It can also pack down into such a small space that almost any cruiser can find room for one on board. Again, a rigid dinghy is permanently ready for use whereas an inflatable has to be pumped up each time you want to use it, and in case you were thinking of towing it inflated, let me warn that it is not always possible.

Thought should be given to what you propose to do with the dinghy when it is ashore. Is there a space at your club where you can leave it, or do you have to take it home each weekend? If you keep your boat in a marina will you have to haul the dinghy on deck (if there is room) or is storage space provided ashore or afloat?

Materials

Plywood is still a very common material for tenders as it is easy to work with and therefore ideally suited to amateur building. It is light and durable but must be protected by a good covering of paint or varnish to prevent delamination. The minimum standard for marine ply is laid down in British Standard 1088. Plywood is best suited to hard chine construction and gains a lot of its strength by panels being curved in two directions. Unless fitted with an expanded polystyrene foam, built-in buoyancy tanks may leak unnoticed, and for this reason it is perhaps better to fit inflatable buoyancy bags held in place by webbing straps. With these any leak is immediately visible. Apart from hard chine construction, plywood may be cold or hot moulded in a round bilged hull form. Bow type for a plywood tender is usually transom, but can also be spoon or stem. Approximate weights would be from 45 lb for an 8-footer to 60 lb for an 11-footer.

Conventional timber dinghies have not lost their worth but are not so common now. They are very strong and robust, able to stand many years of hard use and abuse, but they are difficult to build and expensive. They are built to old, well tried designs making them safe, stable and easy to row, but they are rather heavy and water is absorbed as they work thus increasing the weight. Either air bags or blocks of expanded polystyrene should be used for buoyancy. Construction is usually clinker though occasionally carvel, both giving a round bilged hull. Bows are either stem or transom. Approximate weights would be from 100 lb for an 8-footer to 200 lb for an 11-footer.

Inflatables make very safe tenders: if one compartment is punctured the occupants are still supported by the remaining ones. Light weight makes them easy to bring aboard, and when deflated they will stow away in a cockpit locker, or go in the boot of a car. They are unlikely to damage topsides and can even act as an extra large fender. Little maintenance is needed and they have a long life, but its exact extent seems to vary directly with the price you pay for the boat. In a high wind rowing can be tricky as the rowlocks are often too close to the water and the oarsman has to pull with short, stabbing strokes.

The stern often provides insufficient buoyancy for both man and motor, making an extension arm for the outboard necessary when singlehanded. Larger dinghies overcome this problem by having a wooden transom with the side tubes extending well beyond it. Incompletely inflated dinghies tend to perform rather alarming S-bends in waves, and however hard you try, you invariably end up with wet feet. Inflating is slow and awkward on the deck of a small cruiser, and a CO_2 cylinder is advisable for emergency use. Approximate weights are from 33 lb for an 8-footer to 120 lb for an 11-footer.

Boats built from *glassfibre* suffer surprisingly little damage from being pounded on rocks. Repairs are easy and little maintenance is needed for a long life, but hulls score readily. For strength, the boat is likely to be heavy, though foam sandwich construction (a layer of foam material between two thin skins of grp) is lighter and just as strong. Watertight foam-filled buoyancy tanks can be moulded in. Hull forms for grp boats vary enormously: round bilge, hard chine, clinker, semi-catamaran, tunnel, cathedral, and probably others besides. Bows can be spoon, stem, rounded stem, transom, or square. Approximate weights for grp dinghies would be 100 lb for an 8-footer to 250 lb for an 11-footer.

Collapsible dinghies have never really been a great success, though they do have an advantage over other types in that they will stow flat on a cabin top under a low boom. Light weight makes them easy to bring aboard but they are difficult to row in high winds. The fabric must be checked frequently for cracking and splitting where it creases. As with inflatables, they have to be constructed in an emergency and it is difficult to find any way of fitting buoyancy.

Polyethylene boats are usually formed by either sucking or blowing a sheet of the material into a mould. They are impervious to weathering, but colours may fade with time. It is a light material, needing very little upkeep, but it does score readily. Sandwich construction makes polyethylene boats buoyant in the event of holing or swamping. Usual construction is round bilge, clinker, semi-catamaran or cathedral. Bow shapes are rounded stem or spoon.

Expanded polystyrene is widely used as a buoyancy material in the built-in tanks of many dinghies, but a few boats have actually been *built* of the material, making them as close to unsinkable as it is possible to get. They are very light but damage easily, being averse to knocks and spilt fuel. Damage can be prevented by sheathing the boat in glassfibre or nylon. Production is fairly cheap.

ABS (Acrylonitrile Butadiene Styrene) is a lightweight thermoplastic which is strong and very durable, having a high resistance to abrasion. Buoyancy tanks can be moulded in when the boat is being built, and unlike grp, boats can be produced with an equally smooth surface inside and out without recourse to double skins.

Aluminium alloy is light, strong and durable, but it is absolutely essential to use a marine grade aluminium and to avoid mixing metals, otherwise serious corrosion will take place in the form of electrolytic action. Very little maintenance is needed, and several aluminium boats have lived for years without ever being painted. Foam or air buoyancy should be used and an all round fender is needed to save damaging other boats' topsides.

Carrying Capacity

Like all things to do with boats, tenders are a compromise between the feasible and the desirable. Certain limitations are imposed upon the size of a dinghy; it is pointless having one big enough to carry the whole crew plus gear, cat, dog and carrycot all at once, if it's going to create a massive drag on the boat. On the other hand it is equally pointless having one so small that everyone has to wrap their knees round their ears before the oars can be used.

Ideally you want to have a dinghy that can carry the whole crew at once, so that in an emergency they can all pile into it and stay afloat. However, if you choose a 20-footer into

63

which five berths have been crammed, you are not likely to have a tender big enough to take all five at once, for the simple reason that you couldn't tow it (it would probably be better towing you), and you couldn't carry it on deck. A very rough guide to size would be to have a tender just over one third the length of the parent boat. For example a 20-footer would have a tender of 7ft 6in or 8ft. A 24-footer would have an 8ft or 9ft dinghy, and a 30-footer one of about 10 or 11ft.

Given a rigid dinghy and an inflatable of the same external measurements, their carrying capacities in terms of volume would differ greatly. The rigid dinghy has only very thin hull sides and so has almost the same dimensions inside as it does out, while the inflation tubes of an inflatable are several inches in diameter, thus taking up a lot of the internal area. In terms of weight of gear carried, there need not be a lot of difference, but the inflatable will probably carry more. Point to watch: when an inflatable is heavily laden water will tend to wash over the sides, particularly when turning under power.

Dinghies on Passage

Towing a dinghy is not really the best method of taking a tender with you on a passage – even a short coastal hop. In rough weather it will surge about crossing and recrossing your wake, and if you are unlucky it will ride up and bash against the transom. It has even been known for a dinghy to surf right into the cockpit. Then again it can part its tow

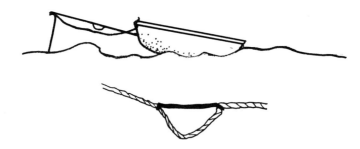

32   *Dinghy being towed on two painters, the primary one having a length of shockcord lashed across a bight (lower diagram). When putting this shockcord in, make the bight just less than the stretched length of the elastic to avoid straining it unduly.*

A strong breeze and the dinghy surfs with all the strain on one painter. In this picture she is apparently quite docile, but on a straight run with anything of a sea she would probably yaw all over the place. Note in passing the way that the horseshoe life-buoy is held by one piece of shockcord – secure but readily available. A floating light is attached to this buoy and is stowed in a funnel lashed to the pushpit.

and disappear into the murk. When the weather is calm and the breeze hardly enough to push the boat along, a dinghy towing astern may mean that the boat *isn't* pushed along. Unfortunately though, for many small boats, the only thing to do with a dinghy at sea is to tow it. There's rarely enough room on the deck of a small boat for such a cumbersome object and it's not a good idea to go without.

Not surprisingly there are various dodges for alleviating the problem. Most obvious is to use two painters, then if one does part the dinghy is still attached to the parent vessel, and they also help to stop her rushing from side to side so much. Keep the tension on the real painter rather than the auxiliary one. The towing point for a dinghy should be low down on the stem or bow transom to lift the bow out of the water slightly. In this way she rides on her after sections, and again her straight running can be helped by fitting a small skeg right at the stern and having runners either side of the keel. Both of these by the way should have holes cut into them so that in the event of a capsize the occupants (or rather ex-occupants) of the dinghy have something to cling to. A length of shockcord lashed across a bight of the painter will absorb much of the snatching, but even so the painter must have a fair lead from the cruiser's quarter cleat and in rough going it is as well to wrap some rags round it to stop any chafing. Oars and any other loose gear in the dinghy must be lashed securely before setting off.

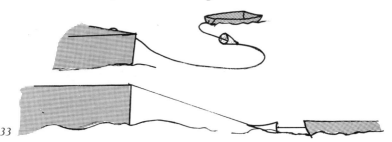

33

If the dinghy does show signs of wanting to join you in the the cockpit then try letting her off on a long painter with another warp trailing over her stern. Alternatively, a funnel can be lashed onto the painter to stop the dinghy running up on the parent vessel (see diagram). A bucket can be trailed over the dinghy's stern when it is bumping alongside at anchor (usually in a wind against tide situation) and you would be surprised the number of people who get underway with it still trailing – until you do!

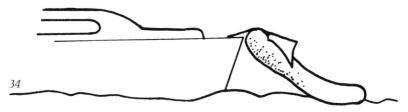

34

Should you decide to tow an inflatable it must be pulled right up so that the bows are out of the water. Many people find the best method is to lash the bows onto the after rail so that only the stern is in the water. The trouble with towing an inflatable is that the wind can get under it and flip it over, at which point it fills with water and is hard to recover.

I realise that all this sounds pretty dismal, but the idea of towing a dinghy is not a good one in general. About the only

66

thing in its favour is the fact that it is already afloat in an emergency, nevertheless the majority of small cruisers are forced either regularly or occasionally to tow their tenders. With a rigid dinghy they just don't have any option.

Wherever possible the best place for a dinghy at sea is on deck. An inflatable can have one end deflated and it can then be lashed down on the cabin top under the boom. In this semi-inflated state it can be launched and it will support the crew's weight until they can completely inflate it. This is

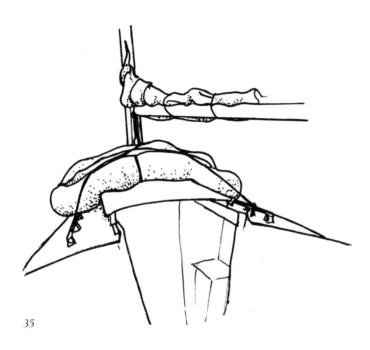

35

the best place too for any other dinghy, but you must make sure that there is still room after you have reefed, during which operation the boom may droop and foul it. The other thing to watch is that the dinghy does not obscure the helmsman's view forward more than can be helped, and he must remember to look round it every so often. Needless to say, I hope, the lashings you put on the dinghy must be very tight and if at all possible should be from a number of eyebolts specifically intended for the job rather than from the grabrails. They must also be quick to untie.

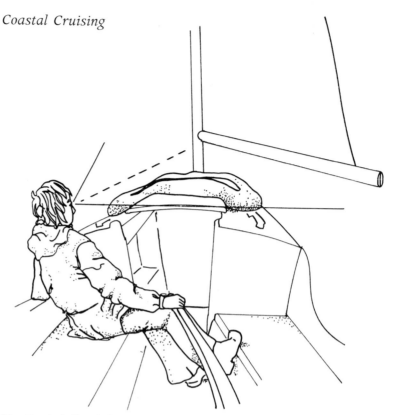

36   *Partly-inflated dinghy lashed down so that the helmsman can still see past it. Even in this situation he must move to leeward occasionally for a proper look.*

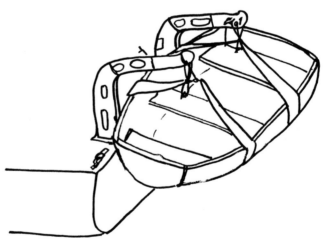

37   *Davits provide a secure stowage for dinghies at sea*

An inflatable can of course be deflated and stowed away in a locker when you go to sea, but make sure that it is not buried under a mass of ropes and fenders. Another alternative to towing is the use of davits. These are like a pair of little cranes usually mounted on the after deck, and which hoist the dinghy out of the water and carry it hanging overboard. Few boats under 30ft have davits, but they are convenient, although they leave the dinghy somewhat vulnerable to attack by marauding seas rushing up from astern or from the quarter. When a dinghy is hoisted in davits it must be hove up really hard against the arms and should also be lashed in tight against the uprights to stop it swinging about and being damaged. In a rough sea a lot of spray will collect in the boat and it is sometimes better to carry her at an angle so that the water can overflow.

Buoyancy

Any dinghy being used as a yacht tender must have sufficient buoyancy to stay afloat and support the crew even when it has been swamped or capsized. This buoyancy may take the form of built-in compartments, air bags, or expanded foam blocks. Built in buoyancy chambers are best filled with an expanded foam plastic to prevent the possibility of an air leak and the chamber filling with water. Air buoyancy bags are arguably better than tanks as any leakage or damage is immediately visible, but care must be taken to ensure that they are fixed in the boat with well-secured webbing straps as the lift given by even a small bag when it is submerged is enormous. In some sailing dinghies with such bags fitted under the foredeck it has been known for the whole deck to lift off after a capsize, but fortunately such cases are rare! Much the same applies to foam blocks, which must be of the closed cell type.

Fendering

An inflatable dinghy is really a big fender, so there is not much to worry about with them, but with a solid dinghy it is necessary to fit a substantial all round fender to prevent damage to other boats' topsides. Traditionally this fender is

69

a tightly stretched length of coir (grass) rope and is still one of the best ideas. More modern materials take the form of a D-section plastic pipe screwed onto the gunwale, but this is a fairly hard material and can still give a nasty knock to paintwork. A length of old canvas fire hose packed with foam rubber, though bulky, works admirably. The hose may be available from a local fire station.

Painters

I said in the section about dinghies on passage that the painter should be lead from a ring placed as low down on the bow as is practicable. It should also be long and strong. I would suggest that a polypropylene 'rough' finish rope is good and that it should be about 8mm diameter and approximately three fathoms in length. This gives you plenty of scope for mooring the dinghy under most circumstances and allows for a fair amount of chafe before it needs replacing. A second painter is always a good idea and it is wise to carry a coil of warp and a small anchor in the dinghy just in case.

Sculling

Sculling over the stern with one oar is a very pleasant means of propelling a dinghy. But it's a knack. It comes from the wrist and is best practised with a second oar in the boat and with no one looking on. The diagrams should make the method clear, but you will have to practise against the day you lose one oar and need to know how.

Dinghies and Outboards

Where your mooring is a long way from your dinghy launching point it is undeniably pleasant not to have to row but to be able to start up an outboard and chug along under power. For a dinghy of about 8ft a 1½ hp motor is adequate and will push you along in most conditions. If you choose a larger motor make sure that it does not exceed the horsepower for which the transom was constructed. To reduce the damage to the transom, wooden pads can be fitted inside and out to

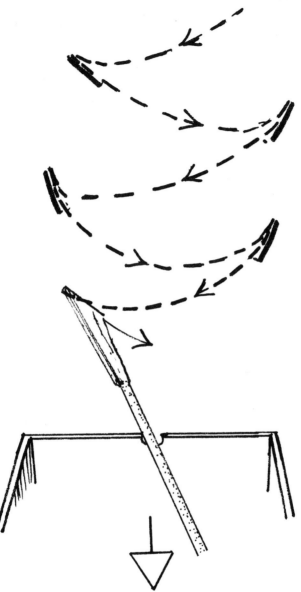

38   Start with the oar blade lying flat on the water, then twist it slightly
and move the loom so that the blade cuts into the water. At the limit of its
swing a quick twist with the wrist turns the blade so that it cuts into the
water as the loom is pushed back the other way. Thus the blade moves in a
series of arcs and is turned sharply at the end of each sweep so that it will
cut into the water on the new arc. Hold the loom from underneath as though
you were going to throw a spear.

71

take the clamps. They need not be very thick but should be replaceable.

Be careful when handling a laden dinghy not to turn too sharply or water will lap in over the gunwales. You will find when alone in the dinghy that you have to move up forward to trim her properly as the outboard tends to push the stern down into the water. To make this easier you can sometimes get an extension tiller that fits on the motor's existing control arm. Finally, never stand up to steer; if you fell overboard there would be nothing between you and the propeller.

39 *Sit well forward when in an outboard-powered inflatable, especially when turning, or water will come aboard over the quarter as in the lower left diagram.*

Rowing Positions

When only one person is in the dinghy a rowing position from the centre thwart is fine, but as soon as you get a second person on board and want to carry dunnage as well, the boat goes out of trim. The best place to carry gear is in the middle where the boat's beam is at a maximum. To make this possible it is worth fitting a second rowing position up by the forward thwart so that one person can row from there, the gear can be stacked in the centre and another person can sit in the stern. Rowing from forward is not quite so easy, as you will probably have to cross your hands on each stroke, but you will soon get used to it.

Life-rafts

In bigger cruising boats it is common practice to carry an inflatable life-raft on deck. This is an excellent idea but alas not a cheap one. The main points to remember are that it must be in a readily accessible place and that the bitter end of the painter or 'trigger rope' should be made fast to a strong point at all times. The life-raft should carry water, flares, food, a torch, a knife and a small first aid kit. When you are undertaking a longer than normal passage it is possible to hire a life-raft and is worth the expense. Whether you choose one

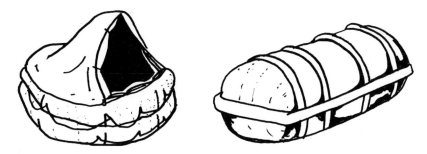

40   Left: *inflated life-raft; right: stowed in a glassfibre case. Ensure that the 'rip cord' is attached to a strong point and keep a knife handy should you need to cut the raft clear once it is launched and inflated.*

of the rafts packed in a bag (valise) or in a glassfibre case is entirely a matter of personal preference, but whichever you choose the raft must be capable of taking the whole crew.

Sailing Tenders

We discussed a little earlier the question of outboards for dinghies. The alternative is to have a tender that can be sailed. The rig will be modest and simple, almost certainly just a standing lugsail, consequently you cannot expect a great

A very simple sailing tender with loose-footed lugsail, leeboard and steering oar. The leeboard has a line from its top to the centre thwart of the dinghy and, when tacking, it is simply lifted across and dropped over the new leeward gunwale, the water pressure being all that is needed to hold it in place.

windward performance, but it is very pleasant to be able to reach a quiet anchorage and then potter round in the dinghy under sail. If you go to visit another boat you always feel slightly superior if you come alongside under sail. Also it is cleaner, cheaper and quieter than having an outboard, but there, I'm prejudiced.

Servicing Inflatables

Both inflatables and life-rafts must be serviced regularly, particularly life-rafts, for which it is only common sense to have a current service certificate. Check with the manufacturer how frequently it should be done and make sure to get them sent off straight away at the end of the season. Many people don't bother to service inflatables and wonder why they eventually drop apart. Don't follow suit.

Have a Care

Don't overload a dinghy – better to make more than one trip than to swim and lose all your gear.

Life-jackets should be worn at all times; they take up very little room in a car and may save your life when there is no one about to help you if you get into difficulties.

Oars and rowlocks should be tied to the dinghy, as their loss can be very troublesome, and at least inconvenient.

Take a look at the painter occasionally to see if it has chafed. If you are underway when chafe is noticed near the parent vessel (usually at a sharp-edged fairlead), and you cannot attend to it immediately, haul some of the rope inboard, otherwise the dinghy will be lost should the line eventually break.

Make sure the painter has been made fast before you step out of the dinghy.

When stepping into a dinghy step into the centre and sit down straight away. Transfer your weight *slowly and smoothly* to or from a dinghy.

Have a couple of propeller sheer pins ready for the outboard, they could save you a long row.

CHAPTER 7

Weekending

Inevitably people living in the confines of a small family cruiser have many more opportunities for getting on one another's nerves than they normally do at home. Tolerance is one thing you can't buy in a shop: you've got to take enough with you to last the whole weekend. As a parent you have a difficult job, you have to command instant obedience from your children to keep them out of danger in an emergency, yet you must not shout at them every five minutes to get out of the way or pull on that rope, or else they won't recognise when some situation is a real emergency. Parents must not try to be joint skippers either. A small boat is very much a dictatorship, but it must be a considerate one tempered by love, thoughtfulness and a good insurance policy, otherwise the 'Mate' will pretty soon tell the Skipper what he can do with his little yacht. Children of course suffer from their normal problems of keeping their parents under control with the additional factor that Dad for once really does know best – at least he most certainly should, and even if he doesn't, he has got to make everyone believe that he does.

Catering

As my cooking has never progressed much beyond Katharine Whitehorn's *Cooking in a Bedsitter,* I would not presume to lay down rules for Mrs Chef, but for those women used to a big, modern kitchen, the galley on even the larger family cruiser may come as a shock. Certainly for smaller boats where the cooker is a simple two-burner affair I would strongly recommend doing as much preparation of food at home as possible. Things like stews can be made up and cooked at home then placed in Tupperware sealed containers so that

Peaceful sailing on a quiet weekend sets you up for a new week in the office.

they need only be heated up on the boat. Jellies with plenty of fruit in them can be taken straight from a fridge (in a Tupperware container) to the boat and if eaten the same evening will still be set.

Should you be thinking of making a longish passage over the weekend it is advisable to take quantities of chocolate, boiled sweets and sandwiches; all stuff that can be dipped into for a snack without any need for going below to prepare it. This really is the crux of the matter, to keep work in a small galley to an absolute minimum with the possible exception of the Saturday night nosh up. For this meal you can really go ape, or as much as the two burners will allow, since you are likely to be at anchor. A wonderful piece of cooking equipment on a boat is a pressure cooker; it can be filled and put on the stove while you clear up and sort out the boat, then when you have finished you have a hot meal ready. Soup of course is always an excellent drink. If you make up a Thermos flask of it before getting underway you can just pour it out when you want it, and it's both warming and nourishing.

Galley Slave

I don't know if I should address this section to Mums and tell them not to let themselves become galley slaves, or to Dads and tell them not to let their wives spend their whole time cooking. All right, some women are perfectly content to do nothing except cook, but it is not really a good thing. A wife should be competent to handle the boat in case of emergency, and in any case it is to be hoped that she can find other pleasures in sailing besides turning out three-course meals going to windward in a Force 6.

Husbands should make every effort to take some of the burden on themselves. A cold lunch doesn't take great culinary skill, but it is one less chore for Mum if someone else does it. Whoever cooks the evening meal should not have to wash it up, even if she does at home. The 'slaving over a hot stove' cliché is rather apt on a boat where you may well have to hold a saucepan in place with one hand, hang on with the other and stir the pot with your teeth. Even if you think you've done your bit with bringing the boat safely to anchor and feel you want to put your feet up and relax after a hard week at the office, remember that someone else has probably had just as hard a week tidying up after the kids and making sure there is a hot meal ready for you when you come home. So be fair and give her a break too.

Point to remember: boiling liquids can scald. Don't work wearing just a swimming costume, always cover up, even if it's with a suit of oilskins.

Dunnage

Dunnage is the seaman's name for his luggage, and like anyone else he has to bring it aboard in something. Most of us were raised in the belief that you should never take a suitcase on a boat, but should pack everything in a soft bag that can be stowed away in a locker. Because this is such a widely accepted idea I would advise you to go along with it on other people's boats, but on your own you can do what you like and that may well be to use a suitcase. Although a case cannot be stowed easily in a locker, it is in effect a locker itself, a portable one. During the day it can be stowed in a quarter berth and during the night at anchor it can stand on the cabin sole. You can sit on them, kick them about and they'll still keep their contents intact. If you insist on taking tidy clothes with you then they usually stay tidier longer in a suitcase than they do in a hanging locker where they will probably spend much of their time rubbing shoulders with salty or even muddy oilskins.

Each person should aim to bring the minimum he or she needs in the way of gear. This may consist of an extra jersey and a change of clothes in case you get wet, but people manage to add a fantastic amount on top of that. It really depends what you keep permanently on board. For instance there is no reason why you should have to cart washing and shaving gear on board each time you go, or even a make-up bag, as these can quite well be kept on the boat for the season.

One of the most useful things you can have is a ditty bag into which you drop loose change, car keys, house keys, wallet, etc and know they won't get lost. A small pouch with a Velcro fastened flap to close it is adequate for the purpose.

A Place for Everything

Hackneyed as it may sound it really is necessary to decide on a place for everything and then to keep it there, otherwise you will get in a real mess. It is no good at all if you have to rout round in a locker by torchlight trying to find a shackle spanner or the baby's clean nappies. Where a locker is not perfectly easy to see into it is as well to tape a list of the contents on the door. This, by the way, is not a bad job to get the children to do one day when you're at anchor waiting for the tide. It's not a difficult task for them, but they will be making a real contribution to the running of the boat.

In very small cruisers it is useful to make up some netting which can be fastened either to the deckhead or hull sides to act as extra stowage for charts or clothing. Flares can be strapped to the bulkhead with shockcord, binoculars can be stowed in a specially made box also fastened to a bulkhead within reach of the cockpit.

Clothes that are to be stowed in lockers are best wrapped in big polythene bags of the type sold in launderettes. A packet of silica gel stops them getting damp and mildewed. In fact it is difficult to have too many plastic bags and containers on a boat, but *don't ever throw them overboard*, for they do not decay and can foul propellers.

The Loo

A few years ago virtually all small cruisers had a simple bucket in a wooden box arrangement, but this meant appearing on deck accompanied by the bucket under the combined stares of the rest of the anchorage. It needed a stout heart. Nowadays all but the very smallest boats have a toilet installed which avoids much of the embarrassment, but even if it is in a separate compartment it is still very much a central character. For this reason it must be generally polished, powdered and pampered with as much care as a prize poodle.

If it is not in an enclosed compartment the cabin will have to be evacuated when it is to be used – not very popular in the middle of the night. From the outside it can be amusing to note the bursts of song and the soft shoe shufflings going on 'in there' during lulls in round-the-lamp conversation. Getting used to having such a normally private place right in the midst of the living quarters is a part of the process of learning to live together on a small boat. The one thing not easily forgiven is a blockage in the loo. In fact I was once lent a boat on the sole condition that we didn't block it up.

Where to Go

When deciding where to go for a weekend or for that matter a week, a fortnight or any length of time, you have various factors to take into consideration.

1 First and foremost is the capabilities of the crew. Should you have very young children on board you can only hope to make passages of a few hours duration. It's not much fun for them being told to sit still, even with the dubious promise of being allowed to 'help' with steering or sail trimming. A picnic on a beach somewhere probably holds far more attraction for them, and why not? This is supposed to be an enjoyable sport for all the family.

Carrycot sized babies are in some ways less of a problem as they can be wedged securely where no one is going to tread on them and then left asleep for a bit. At least, that is the theory. If you must make a long passage with children aboard, then it is often better to do it at night in the hope that they will stay asleep. With the aid of an anti-seasickness pill (which often causes drowsiness anyway) this is quite likely. In fact many children trot off to their bunks without being told when the wind pipes up and the sea gets a bit rough. An excellent thing for everyone.

Apart from the children, it is likely that there will only be two of you aboard and you must recognise your limitations and plan a weekend cruise accordingly. If the weather is rough you are obviously going to make a shorter passage than you might otherwise do, and you will not choose to go to windward, which leads onto the next point.

2 Whatever sort of cruising you do a careful watch must be kept on the weather and on weather forecasts, particularly the Shipping Forecasts. I will say more about all this in Chapter 16, but for now let me say that if you are planning to head, say, Northeast and the forecast is for a rising Nor' easterly, then you are probably going to have to go somewhere else. This adapting of plans according to prevailing conditions is an integral part of seamanship and certainly not something

to be looked down on. After all, you are cruising, not competing in a race round a set course.

3 Last but certainly not least comes a consideration of tides. If you keep your boat on a drying mooring then before you do any planning of where to go, you must consult a set of local tide tables and see when you will be able to get away. In a small cruiser there is very little to be gained by trying to make progress against a foul tide, particularly against a foul tide and head wind. It's a fact that you discover very quickly if you try it. Always aim to carry the tide under you, and be prepared to change your plans if need be.

Back Home – On Time

One other calculation comes into the question of where to go, and that is the time at which you have to be back. As with time of departure, time of return to a mooring may be restricted by tide and you must be sure that you can get back when there is still sufficient water. Few of us can say 'To hell with it. I'll skip work on Monday and go in on Tuesday'.

In order to catch the right tide home it may well be necessary to get up at some apparently ridiculous hour, but once up and doing you'll usually feel a sense of satisfaction. Boats today are being fitted with much more powerful and more reliable engines than has previously been the case and with their aid returning to base on time is not so much of a problem as it used to be. If there is a flat calm you can motor at least most of the way, and if the wind fills in from dead ahead you can always help yourself along by motor sailing.

Keeping the Log

Apart from its primary function of providing the navigator with all the information about courses, wind, speed and so forth that he needs to keep track of the ship's position, the logbook also acts like a diary. It forms a day-to-day record of where you have been and what you have done, making fascinating fireside reading on cold winter nights when the summer seems so far away. Even when you are not really navigating, only ticking off marks as they pass, it is still worthwhile keeping up the log. If you do so and the weather suddenly closes in, you have at least some idea of where you have been and a chance of working out your position.

Yacht Clubs – Use and Abuse

Many yacht clubs have showers and a drying room for the use of their members and they are usually generous enough to allow visiting members of other recognised clubs to use them. The normal practice is either to make a visiting yachtsman a temporary member of the club, if he is to be staying some time, or else to charge him a nominal sum for the use of the facilities. If this is the case then it is assumed that after he has signed the visitor's book he and his crew will contribute to the club's funds by having a drink or two in the bar. Which, I am sure you will agree, is not a very onerous task, and yet the number of people who abuse the host club's courtesy is quite staggering. You don't like finding a bath or shower covered in dirt and scum, so why leave it like that? Likewise if you go into the bar it is not very hard to have a drink and be sociable with whoever else is there without getting drunk and singing bawdy songs, yet people do. Really all that is called for is politeness, commonsense and a little gratitude. One day you may return the courtesy and then you'll expect your visitors to behave, won't you?

Adding Up Weekends

We saw earlier that there are a lot of factors limiting how far you can take a small boat in a weekend having in mind the need to return to base on Sunday night. However, if you want to go further afield but can still only spare weekends to do it in, don't worry, you can. Instead of going out on Saturday and back on Sunday, all you do is to go out on both days leaving your boat at the port you fetch up in. This means putting the boat in someone's charge, and if it is a marina it may be expensive, then returning home by public transport. If you have three or four in the crew, travelling further and further each weekend, it can be a bit costly, but it does get you away into new waters. In fact should you want to cruise some new area during your summer holiday, this adding up of weekends can win you extra time in the chosen cruising grounds since it is only the return passage which is actually taken out of your holiday time.

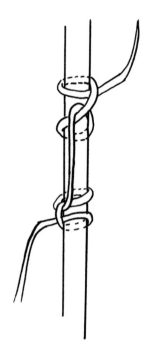

41   A burgee halyard should be attached to the stick with clove hitches spaced as far apart as possible. This holds the stick vertical allowing the burgee to fly clear of the masthead. Etiquette dictates that you hoist your club burgee as soon as possible after boarding your boat, and that you never allow the halyard to slacken and the stick to loll.

CHAPTER 8

Seamanship

Seamanship is the practical art of working and handling a boat. Good seamanship is something to be proud of. It's not just sailing the boat from port to port without mishap, it's knowing your boat and how she will behave in every situation, and applying that knowledge to advantage. We can never hope to be complete seamen, we are forever learning, but we can go a long way towards it, and part of that journey is accomplished by watching another man and recognising his seamanship.

Sail Handling

Making and handing sail involves working around the foot of the mast and on a small cruiser at sea this is not a safe place to be. The safest way to work on the foredeck is to sit down, though many people opt for kneeling instead. Try to stand up as little as possible, and when you have to, for instance to swig on a halyard, then first hang on and second put one foot behind you just in case something slips or carries away and you find yourself going backwards. The bitter ends of all halyards should be made fast either by passing the end through a hole in its cleat and tying a figure of eight, or better by making them fast to swivel eyes specially located round the mast step.

Doing up or undoing shackle pins can be the very devil of a job when the boat's movement is at all lively or your hands are cold, and it's as well to avoid their use on sheets and halyards as much as possible. Snapshackles with piston action pins are far better although it is not completely unknown for them to come undone. Alternative clips to use are Inglefield clips (see illustration), but these should not be used on sheets

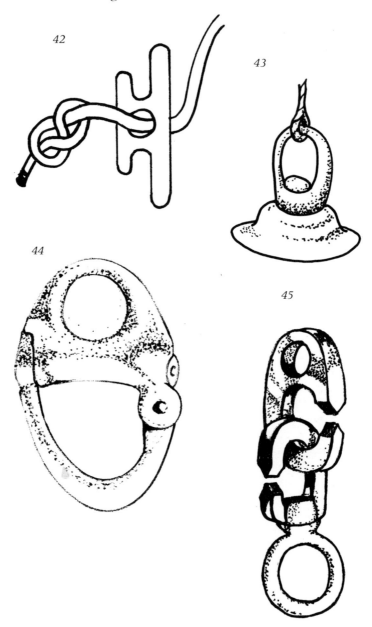

42, 43, 44, 45   *Halyard falls secured (upper left) by a figure of eight and (upper right) by seizing to a deck swivel. Above: a snap shackle, and right: a pair of Inglefield clips.*

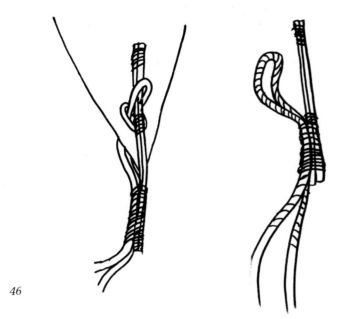

46

as it is possible for them to shake apart, but they are fine under load, for instance on halyards. My own favourite method of attaching sheets to the clew of a headsail is the one shown in diagram 46, where a bight of the sheet is passed through the clew cringle and a doubled length of rope seized to the sheet is passed through that. It won't come undone and if it clouts you round the head it does far less damage than any metal shackles or clips.

Lightweight Terylene blows and billows around alarmingly and the only easy way to handle it is when it is in the bag, so as soon as you take a sail out, smother it, and when dropping a headsail lash it down with shock cord or a tier quickly. Never get to leeward of a sail that is being set or handed as it can push you overboard and the flogging thimbles, hanks and shackles can cause serious injury. Look out too for standing on a lowered sail as the cloth slides readily across decking.

When you go to hoist a foresail, clip on the tack first and then run your hand up the luff clipping on each hank as you come to it until you reach the head. After you have attached the halyard (checking it is not twisted round the forestay), go back to the tack and run your hand along the foot till you come to the clew and attach the sheets. All this is intended to avoid any twists in the sail, and if it is always carried out, it will. Always watch the sail when hoisting to avoid snags. Come time to take the headsail off, drop it, lash it down and as soon as you unshackle the halyard, clip it onto either the guardrail or a rope becket attached to the deck for this purpose.

The question of when to reef looms larger in many people's minds than it really needs to. What you must remember is that she is *your* boat, they are *your* sails, mast and rigging, and the crew is *your* responsibility. Always reef early, and never be afraid of looking stupid with three rolls in the main when everyone else is bending on genoas. You may have heard the forecast that they missed and anyway your boat is not their boat.

Small cruisers are generally rather tubby and the only way they can hope to get to windward reasonably well is by being sailed upright. If they are pressed over on one ear they present a massive area of hull to the wind and lose all drive from their sails. For this reason it pays to tuck in a reef as soon as she starts to be hard pressed. She will sail better and you will be more comfortable.

If you have to reef at sea, don't try to do it with the boat still crashing along, slow her right down and preferably heave to. Then you can take your time to tuck in a neat reef so that the sail still sets nicely. If you have the chance of reefing before putting to sea so much the better, and remember that it is much easier to shake a reef out than it is to take one in. Generally it is better to reef the mainsail before changing the headsail for a smaller one as this often lessens the increasing weather helm, and with a masthead rig, it keeps the driving sail area large.

Leaving Moorings

Just to add a little extra spice to the sailing life, wind and tide always manage to combine in a new way each time you come to or leave your moorings, and for that reason it is impossible to be dogmatic about how it should be done. The situation must be weighed up afresh on every occasion with due allowance being made for the prevailing conditions.

To reef or not to reef? At the start of a potentially rough passage this crew has made the wise decision to take a good reef in the main and to set a small jib while still in sheltered waters. That is good seamanship.

Before you make any hasty moves to cast off, sit back for a minute and take a look at what the wind and tide are doing and how the boat is lying in relation to them and to other boats in the anchorage. With the wind and tide there are three basic situations: wind with tide, wind against tide, and wind across tide. Conspiring against you in conjunction with the wind and tide are the four possible types of mooring: a deepwater swinging mooring (the easiest of the lot), fore and aft buoy moorings, fore and aft pile moorings, and marina berths. Please don't get frightened yet; a degree of seamanship is required to clear a berth of any kind, but there is seldom any very great problem in a small boat.

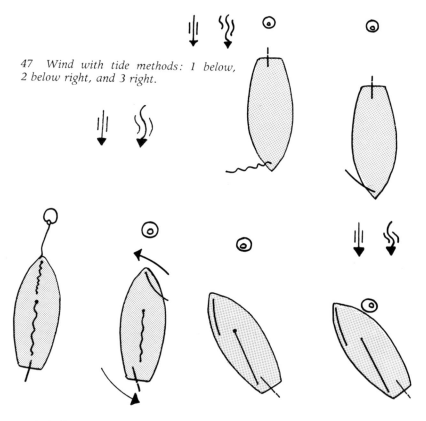

47 *Wind with tide methods: 1 below, 2 below right, and 3 right.*

Wind with tide: swinging mooring. This is the easiest situation of all. First decide whether you want to beat up against wind and tide after you have fallen clear of the buoy or whether you want to run off downstream. Assuming the former, choose the tack that gives you a slant clear of other craft, then hoist sail with the sheets eased right off. When all is ready the buoy can either be chucked over straight away, if there is clear water astern of you, and the jib backed to cast her head round onto the desired tack, or the buoy can be walked a short way aft allowing the tide to turn her head onto the right tack. If you want to run off downtide your best bet is to walk the buoy aft so that the boat turns on the buoy rather than making a rather large and sweeping turn close to other craft.

Wind against tide: swinging mooring. Not quite so easy this one. The boat will probably lie across the tide at some angle determined by her hull and keel shape. In most cases the best bet will be to hoist a jib, cast off and get clear of the mooring by running downwind into open water, then round up and hoist the main before returning to a run or beating back upstream.

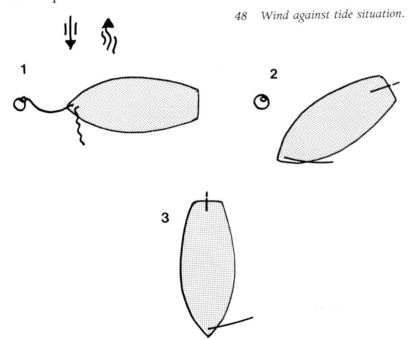

48   *Wind against tide situation.*

Wind across tide: swinging mooring. Here again the boat will more than likely lie at an angle to both wind and tide, but you will probably be able to hoist both main and jib without the boat careering about fouling the mooring. If you

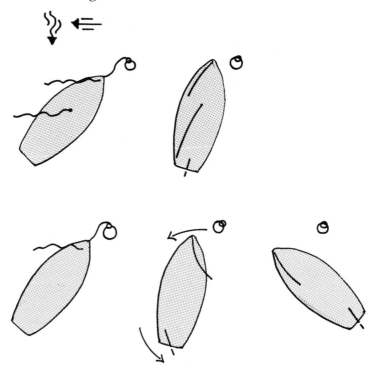

49   Top: *a boat getting away simply under main and jib; lower: showing the more complicated alternative.*

can set both sails then you can proceed as though the wind were blowing with the tide, but if you can only get the jib up then you are in for a wind against tide manoeuvre.

Wind with tide: buoys fore and aft. In this situation the boat will be lying with all the strain on one mooring. If this is the bow mooring then all you need to do is bring the stern mooring forward outside everything and tie it to the bow one and treat the whole thing as you would for a swinging mooring, casting the pair off together. Where the strain is on the stern mooring, you can either make the bow one fast aft and run off under jib alone until you reach clear water and can round up to set the main, or you can turn the boat end for end. To do this one person takes the bow buoy aft outside everything while the other person leads the stern buoy forward. When she has settled down you can take the slack mooring rope forward and cast the boat's head off on either tack with all sail set.

92

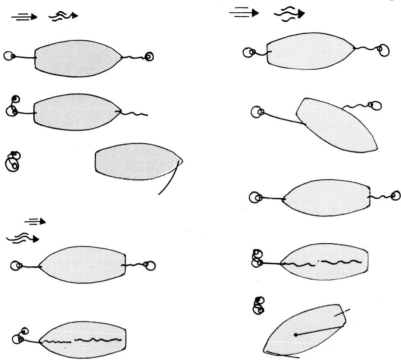

50 *Wind with tide: buoys fore and aft. Lower left: bows to wind and tide; upper left: stern to both, method one; right: stern to both, method two.*

Wind against tide: buoys fore and aft. Again what you do depends on which way the boat is lying and whether the wind or tide is the stronger influence. Assuming that wind and tide are about equal you can usually bring the buoys together at either bow or stern and move off as you would from a swinging mooring. If they do not balance you are usually better off turning the boat's head into the stronger one.

Wind across tide: buoys fore and aft. First make sure that the boat is downwind of the mooring warps else she will foul them when you cast off. The best bet here is usually to bring the buoys together either at bow or stern depending on which way you want to leave the moorings. But do be careful not to sail over the ropes or you will get them wrapped round the keels or rudder. Always bring buoys together on the windward side and if you give up sailing and motor out, get clear before engaging gear.

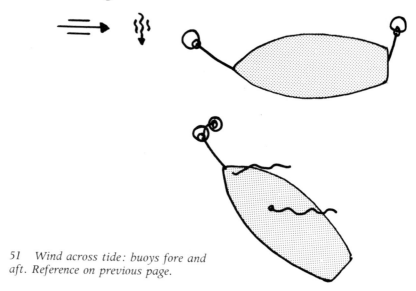

51   *Wind across tide: buoys fore and aft. Reference on previous page.*

If you are moored fore and aft to pile moorings you do not have to worry about bringing the moorings together, you can moor the boat to one pile or wind her (turn her end for end) just as you please. There may however be another boat moored alongside, in which case you are virtually in the same position as being in a marina berth alongside a pontoon. Certainly with a marina berth, and unless the wind is blowing you off the boat alongside, I would suggest leaving such a mooring under power, turning the boat or moving her out using warps, springs and fenders.

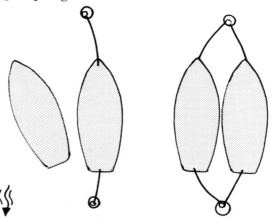

52   *Clearing an alongside berth using the current.*

Unfortunately this all sounds very complicated. In fact it need not be a difficult manoeuvre leaving your moorings, but you must think out a plan with the crew before you make any move. Take things slowly. If you want to and have room, just drop the moorings and drift clear before making sail, but once sailing remember that a boat will turn more tightly (and slow up in the process) if you luff her up. If you are running into trouble and try to bear away you will speed up, swing round in a wide turn and probably end up in a far worse situation.

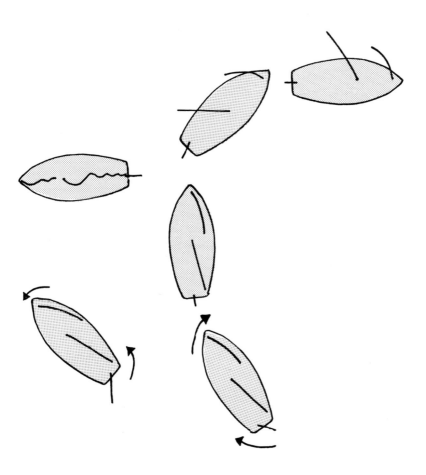

53 On the left the boat luffs up and stops, on the right she bears away, gybes and continues in a wide sweep, often speeding up.

95

Picking Up a Mooring

The boat approaches her mooring into the tide under jib alone and as she nears the buoy her helmsman lets fly the sheet and allows the sail to flap. The boat loses way and is virtually stopped when the pick-up is made – in this case with a Grabbit boat hook from the cockpit.

It is scant comfort when it happens to you for the umpteenth time, but everyone misses their moorings sometimes, even people with years of experience. What the experienced man does though is to recognise the fact that he is not going to make it and go round for a second attempt while the boat still has way to manoeuvre. The whole aim with picking up a mooring is to bring the boat up to the buoy with as little way on as possible – ideally with none at all. Of course you can only hope to do this by practising and learning how much way your boat carries under various wind and sea conditions. Here is a chance to use a bunch of empty washing up liquid containers moored with a half-brick in clear water. Approach them from all angles, upwind, downwind, across the tide, with it and against it, trying always to stop the boat as close to the buoy as you can. Don't say 'blow this for a lark' and start up the engine; a sailing cruiser is designed to be sailed, and unless you are entering or leaving a tight marina berth or laying alongside, you will usually do better under sail keeping the engine as a last resort. However, if the moorings are crowded and you feel more in control under power, then don't be afraid to motor. You would be displaying discretion and therefore good seamanship.

As with all mooring problems, the easiest to deal with is the deepwater swinging mooring, but in fact when it comes to picking up a mooring as opposed to laying her alongside either a wall or another boat, they all have to be treated in virtually the same way.

Wind with tide. This is once more the easiest situation. Approach from downwind and either tack up to the buoy, luffing at the last moment to bring it under the bows, or perhaps better if space allows, reach across to it. This way you can start the sheets and take way off the boat early, but still be able to harden in and keep steerage way, or even sail clear of the buoy and go round for a second attempt. As you approach, line up the buoy with a mark on the shore beyond; if it stays in line you will hit the buoy all right, but if it moves you will miss and you must change your course accordingly.

These pictures show only one case of picking up a mooring, but they show how it can be done without fuss or great exertion if the whole process is thought out in advance. Forward thinking is a big ingredient of the brew called seamanship.

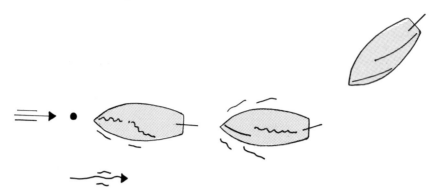

54 *Ideally, when shooting up to a mooring, the boat should come to it with no way on. Reach across tide at a controlled speed (see previous page), then luff to the buoy.*

Wind against tide. Unless either wind or tide is very much stronger than the other you have only one option in this case. Get up wind of the buoy and drop the mainsail before running down under headsail only. As you approach the buoy take some of the way off by starting the jib sheets and letting the sail flog; you can always harden in if the boat falls short. If you have fore and aft moorings and have left the buoys tied together, you must take care not to let the boat swing over the slack line.

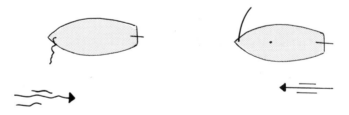

55 *Wind against tide: run downwind for the buoy under a headsail only.*

Wind across tide. Approach from down tide controlling the boat's way by hauling in or slackening off the sheets. If you like you can drop the jib and approach under main only, giving yourself a clear foredeck, but this depends on how the boat handles without a jib. With fore and aft moorings try to pick them up to windward so that the boat does not foul them as she swings round.

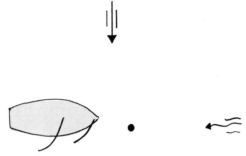

56, 57 *Wind across tide: approaches under full sail (above) and mainsail only.*

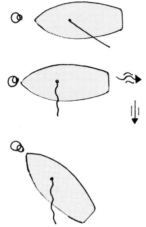

The ideal, as I said before, is to bring the boat to a dead stop at the buoy, but this happens rarely so aim to overshoot very slightly. By doing so you maintain steerage way and if the buoy is missed you can cast the boat's head off on a safe tack. It does however mean that the foredeck hand must take a quick turn as soon as he gets the buoy on deck. In many ways it is better to have an experienced person on the foredeck making the pickup and the less experienced hand on the helm rather than the other way round, as the experienced one can then call out helm orders and can judge whether or not the 'shoot' is going to come off.

With a small cruiser where the freeboard forward is quite low it is usually possible to do without a boat hook and just lean over and pick up the buoy by hand. Heretical as it may sound I strongly favour this procedure because it means that if the boat is making so much way that you can't hold on, all you have to do is drop the buoy whereas with a boat hook you are fiddling round trying to unhook it and will perhaps lose it. Also you can bring the buoy on deck and take a turn without having to hold on with one hand while you grope round behind your back trying to find a place to put the boat hook down and know it won't roll overboard.

If you don't like the above method or if you are short-handed, an excellent device to use is the Star Grabbit boat hook (see illustration). A line is run from the hook to the samson post, so that when the buoy is hooked the pole is pulled out, the spring snaps shut across the hook and you are made fast to the buoy and can get the sails off at leisure. A refinement of this technique is particularly useful for single-handing. Run the line from the hook through a snatch block at the bows thence aft outside all to the cockpit. The buoy is then picked up from the helm and hauled forward to the bows, which allows you to bring the boat right up to it without a mad dash from tiller to foredeck.

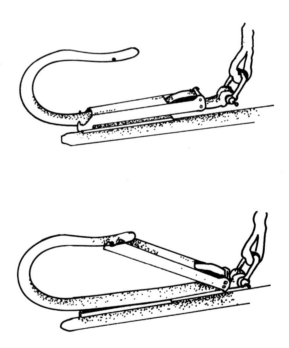

58   Top: *Grabbit boat hook correctly loaded into the slide with the hook open;* lower: *wrongly loaded with the hook closed. The latter might work, but it is not recommended.*

100

Anchoring

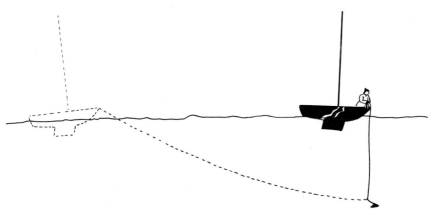

59 *By anchoring and veering a scope of chain equal to three times the depth at HW, our example boat settles back a distance of five boat lengths.*

The problem with coming to an anchor is dropping it in the right place so that your vessel lies snug on the right scope of chain but clear of any other anchored boats. If your proposed anchorage is fairly full when you arrive it's not a bad idea to sail through it taking a look round before deciding where to lie. Note how other craft are lying and try to work out where their anchors are so that you don't drop yours nearby. Also as you pass through check the depth so that you can work out how much cable you will need. The minimum recommended is three times the depth of water at high water for all chain cables, and five times the depth for warp and chain.

Try to approach your anchoring point in the same direction as other boats are lying, which is normally with their bows into the tide, though if the wind is stronger then they may be wind rode. To do this the alternatives are really the same as for picking up a swinging mooring. Aim to let go when the boat has come to a standstill and is just beginning to gather way astern, then you can snub the anchor in to make sure it bites and lay the chain out clear of it.

Choosing the exact spot to let go is largely a matter of experience and a deal of trial and error, but a useful guide is to let go at a distance ahead of where you want to lie equal to three times depth at HW measured in boat lengths plus one boat length. For example if the depth of water at High Water is 4 fathoms, you will need to lay out 12 fathoms of chain, and if the boat is 18ft or 3 fathoms, you should drop anchor 3 × 4/3 + 1 = 5 boat lengths ahead of where you want to lie.

Where there is a foul bottom you may decide to bend a tripping line onto the crown of the anchor in the hope that if it fouls some obstruction you will still be able to retrieve it. For this purpose a line equal in length to *at least* the depth at HW should be bent onto the crown with a float at the other end. When you drop anchor you also have to throw over the line and buoy, making sure they go clear of the chain.

Once you have settled to your anchor and if the anchorage is at all bouncy it helps to make for a quiet night if you run a heavy weight part way down the cable (on the end of a line) to absorb some of the snatch in it. Multihulls will also ride more quietly if a bridle is run from the cable to each bow so that the strain is spread out and to stop her sheering around. Any boat will lie more comfortably if she is given more than the minimum scope.

Come time to weigh anchor you are faced with two main situations, one where there is plenty of room to leeward or down tide of you, and the other where there is not. If there is plenty of room you don't need to worry too much, you can get sail on, preferably mainsail only to leave the foredeck clear, haul up short, break out, and as you gather sternway, reverse the helm to bring her head round then correct it

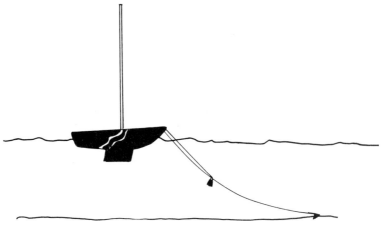

60   A weight slid down the anchor cable.

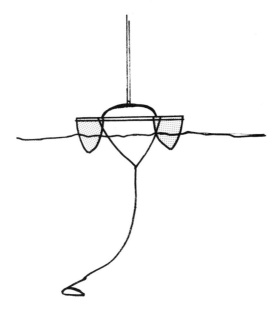

61   A multihull riding to a bridled cable to reduce sheering about.

when the sail fills and sail away. On the other hand if the next boat astern is a bit close you must either haul up short and just as the anchor breaks out cast her head off on one tack, or else run up a jib and when the anchor breaks out back it, reverse the helm and spin round tight to run out of the anchorage. The trouble is that you can't guarantee success with either of these manoeuvres, but you can pat yourself on the back when they come off. I suppose if you don't fancy trying it to begin with you can always start up the motor – and in fact with a really crowded anchorage it might not be a bad idea to have it running in neutral even when sailing out.

Occasionally an anchor digs in too hard to be broken out by hand and you have to sail it out. To do this, get sail on and begin to sail closehauled. When you reach the limit of the cable tack smartly and haul in slack cable. This board should take you either over or close to the anchor, and as you pass the chain must be snubbed so that the anchor is broken out by the boat's way. *But mind your fingers when snubbing.* Once the anchor is free the helmsman must slow the boat down to avoid damage to the bottom or topsides by dragging the anchor and cable over them. An anchor can also of course be broken out under power by motoring straight up to it, gathering chain on the way, and snubbing as you pass over the anchor.

62   *The pattern for sailing out an anchor.*

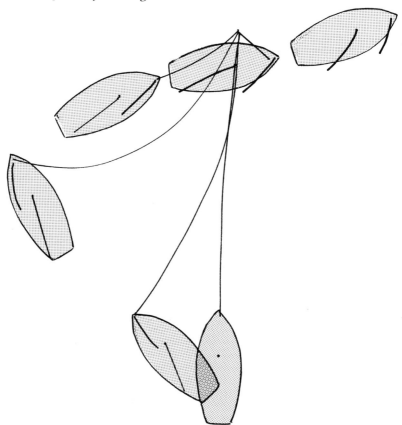

Berthing Alongside

The two primary rules here are to come alongside *slowly* and to get a stern line ashore *quickly*. The commonest occasion for berthing alongside is on entering a marina, and here you have no choice as to which way you approach the berth

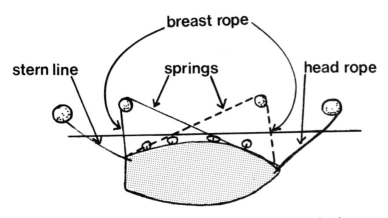

63 Top: *names of the various warps that can be used when mooring alongside; lower: when mooring alongside pilings or a staging it is a good idea to lay a plank between them and the fenders to prevent the fenders sliding in between the piles (as they inevitably will) and the topsides getting chafed.*

and very little room for error since there will either be a glossy stern or a hard pontoon looming up close ahead. Obviously in such a situation it would be foolish to try to sail into the berth; much better either to motor in dead slow or even to warp the boat in.

Before trying to berth you must take a careful look at what the tide is doing – carrying you into the berth, holding you out or what? Then with due allowance made for it, head into the berth at an angle with a man on the foredeck ready to take a *stern* line ashore as soon as possible. This line should be lead from a quarter cleat outside all to the bow and the bow man should be urged to avoid falling in by jumping too soon, but to take a turn on a mooring bollard immediately he does get ashore. Even the smallest boat is a heavy object to stop and if he simply leans back and takes the strain there'll be a sudden splash.

With a stern line checking her way you can help with the engine in astern gear, not only to take way off but also to straighten the boat in her berth. Once alongside you can make up with bow line and springs as necessary. A spring incidentally is a line led from one quarter to a mooring point by the bows, or from the bow to a mooring point by the stern. They stop the boat surging about, hold her close and parallel to the pontoon or quay, and can be used to turn the boat end for end.

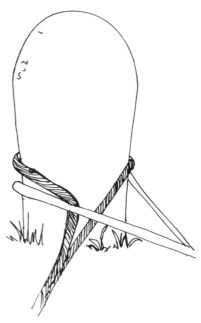

64 *When securing a mooring line to a bollard, always dip the loop under any others already there. By doing this everyone can free his own lines without disturbing the others.*

When the time comes to leave an alongside berth another study must be made of the tidal current to see how best to make it help you. If it is directly off the pontoon you're in luck as you can more or less cast off and drift out, but it more usually runs along the berth in one direction or the other. The wind must be assessed in the same way. If it is in any part off the berth then it's all to the good, but if it is holding you in you may have (in an extreme case) to lay out an anchor to haul off to.

Let me hasten to say that there is rarely much difficulty in leaving an alongside berth, particularly a marina berth. In this case there are plenty of other craft around and plenty of places warps can be led to haul off on.

Where the tide or current is running along the berth, much

use can be made of it to sheer your bows out and let you sail off. If for instance the current is from ahead, and the wind is roughly the same way, you can cast off the bow line, stern line and forward spring so that the boat can pivot on the after spring. The current will push her head out at an angle to the berth and then sail can be set and a neat exit made. Have a fender ready on the quarter though, to avoid damage as it swings in.

Running, Reaching and Beating

To my mind running wing and wing dead before the wind is not a happy way of sailing. One moment's missed concentration by the helmsman, or the slightest wind shift, and the boat is running by the lee in imminent danger of a gybe. Nor is it a very fast point of sailing as the apparent wind speed is greatly reduced. No, I would say that it was much better to luff up a little and sail on a very broad reach. By doing this you make the helmsman's job far easier and may increase the boat's speed.

Where your destination lies directly down wind, haul the wind slightly and then every so often gybe round and bring it onto the other quarter. In this way you progress downwind in a series of gybes along a zigzag course, the whole process being called, logically, tacking down wind. As I said, a very broad reach is faster than a dead run, and this increase in speed combined with the reduced strain on the helmsman more than makes up for the slight increase in distance actually sailed.

After you have spent some time slogging to windward in a short head sea, or rolling downwind it is quite remarkable the feeling of peace and steadiness gained when you come round onto a reach. Suddenly everything is quiet and the boat runs smoothly along, a compass course can be set, with some hope of its being kept, and all is well with the world.

Reaching is probably the point of sailing on which a boat will do her best, or can do her best, but careful sheet trimming is needed to get her going well. Bone idle people like myself tend to adjust the sheets to a position where the boat is driving along reasonably well, and then sit back to enjoy the view, while others – mostly with a bent towards racing – will leap wildly round the deck muttering that the halyard's set up too hard or the jib's too flat. A half-way position is really what you want. Tend the sheets but don't let playing with them become a fetish.

Working up to windward in a small, possibly tubby, family cruiser is, alas, a slow business. The distance sailed through the water is far greater than that made good over the ground in the right direction, and the physical discomfort of punching into a head sea can be most unpleasant. The wind always seems much stronger when you're beating into it than when running before it. Be that as it may though, we spend a lot of time beating and we always come back for more, so it is worth looking at some of the techniques involved.

Not surprisingly the first thing to do is concentrate. The direction of the wind is changing constantly, as are the boat's heading and the relative direction of approaching seas. All these forces have to be kept weighed and balanced, and the boat must be kept driving. This is the big point, the kind of boat we are talking about must never be pinched or she will stop dead and you'll probably lose hard won ground in trying to get her sailing again. A family cruiser suffers badly when going to windward from her light displacement and large area of tophamper. A puff of wind heels her over, she presents a larger area of topside to the wind and is blown off to leeward, while at the same time she is probably griping up into the wind and meeting a wave right on the nose.

The aim must be to keep her sailing the whole time even if it means sailing her full and by rather than right up hard on the wind. Don't haul the sheets in so far that all the belly is taken out of the sails – this may be alright with specially cut racing sails, but it certainly won't work on these boats. When she is sailing nicely, watch the luff of the jib and always keep it just asleep. As soon as it starts to lift, and before it can start to flutter, bear away a shade until it goes to sleep again. Do this the whole time and keep an eye on approaching waves as well.

Even a seemingly small wave can stop a little cruiser dead in the water and she will simply hobby horse up and down in the same hole until the helmsman can get her to bear away and pick up speed again. The art is to anticipate a wave and make sure she has plenty of way on when she meets it, even if this means bearing away beforehand. The ground lost to leeward in so doing will be offset by constant progress to windward.

108

There is rarely any point in trying to insist that the helmsman steers a particular course to windward. Give him a course to act as a guide by all means, but after that let him steer the best course he can and keep a note of what it is.

When sailing with your family as crew remember that they probably aren't muscle-bound gorillas and that even a fairly small headsail can take a lot of sheeting in, winches or no winches. Consequently it is sensible to have a 'team tacking' system, where one of the crew lets fly the lee sheet as you put the helm down and then takes the tiller to settle the boat on her new heading while you harden in the opposite sheet. Once you have done it you can return to the helm. Don't try to spin the boat round on a sixpence and have everyone leaping about tripping over their own feet, rather sail her round slowly without panic. With heavier boats you can forereach dead into the wind for some distance in smooth water to eat a little extra to windward, but many small boats are too light for this and will end up in stays.

Boats with small cockpits and large crews benefit enormously if the tiller is made so that it can be lifted to a vertical position while tacking and then dropped back again afterwards. Not all boats by any means have this arrangement and it is something that can be done in the winter, but it is worth converting a fixed tiller into a lifting one.

Man Overboard

There are three main problems to be dealt with here. The first goes right back to basics: how to stop a man going overboard. The second is to find a person in the water, possibly on a dark night, and the third is how to pick that person up. It may seem trite to mutter about prevention being better than cure and to say that no one should go overboard in the first place, but it *is* infinitely better to take all possible precautions against its happening.

When working on the foredeck of a small cruiser it is always advisable to sit or kneel. The helmsman should be attached to the boat at night with a harness and anyone going forward in rough weather should wear a life-harness and *clip it on*. It may not actually stop you falling into the water, but you are still attached to the boat and if she is kept moving you will surf alongside and can usually pull yourself back

109

Bouncy weather and the helmswoman on the left wears a life-harness, as should anyone going on deck in such conditions. The twisted neckstrap may be uncomfortable but will not weaken the harness. The important point is to wear it fairly tightly, with the point of attachment for the life-line well up on the chest.

One of the things that prevents many people wearing a life-harness is the time taken to put it on – sorting out and adjusting straps, untangling the line. This Haward waistcoat harness goes a long way to relieve the problem as there are no straps to adjust (apart from the chest one which only needs to be done once), it is hard to tangle and quick to put on. So people are encouraged to wear it. The other thing I like is the carbine hook halfway along the line which allows either a long or short line to be used – always make sure to hook on to the strong point with the end hook.

aboard with very little effort. Avoid standing (or kneeling) on wet Terylene sails, they are extraordinarily slippery. Be very careful if you have to walk along narrow sidedecks. And so on, the list is almost without end, but assuming that someone does go overboard, what then?

The immediate problem is to find the person and get a buoyancy aid to them, whether it is a life-buoy, a life-jacket or a floating cushion. You must have a *practised* plan both for finding and recovering a person from the water: different boats different ways. The old rule of chucking a life-buoy, gybing round and making a quick lunge with the boat hook just does not work. The gybing part is all right as it is the beginning of a plan, but there is no point in throwing a life-buoy from 50 yards away so that the person overboard has to

Here a man wearing a harness has gone overboard from a boat moving at between 4 and 5 knots and he tows alongside quite safely and comfortably. Under normal conditions it should be possible for him to climb back aboard, as shown in the right-hand picture, if sufficient way is kept on the boat to allow him to float without swimming. When a life-jacket is worn, as in this case, care must be taken to ensure that it and the harness do not interfere with each other.

tire themselves swimming for it. Much better is to turn the boat round quickly, sail back on any point of sailing and drop a buoyancy aid close to them as you pass. *Then* you can think about picking them up, once you know that there will be something to pick up. One thing about life-buoys: the choice is between a ring and a horseshoe shape – I would suggest the use of a ring because, although the horseshoe is easier to get into, it is also rather easy to slip out of.

In rough weather when a head is virtually invisible in the waves, or at night when you can't see much anyway, finding a person in the water is a tricky job. Never flash a torch about at night – it destroys all night vision. If you see a person go overboard and there are several people on the boat, give one of them the sole task of watching the man in the water. When

111

As soon as the man overboard can be located, the boat is sailed close past and a life-buoy is thrown to him. Once that has been done, the remaining crew can set about picking him up.

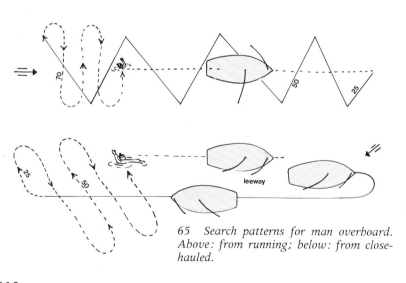

65 Search patterns for man overboard. Above: from running; below: from close-hauled.

on your own or when no one can see the person in the water, you must follow a search pattern strictly. By following a pattern you stand a far better chance of finding the person than you ever will by blundering around wherever instinct misleads you.

If a man goes overboard on a dead run and you sail on before noticing he has gone, you will have to beat back towards him on timed tacks. Gybe round and haul your wind then count say 25, tack and count 50 before tacking again. That will mean you cross your original track and go out on the other side. Count 50 on each tack until you feel sure that you have beaten up past the place where the man went overboard. If you have not sighted him then bear away onto a broad reach for a short way, gybe round and sail back to a count of say 70 before gybing and repeating. By this means (assuming that you had beaten up past him) you will almost certainly find the man in the water.

When a boat is on a close fetch she will make some leeway, and this leeway combined with the downwind component of a gybe will put the boat to leeward of a man in the water. It is always a good thing to *know* that you are down or up wind of him. OK, so you are on a close fetch, man goes overboard and you notice he has gone. Gybe the boat round and run back on a broad reach. As I said, you are unlikely to run back along your outward track, so you may not sight the man. When you are sure you have gone past, bring the boat up onto a broad reach and count 25. By the way, all these numbers I have given must be altered according to what speed your boat is making and how fast you count, but they act as a guide. Tack round this time and count 50 before tacking again. This broad reaching pattern should ensure finding the man.

After a man goes over the side with the boat on a broad

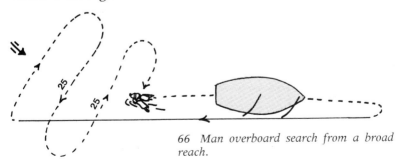

66 *Man overboard search from a broad reach.*

113

67 *A strop to step in·may aid recovery.*

reach you will have to gybe round and sail back as close to the wind as you can. By doing this you will again be sure of being down to leeward of the man. When you are sure you have sailed past him and haven't seen him, tack round onto a broad reach and count, say, 25 before tacking again. Reach and tack, reach and tack. This process should again bring you up with the swimming man.

I have not mentioned motoring back to find someone because of the extreme danger of injuring him with the propeller. Of course there may be times when you decide to motor, but do *cut the engine* well away from the swimmer and drift up to him. Putting the engine in neutral is not sufficient safeguard – some propellers still rotate slowly.

All right then, you've found the man overboard, now you have to get him on board again. Perhaps the most difficult situation is when a light wife is trying to get a heavy and exhausted husband out of the water. In contradiction to all the rule books I would suggest that it is much easier to pick someone up to leeward than to windward. Although the boat is drifting down on them, even the slightest angle of heel reduces the freeboard and makes the rescuer's job easier.

First of all get a line attached to both the man in the water and the boat. Second, drop all the sails and lash the helm hard a-lee. Now you can start to land your fish. If he is still in a state whereby he can help himself, then a bight of rope to put his foot in or a boarding ladder or a set of steps up the transom, anything will help him. If he is slightly less capable an excellent idea is to launch an inflatable dinghy – assuming of course that you carry one – with one end inflated but not the other. With this attached to the boat you can pay out the line to the man and he can half float half push himself into the dinghy. He can then rest there until he has the strength to climb aboard the cruiser.

Failing that, if there are two or more people aboard, even a mother and child, they can take the mainsail out of its mast track and drop the bunt of it into the water for the man to climb into. He pushes the sail under himself with his feet and lies flat in it, then the people on board haul on the halyard and roll him up the topsides. This is pretty cruel on the sail, but it does work.

The real point about all this is that it *must* be practised by the whole crew. Shooting up to a mooring is some practice, but it is not enough. Everyone must be able to work the boat back to a person in the water *and stop her there*. They must also have some idea of how to help bring the person on board again.

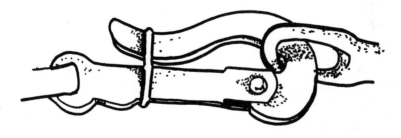

68   A Pelican hook is often used to secure the ends of guardrails to the pulpit or pushpit. They can be released fairly quickly by sliding the ring over the nose of the hook, but it is arguable that lanyards are better, as these can be cut in a trice if you need to get the guardrails out of the way when helping someone back on board.

Three ways to recover a man gone overboard. If an inflatable dinghy is available and the man can help himself, then he can best get back aboard by working his way into the part-inflated dinghy and taking a short rest there in safety before being helped on board the parent boat. Alternative methods

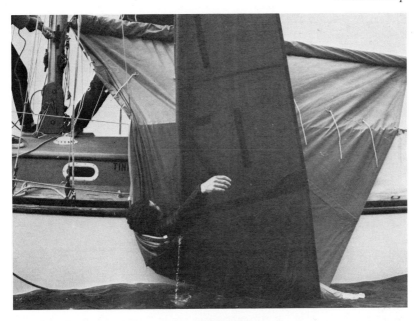

of recovery are not so kind to the boat's gear, particularly the one shown here with the man being hoisted out of the water in the bunt of the mainsail. It is not so easy to keep a tired man in a strop placed around his chest, as he has to keep his arms forced down by his sides. Whatever method you opt for, it will be easier if it has been practised before.

117

Running Aground

This is almost a hobby in itself for some people. They seem to hop gleefully from mud bank to mud bank. There can't be anyone who has done much sailing and not run aground, but don't be a glutton for it. In a quiet backwater where the bottom is soft mud the boat won't come to much harm, but if you ground on an offshore sand bank with a rising wind you could be in trouble. There are times though when running aground intentionally can be a perfectly reasonable way of getting out of trouble. Say for instance that you are running into an anchorage and just as you go to drop the main you find the halyard has jammed and you have the option of careering into a moored boat or running aground, I know which I would choose. There is certainly no surer way of slowing the boat down.

Trying to get off in the direction you went on is a fairly straightforward plan, but if the bottom shelves gradually and the tide is ebbing you will have to work quickly. If you went aground with a following wind get sail off immediately to stop her driving even further on, then either try to motor off astern or pole her off with oars taken from the dinghy, or lay out a kedge into deep water and haul off on that. Boats with a single keel can have their draught reduced by getting the whole crew to one side and if necessary leaning overboard holding onto a shroud to heel her over. A bilge keel boat is a pretty hopeless case unless you fancy jumping overboard and shoving her off with your shoulder under the stem.

Despite the presence on board of an echo-sounder it is quite common to run aground when beating up a narrow channel, in which case you can often back the jib to turn her head then let draw and distribute the crew's weight to lift the heel out of the mud. On the windward shore with a rising tide all you really have to do is sit back and wait, because as the tide rises you will simply blow off and you can then continue on your way. Be careful how much you rely on the echo-sounder; remember that it will tell you when you *are* aground, but won't give much warning of when you are *going* to go aground. Centreboarders of course are cheats when it comes to running aground as they can very often just hoik up the plate and sail off. Convenient but not really 'cricket'.

Kedging

A kedge anchor can be used in two main ways, one as an anchor to lie to, either by itself or more usually in conjunction with the bower anchor, and the other as a fixed point to haul off to, either from a berth or a mudbank. Ideally the kedge should be of sufficient size to act as a bower anchor but be of a different type. In practice though most people carry a smaller anchor as their kedge, which means that conditions must be light before you can lie safely to it with no other anchor down. On the other hand it does mean that it can be taken off in the dinghy and laid out easily in the event of say a grounding.

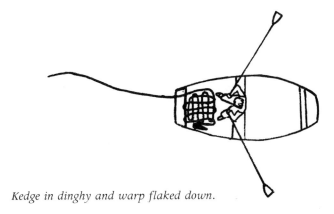

69   *Kedge in dinghy and warp flaked down.*

When you lay out a kedge using the dinghy, always carry the anchor and its warp in the dinghy. Make fast one end to the bitts then put the anchor in the dinghy and flake the warp down in the stern. Don't try to coil it as it will then inevitably snarl up as you row off. Alternatively, if you want to take the bower anchor with its chain, make a bowline round the crown of the bower the same length in the bight as the depth of water, then row out with this line flaked down in the dinghy. Anchor the dinghy and haul out the bower with its chain. This you will find is infinitely easier than taking the bower and chain in the dinghy.

If you use a warp on the kedge you must have about 3 fathoms of chain between the anchor and the warp to keep the angle of pull low and to ensure that the anchor stays well dug in.

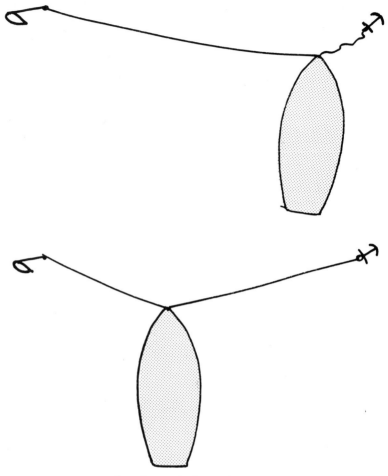

70 *Laying out a second anchor at the limit of a double scope on the first (top) and then centring on the pair.*

Lying to two anchors is often a safeguard in a rough anchorage, provided you can be sure no one will foul you. Drop the main anchor to one side of where you want to lie and paying out twice as much chain as is required to lie to, sail or motor away at right angles to your desired berth until you reach the limit of the chain. Then drop the kedge and pay out its warp as you haul in half the length of the chain. This now is your berth, centred between the two anchors. Secure the kedge warp to the main anchor cable with a tight rolling hitch and lower it down below the keel so that when the tide turns the boat can swing clear of it.

Occasionally you want to keep the boat lying in the middle of a creek (or some other gap) and to do this you can use an anchor from the bow and another from the stern. As you run into the berth let go the kedge from the stern and run on, paying out twice as much cable as is needed having regard to the depth of water. Bring up hard on this anchor to make it bite deeply and then let go the bower anchor. Pay out cable and haul in on the kedge until you are moored in the middle of the two anchors. Come time to get underway, buoy and let go the kedge warp, haul up to the bower anchor and get that, then sail round and pick up the kedge. Alternatively, reverse the anchoring process by paying out on one cable and recovering the other anchor, then hauling up to and breaking out the first.

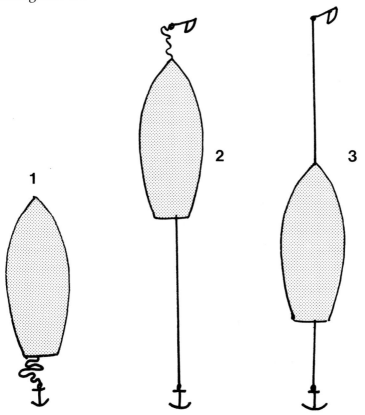

71   *A running moor. Drop anchor (kedge) 1, run on and snub it in as you drop the bower anchor 2, then centre 3.*

Manners for Mariners

Anchorages are crowded places these days and marinas are a commonplace, so that boats are mooring overnight in close proximity with others. This means that consideration must be shown towards others not only in the way we moor (that is to say without fouling or lying too close to another boat) but also in what we do and how we behave.

DON'T

> Play transistor radios loudly whether listening to pop music, the Proms or the Shipping Forecast.
> Chuck litter overboard, especially plastic materials.
> Let men relieve themselves over the side in daylight.
> Shout and swear, even when getting the anchor up.
> Run generators in the middle of the night or let exhaust fumes blow across neighbouring boats.
> Hold noisy parties late at night when children may be trying to sleep.

DO

> Be friendly, pass the time of day with other people and if you make friends with other crews invite them aboard for a drink or for coffee.
> Stop halyards slapping on metal masts. Few noises are more irritating.
> Pass on (accurately) the latest weather forecast if asked for it.
> Lend a hand if one is needed.
> Think.

Competent Wives

Aboard many small family cruisers the husband does the majority of the actual sailing while his wife cooks, looks after the children and occasionally takes the helm when instructed to 'head for that buoy'. But what happens if the husband hurts himself, or worse if he falls overboard? Fair enough there are certain jobs aboard, like hauling up a recalcitrant anchor, with which a man is better able to cope by virtue of his greater physique. But I think it is incredibly foolish not to make sure that the woman aboard is competent at least in the basic handling of the boat in case of loss or damage to her husband.

Wives should certainly be capable of making and taking in sail, of reaching, running, beating, *heaving to,* starting the motor and operating its controls, rounding up to a buoy and, on smaller boats, of dropping anchor. I emphasise heaving to not only because it is a manoeuvre that many husbands neglect to teach themselves, but one that can be very useful in all sorts of situations where you want to stop the boat. When practising any manoeuvre, be it mooring or man overboard drill, try to ensure that your wife can carry it out at least competently – and don't be disheartened if she is better at it than you.

I am not trying to preach about marital relationships, but judging by the number of cross words I have heard flying between foredeck and helm, I would warn you not to get angry, or else the lady will go off in a huff and refuse to try any more boat handling. And one day she *could* be called upon to save your life. Think before you shout.

Rules of the Road

More correctly these are the 'International Regulations For Preventing Collisions At Sea', which are drawn up by an international committee. These rules must be learnt and understood by all who go to sea. The complete regulations are far too long to reproduce here, but they can be found for example in *Reed's Nautical Almanac*. The rules govern navigation lights, and sound and light signals besides telling you what to do when two vessels meet.

Points to remember: if you have to alter course do so *positively* and in *good time*. Also something that many people forget – as soon as you start your engine, *even if you are motor sailing,* you become a *power driven vessel* and are then governed by the rules for such vessels. Never dice with big ships, and if in doubt get out.

CHAPTER 9

Pilotage

Without the proper chart table and working space found on larger craft, the navigator of a small family cruiser spends much of his time doing what is called 'coastal pilotage' rather than more formal navigation. He learns to look at a chart and see it as a three dimensional shoreline, and to look at the land and visualise it as a flat chart. What he is really doing is nautical map reading. Far be it from me though to suggest that it is unnecessary to learn the more formal navigation methods. On the contrary, to cruise safely and successfully a sound knowledge of coastal navigation principles is essential. But it is as well to realise that while you can keep up an accurate plot in fine and settled weather, as soon as a bit of a sea gets up, or the weather closes in, in fact just when you most need a good plot, you are likely to have your hands full coping with the boat, and all you will be able to do is sail by eye.

Reading the Chart

A chart is not just a pretty picture to look at, it is a mine of information about both the sea and the adjacent coastline. All you have to do is learn to read it. Building up a picture in your mind from a chart is a bit like 'painting by numbers', the chart is the numbered canvas, and the land and sea the finished painting. Just as an Ordnance Survey map uses contour lines to show heights and gradients of land, so a chart uses contour lines on the land parts and sounding lines on the sea. The closer the contour lines the steeper the land, or the more quickly the seabed is shelving. From this information alone you can start to visualise the coastline: whether it consists of cliffs and steep hills with deep water close in, or low, undulating land with shallows extending well offshore.

Of course some parts of the coast are easier to navigate by eye than others. Where you have a rocky coastline with well defined bays, headlands and hills, even perhaps an offlying island, it is fairly easy, but if the coastline is low with undulating features, and shallow water to keep you well offshore, it is not so easy. Features such as there are must be kept under close surveillance and good use must be made of buoys, beacons and depth readings.

On particularly hilly coasts the direction of sunlight can be tricky as it may for instance throw into prominence a hill that is perhaps some way inland, and tone down a hill closer to the shore. Then again it can get behind a hill and shroud an otherwise prominent landmark in shadow. Sunlight on a low-lying coast can make it difficult to see where the land becomes sea, and a river mouth can be all but invisible until quite close in. Here in fact, the cruising man becomes a buoy-hopper, ticking off each one as he passes it, but he must steer an accurate course between them and must be sure to *identify* all marks. The danger is to assume that a buoy or mark is the one you are looking for without any positive recognition. That way you can come badly unstuck.

Transits

Many of the more difficult creeks and harbours are provided with what we call leading marks to guide boats in. These marks usually take the form of two shore beacons, which are lit at night, one being kept directly in line with the other. That is to say they are kept 'in transit'. Such transits are common and of great value, but the coastal topography in any area provides many natural transits. For example a head-land may line up with a particular off-lying rock, or a church with a hilltop or clump of trees.

The beauty of transits is that they give an incontrovertible position line. There is no possibility of compass error or misreading or anything else, and if you can find two transits that form at the same time (come 'on' at the same time), then you have an absolute fix of your position. This of course is seldom possible, but when it does happen it is a great source of comfort. One thing to be taken into account in areas of great tidal range is that at low water (or thereabouts) a buoy

A good, easily identifiable landfall, but what is the distance off? Remember that the charted height of a lighthouse is actually the vertical distance between High Water mark and the centre of the lantern.

may well be out of position, blown off station at the limit of its riding chain, or carried down tide. This will not make a great deal of difference to its position, but it could be enough to throw a transit slightly out.

When you are planning a passage look out for possible transits on the chart and make a note of them to use as one more check on your boat's position. You may not need them in the event, but if you are stuck at the helm for some reason and only have such a list at hand, then at least you have something, you are not completely reliant upon 'guess and God'.

Distance Off by Eye

Judging distances at sea can be extraordinarily difficult and is something that comes only with practice, but there are one or two tricks that help and hardly require any instruments. The real criterion for judging distance off is what you *cannot* see rather than what you *can* see. For instance you can get a far better idea of how far off the coast you are by the fact that you cannot yet see the windows of a house than by the fact that you can see them though they are 'not too clear'.

The following table gives a rough idea of distance by observation rather than measurement.

Distance	Details Visible
100 yards	Face of person on shore is seen as pale shape with dark lines for eyebrows, and possibly line of mouth can be seen. Guard-rails and rigging visible.
200 yards (Approx 1 cable)	Face now just a pale blur, tide seen to ripple round buoys, staging piles quite clear.
400 yards	Person now generally blurred, but leg movements visible. Just about see rigging.
500 yards	Person seen as dark splodge, cross-bars on house windows just detectable, uprights plain to see.
1 mile	Large buoy shapes clear, small ones shape-less, windows recognisable, traffic clear, people just dots if seen.

Buoys give a very useful indication of the direction and strength of tidal streams, though they are not always as strong as this one.

2 miles	Small buoys usually lost, large ones little shape, windows seen as dots, traffic visible, ship's sidelights first seen at night.
3 miles	Bow waves of ships seen from cockpit and waves breaking on shore.
4 miles	Hedges, individual trees, houses and wet roads, but little detail. Beach dipped below horizon and colours tending to assume uniform bluish grey.

You can also get quite a good idea of distance off with a couple of very basic instruments, namely a pencil and a clear plastic ruler. Hold the pencil at arm's length and line the tip up on some object viewed through the right eye. Close the right eye and open the left. The pencil will jump to the right. Note this distance and using it as a unit, measure off four such units to left of dead in front of you and four to the right: the distance so covered is your distance off. In fact the number of units needed seems to vary from person to person between 7 and 9, but this can be found by experimentation. The shoreline should also be as straight as possible, but it does at least tell you if you are 'far or near'.

Taking the ruler, attach a piece of string to it and make a knot at exactly 60 centimetres from it. Holding the knot against your nose and the ruler at full stretch, measure the apparent height of a prominent object of known height (say a lighthouse). The height of the object in feet divided by the apparent height in millimetres equals your distance off in cables (1 cable approx 200 yards). For example a 60ft tower apparent height 30 mm is 2 cables distant.

These are rough and ready methods but they are better than nothing and with practice they can become quite accurate.

72 *Distance off by holding a ruler 60 cm from your nose and measuring the apparent height h.*

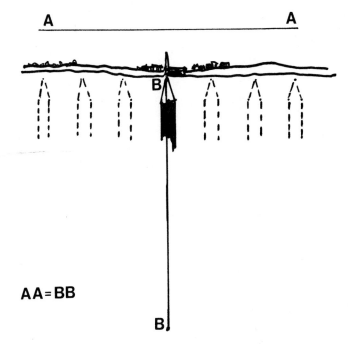

73 *Distance off by the 'jumping pencil' method.*

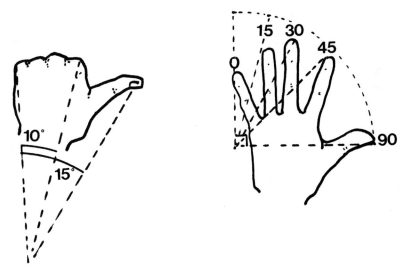

74 *Natural angles created by hand and fingers are useful to the coastal pilot.*

129

Signs in the Sea

Sailing by eye is rather like a detective game in which clues are scattered liberally about the place, but are mostly in code. To make matters more interesting, the code can be wildly misinterpreted if you don't have a pretty accurate idea of your whereabouts. The sea herself is full of such clues, and a study of them is both fascinating and invaluable. If you don't know quite where you are, then every wave and ripple seems to indicate a shoal or submerged rock, but if you are sure of your position they may take on a completely different and happier meaning.

Wave form depends a great deal on the depth of water and the nature of the bottom they are passing over. There is a very distinct change in wave form when ocean swells cross the continental shelf for instance. There is also a great deal of difference between waves in a deepwater channel and those over a shallow patch. The detective work is in deciding just what the water is telling you.

In shallow, muddy water where the water is perpetually discoloured it may appear to be just the same in 'texture' where the depth is a few fathoms as it does over a patch just a couple of feet deep. However, in rocky waters the colour changes from a dark blue in deep water to a pale green over shallows, with the odd rock marked by an almost black shadow.

The sea offers an indication of two things: deepwater channels and underwater obstructions. When the wind is against the tide, a nasty choppy sea can build up, and this will be greater in a deepwater channel than it will over the shallows. This is because the tide flows faster down the main channel and offers more resistance to the wind: like a cat it doesn't like being stroked the wrong way. On a very calm day when the sea is glassy, then the main channel is likely to be marked by slight rippling, again because the water there is moving faster than it does over the shallows. However, if the wind is with the tide (in the same direction as the tide) the channel will be smooth and the shallows will be rippled, since the stream in the channel is fast enough to reduce its resistance to the wind.

A bar at the entrance to a port is usually marked by some disturbance of the water, and with an onshore wind there are often breakers. These signs tell the navigator quite clearly that there *is* a bar, but they can be deceptive about its precise location. With an onshore wind the seas will in fact pass over the bar and break a short distance inshore of it, so that from seaward you see the backs of breakers *beyond* the bar. A point to remember: the same thing can happen with overfalls and tide rips where a rock or sharp rise in the seabed causes the tidal current to shoot up to the surface at some distance from the obstruction. Never sail too close to such disturbances unless the exact depth of water there is known.

In areas of deep water and very fast tides you find 'tidal races'. When there is anything of a sea running these tidal races are best avoided, for a passage through them can indeed be frightening. On a calm day the sea seems to boil with huge smooths or slicks forming on the surface. I know that I have on many occasions found myself sailing into such areas and had to take a close look at the chart and echo sounder to reassure myself that there really was deep water there.

Just occasionally you come across a line of foam and debris on the water where two tidal currents meet, each bringing its own flotsam. Again these can be a disturbing sight if you don't recognise them for what they are.

Dirty Weather

However carefully we listen to and take note of weather forecasts, there comes a time when we get caught out with a rising wind or fast reducing visibility, and at such times we have to make a snap decision as to whether or not we are safe to make port. Even a moderate wind against say a spring tide can kick up a nasty sea for a small boat, and a heavy rain squall or a light sea mist can blot out the land, any of which may be a local phenomenon that couldn't be expected from the overall forecast.

I have tried to stress the importance of keeping a constant check on your position and progress along the coast, for it is when the weather turns dirty that you really need to know where you are. If you have been checking off buoys and landmarks and can say with some confidence 'the river mouth bears about nor'east from here and is distant about two miles', then you are in a strong position to decide your next move.

The questions you have to answer are threefold: is the

Even on quite a calm day the tide running across the entrance to this harbour makes entry a tricky operation. Think what it would be like in a real blow.

weather going to worsen, are you safe to make a dash to the nearest refuge, or should you stay at sea and ride it out? The idea of 'staying at sea and riding it out' may be highly romantic and may in the end make a good clubhouse yarn, but with your wife and children aboard it can be an extremely harrowing experience – and yet it could be the safest course to take. If you have a safe anchorage close at hand with an easy approach and you think you have time to get in before the weather worsens, then you will probably decide to put in, even if it means scrabbling down a deep reef and motorsailing. If on the other hand there is a rocky, harbourless shore under your lee and you are not dead sure of your position, then you may have no choice but to claw your way to windward, get a good offing and stay there. We will look more closely at handling a small boat in heavy weather later.

You may find of course that as you approach your chosen port you are bucking a foul tide and making no progress. Here again a knowledge of your position can save you. It could be that the tide will turn fair in an hour or so, in which case you decide to plug on, or again it may be against you

132

for ages, and you'll look to another anchorage for refuge. But it all depends on this knowledge of the boat's position, which is what pilotage is all about; a probably unplotted, but *known* position.

How Deep the Water

One of the most useful aids to inshore pilotage is an accurate measurement of the depth of water under the boat's keel. This is not simply to confirm that you are either afloat or aground, but to help you pinpoint your position. For example, if you are running in towards an as yet unsighted harbour, you may be able to fix your position with some accuracy by finding the depth of water. Say you look at the chart and find that at $1\frac{1}{2}$ miles off there is a four fathom line marked on the chart, and at one mile there is a two fathom line shown. A watch on the depth will show when you pass over these lines and combined with your compass course, this information will give a rough guide as to your position, assuming that the four and two fathom lines don't run parallel to the coast in the same way for very far either side of the harbour. This by the way is called taking a chain of soundings. Of course it is only a rough guide, but it is something, another piece of evidence.

The commonest way of measuring the depth of water these days is to use an echo sounder. This is an instrument that sends out a sonic impulse from a transducer mounted on the hull underwater, and that times how long it takes to bounce back off the bottom, thus calculating the depth of water. The display of this information can take the form of a flashing light on a dial, a needle pointer on a dial, a digital counter, or a graph. Naturally there are points for and against each display, but they are all good in that they give a continuous reading (thus making a chain of soundings simple), but it must be remembered that they tell you the depth of water *under the transducer,* and take no account of the boat's draught.

The two other methods still in use, though not as common as they used to be, are the handlead and the sounding pole. The handlead consists of a plaited or left hand-laid line several fathoms long with a lead weight on the end, which is held (see diagram) coiled in one hand while the lead is swung and thrown clear ahead of the boat with the other, then when

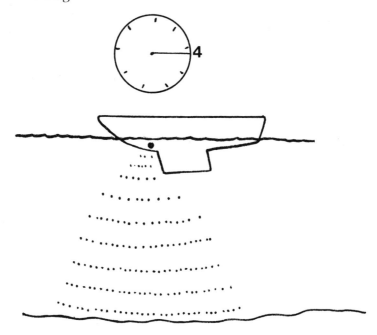

75 *An echo sounder bounces sound signals off the bottom and shows the depth on a dial.*

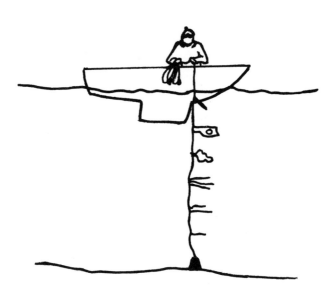

76 *The leadsman calls the depth from marks on his leadline.*

the line comes up straight, the depth is read from the markings on the line. Traditionally the line is 20 fathoms long, but for a small cruiser 10 fathoms should prove ample. Again traditionally, markings were not put on the line every fathom, but I would suggest doing so on the shorter line; perhaps like this:

1 fathom	cord with 1 knotted tail	
2 fathoms	cord with 2 knotted tails	
3	,,	cord with 3 knotted tails
4	,,	white rag
5	,,	piece of leather with hole in it
6	,,	white rag two tails
7	,,	leather 1 tail
8	,,	leather 2 tails
9	,,	leather 3 tails
10	,,	white rag knotted

The point about this system is that all of the markings can be identified by feel, making use at night much easier, but you may well prefer to work out your own markings. The lead itself has a hollow base which can be filled or 'armed' with tallow to bring up samples of the seabed. Such samples are of great value as yet one more clue to your position, and are something that an echo sounder can't give you. An echo sounder of the flashing light variety can tell you if the bottom is hard or soft, but that's about all.

Bringing tradition right up to date there is now a metric leadline, marked thus:

1 & 11 metres – one strip of leather
2 & 12 metres – two strips of leather
3 & 13 metres – blue bunting
4 & 14 metres – green and white bunting
5 & 15 metres – white bunting
6 & 16 metres – green bunting
7 & 17 metres – red bunting
8 & 18 metres – blue and white bunting
9 & 19 metres – red and white bunting
10 & 20 metres – piece of leather with hole in it.

These markings are the ones used by the Hydrographic Office. It must be remembered that a metre is about *half* a fathom.

At one time not so long ago, it was very common on England's East Coast to see black and white banded poles lashed to a yacht's shrouds – sounding poles. On this coast where a cruiser often has just inches of water under her keel, a pole of about 12ft, which often doubles as a whisker pole or boat hook, is all that is really needed. The bands are 1ft in length, and one end of the pole is weighted to make it sink. All you do is lean out of the cockpit and take a sounding over the side. The end of the pole can be armed in the same way as the lead and because the pole is rigid it allows you a better 'feel' of the seabed.

All of these methods are valid in their own way, but it must be watched that in each case the boat's draught is not taken into account by the instrument itself and you must make the appropriate allowance. Also they all tell you the depth of water you are in, not what you are approaching. The sounding pole is rarely seen today and leadlines have lost popularity to the convenience of echo sounders, but they are still much cheaper and perfectly effective for pilotage.

Harbour Signals

Because harbours are sheltered and protected areas, their entrances are generally very narrow, and where there is much commercial traffic, or where there is a blind corner, they usually have signals to tell you when it is safe either to enter or leave. Unfortunately these signals are by no means the same in every port. Why a standard system has never been worked out is difficult to say, but it means that if you are planning to put into a particular harbour you must be careful to check up first if there are any harbour signals, second (assuming that there are) what they are, and third where they are displayed.

Reed's Nautical Almanac (published by Thomas Reed Publications and available from chandlers) is the bible for British yachtsmen, and this gives the harbour signals for each port around the UK and Continental coasts. Other local sailing directories will also provide the necessary information. But do check and do be careful as you could otherwise find yourself bows to bows with an ocean liner!

Landfalls and Accumulating Errors

Although when coastal cruising you are not normally out of sight of land for more than a few miles, even this can be disturbing the first time. Particularly so if you stop to consider the possibility of not being able to recognise your landfall when you make it. On short coastal passages you aren't going to be far out, but a headland viewed from only slightly different angles can be quite unrecognisable as the same place. Strong light throws up minor hills as stark mountains to eyes looking for low hummocks. A bay that appears large on the chart can mysteriously fade into the rest of the coastline and be invisible to the navigator until he is quite close inshore. Buoys can appear to be way out of position according to the chart, simply by being approached from an odd angle. All of these things are disturbing to say the least, and the worry is increased if the navigator is not dead sure of the boat's position.

Generally speaking a large yacht is likely to make a better landfall than a small one, not only because the navigator can sit down at a proper chart table with all his instruments to hand rather than trying to perch with a piece of plywood on his knees, but also because the boat is moving faster (and is therefore out of sight of land for a shorter time), and the helmsman is able to hold a steadier course in the larger yacht. But of course, it is the smaller boat with the tired crew that needs the good landfall. Marvellous isn't it?

We will be taking a look at some of the intricacies of navigation in the next chapter, but it's as well to know some of the things that can contribute to error when undertaking coastal pilotage. Perhaps the biggest source of error, and usually the most embarrassing, is the helmsman who does not admit to steering anything but the set course. You soon learn at sea that (in open waters) the navigator sets a course as a *guide*. If he's any good he will not mind you steering a course on which either you or the boat is happier (within a few degrees of the set course), *provided that you tell him*. A one degree error over 60 miles only means an error of one mile at the end, but a helmsman who steers 5 degrees off, doesn't admit it, and a navigator who says 'the tide's running at 2 and a bit knots, we need a touch of leeway to add spice' and so on, are combining to create a big mistake. Occasionally of course a mistake is made and some other one cancels it out, but you can never rely on this to happen.

The other thing a navigator has to do is study the helmsman (without his knowing it) and see to which side of the course he is tending to steer. Going to windward some men steer free, others pinch up. Boats too have their foibles. Some carry a lot of weather helm and will tend to gripe the whole time. Running dead before the wind is the worst time. Start two boats off together on opposite gybes and you can guarantee that they won't stay parallel for long; either they'll diverge or they will collide. Far better to set a safe course without fear of a gybe and tack downwind.

Logs too can be a source of error by over or under reading. It must also be remembered that they only tell you the distance run *through the water*. A boat making 4 knots against a 2 knot tide is only going to cover half the distance over the ground that she records through the water.

All of this really adds up to the old question of whether it is better to head for a point and try to calculate which side of it you are if you miss, or to put in a known error by aiming well to one side right from the start. I prefer to head for a point and try to keep a check as I go along of what could be in error. The point is though to realise that the landfall you make won't always *appear* to be the one you want. Be prepared for this and try not to panic, take it easy, even if you sight land at only 5 miles off, you probably have over an hour in which to identify it before you have to start thinking about heaving to or anything else.

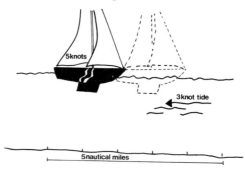

77   *Under tideless conditions the black boat would cover the 5 miles marked at the bottom of the diagram, but against a 3 knot tide she only moves to the dotted position 2 miles ahead. Thus a careful distinction must be made between speed/distance through the water, and speed/distance made good over the ground.*

CHAPTER 10

Coastal Navigation

The last chapter dealt with pilotage or sailing by eye. Now we come to the more formal business of coastal navigation. Whole books have been written on this subject alone so I can only hope to introduce the bare bones of it here and to encourage you to make a separate and careful study of it. In order to navigate or to pilot a boat we need charts, so let's start there.

Charts and Symbols

The main chart publishers in the UK are the British Admiralty, Edward Stanford, and Imray and Wilson, though there are a number of other concerns who publish large scale harbour plans and localised charts. The BA charts are the basis for all the others and are probably the most detailed. The only drawback to them for the navigator on a small cruiser is their size, which can be anything up to 52in by 28in when opened out flat and about 28in by 20in when folded for stowage. The Stanford charts are coloured, have suggested course lines printed on them, fold down to about 10in by 6in, have some useful pilotage notes printed on the back and include large scale inserts of ports. The Imray charts are flat sheets which are coloured, and cover either single harbours in large scale, or else fairly long stretches of coast on a small scale.

Many chandlers stock charts, but the Admiralty ones are best purchased from an Admiralty chart agent who will correct them up to the date of purchase. Which charts you choose is up to you, but the BA charts are the only ones that cover the whole of the British Isles (and indeed the whole world) and are the ones generally recognised as being the mother and father of charts.

139

Until very recently charts measured depth in fathoms and feet, but at the moment we are in the middle of a transition from this system to the metric one of metres and decimetres. For a while this is going to cause much head scratching and a careful check must be made of each chart to discover which units the soundings are given in. Where soundings are in fathoms and the depth is less than 11 fathoms it is shown in fathoms and feet, thus 5_2 represents a depth of 5 fathoms and 2 feet, while on a metric chart a depth of 4.5 metres is shown as 4_5. Figures that are underlined show the height to which a bank or other object dries above chart datum.

Charts provide the navigator with a fantastic amount of information in a small space by using a fairly simple series of symbols. Because the sea and seabed contain such a variety of things – shoals, wrecks, buoys, etc – the list of symbols is quite long, and in fact the Admiralty publishes a complete chart (BA chart No 5011) to display them. Sometimes a magnifying glass will help in reading the smaller symbols inshore on a small scale chart.

Pilot Books

When you hear talk of 'the pilot', as in *The North Sea Pilot* or *The Irish Sea Pilot*, it is the Admiralty pilot books that are being referred to. These volumes are valuable adjuncts to the BA charts and as with the charts there are volumes to cover the whole world. They are intended primarily for big ships and in places tend to be rather 'gloom and doom' in their wording. All the facilities at each port or harbour are meticulously listed, from where to anchor or obtain fuel to the nearest de-ratting point. Approach channels, lights, buoys, beacons and sound signals are all detailed, together with very useful topographical information to aid you in making a landfall. In some of the pilots drawings of 'views' are given to show the navigator for example what a particular headland looks like from two or three different angles. These again are of much help.

Apart from the Admiralty pilots there are several books produced by yacht clubs, notably the Clyde Cruising Club, Irish Cruising Club, the Royal Northumberland Yacht Club and the Cruising Association, whose outstanding Handbook should have a place in every cruiser's bookshelf. For the

Solent and South Coast Adlard Coles' *South Coast Harbours and Anchorages* is the standard work, while for the Thames Estuary it is Yachting Monthly's *East Coast Rivers*.

No book giving pilotage information can hope to stay up-to-date for very long because marks, and in many cases shoals and bars, change quite rapidly, but if care is taken they may prove to be your salvation. While we should always carry charts showing every harbour along our planned passage, we may not always carry one of the largest scale for a particular entrance, and that's when the pilot comes into its own.

Reed's

I have mentioned already a volume called *Reed's Nautical Almanac*, several times with overtones of reverence. If you want to know something about anything 'look it up in *Reed's*' is a pretty fair maxim, for $9\frac{1}{2}$ times out of 10 you will find the answer. Published annually, it is a compendium of tide tables, light lists, weather, navigation, buoyage, radio work, distress procedures; you name it, it's there. All I can really say is that if you intend to go cruising you must have an up-to-date copy on board.

Navigation Instruments

As with so many things in sailing today the number and intricacy of the navigation instruments carried depends entirely on the amount of money you are prepared to spend. It is very easy to spend over £1000 on electronic aids and instruments, but few of them are really needed by the average cruising man, though they are sometimes fun to have – expensive fun. There are however some basic items that you must have, and to these can be added some that are highly desirable and others that are distinct luxuries.

In the *essential* category come a good steering compass, charts, leadline (or echo sounder), radio capable of picking up shipping forecasts, watch or clock (with second hand) of known error, soft pencils, sharpener, rubber, parallel rules or Douglas protractor or Hurst plotter, dividers, *Reed's*, local pilots, log book, note books, and distance log.

The above are not in any particular order because they are

Here the cabin table doubles as a chart table during a night passage.

all necessary. The steering compass I will mention again in the next section of this chapter. The charts we have already looked at, and the same applies to the leadline and echo sounder. Chapter 16 deals with weather forecasts, so I'll say no more now. Always use a soft pencil on charts; 2B is about the best as it can be rubbed out easily and does not leave deep trenches in the surface of the charts. HB pencils are fine for log entries as these shouldn't need to be rubbed out so often and the pencils stay sharp that much longer, though a sharpener is still needed.

Although they are beautiful instruments roller parallel rules are practically unusable on a small boat without a proper chart table and the more common 'walking' rulers are the ones to consider. The Hurst plotter consists of a gridded transparent plastic square with a circle of plastic marked in 360° and a long arm mounted on top of it. The disc can be clamped to show magnetic variation and with the grid aligned with a meridian or parallel of latitude on the chart, the arm can be used to read or lay off a course. Its main advantage is that the arm is flexible and can therefore be used with a chart spread on your knees in dire circumstances. The Douglas protractor is a gridded square of clear plastic with a 360° notation round the sides. To lay off a course the centre hole is placed over the departure point, the grid is aligned with a meridian or parallel of latitude, and a mark is made at the side next to the bearing of the destination (say 030°). The departure point and this mark are then joined up using the edge of the protractor as a ruler.

As to dividers, I would suggest that despite their extra cost, the one-handed type are infinitely preferable to the ordinary geometry set type. But be sure to use them properly (see diagram) or your money will have been wasted. *Reed's* I have already talked about, and so too local pilots. A log book is necessary not only as a record of events but as an integral part of navigation of the vessel, but more of that later in this chapter. A note book saves scribbling calculations on charts and easily lost scraps of paper.

Distance logs fall into two categories: towing logs and through-hull logs. Towing logs, otherwise known as patent logs, consist of a recording head with dials reading in miles

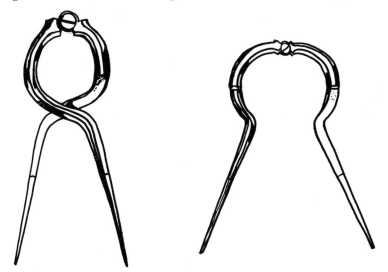

78   *One-handed dividers should be squeezed to open the points (left), and not stretched (right), which usually needs two hands anyway, thus defeating the whole purpose of the design.*

and tenths of miles, and a long line to which is attached a metal sinker and rotator. The rotator spins in the water, twists the log line and the counter translates the number of revolutions into miles and tenths which it displays on its dials. The hull logs have a small plastic or nylon impeller which either twists a wire (in similar fashion to a patent log) or creates an electric current which sensors translate into distance run. The electronic type can have one or more 'read outs', and the impeller on some makes can be withdrawn from inside the hull for weed clearing. The towing type of log should not be streamed until the boat is in clear water and should be handed before entering congested waters. To hand the log, unclip the line from the recorder and pay the line out into the water as you haul in the spinner, then coil it up from the spinner end. This way you avoid kinks and snarl-ups. By the way, a measure of the boat's speed can be obtained by watching the tenths of a mile scale on the log over a 6 minute period (one tenth of an hour) and multiplying by 10. Thus 0.4 miles in 6 minutes = 4 knots.

On top of this list of essentials there are some items that I would class as 'highly desirable'; handbearing compass, radio direction finder, binoculars, and stopwatch.

Not all steering compasses are so sighted that it is easy to take a bearing of something from them unless that object is more or less ahead, and for this reason a handbearing compass is very useful. There are many types of handbearing compass on the market and as usual each has its merits, but one of the best for small boat use is the Mini Compass produced by Offshore Instruments Ltd, which can be hung on a lanyard round your neck and used with one hand while you are at the helm. The great advance with this compass is that the optics allow the bearing to be read with the eyes still focussed on the object, thus making a 'snap' bearing accurate.

Radio direction finders are being used increasingly and some of the smaller sets, notably the Seafix, are giving perfectly workable results while not being exorbitantly priced. The principle is that you pick up the signal transmitted by a shore station, record its direction from you and cross that bearing with ones from other stations.

Binoculars have such obvious uses as spotting buoys and landmarks, but don't go for a pair with too great a magnifying power as it will be difficult to keep sight of the object in the narrow field of view. It's much better to go for a pair with a lower magnifying power and larger object lenses (the big end ones) as they will be manageable and will let in a lot of light – especially useful for night work. A pair of 7 or 8 × 50 glasses would be ideal.

Accurate timing of sequences is of the essence when trying to identify a light, and to this end a stopwatch is an enormous help. It need not be expensive, but it must be easily operated.

So we come to the luxuries in the navigator's repertoire. Barometer, sextant, speedometer, wind speed and direction indicator, and other electronic instruments.

A barometer provides a check on local pressure systems and can make interpretation of the weather forecasts much more accurate. It also gives the whole crew something to tap and shake their heads gloomily over when they want to stay in port an extra day.

A sextant we will see later is not the mysterious instrument it is made out to be, nor is it one to be used solely for astro navigation. It has a definite place aboard all coastal cruisers as well as those venturing out on longer voyages.

Sophisticated electronics in the form of speedometers, wind speed and direction indicators, anemometers, course computers and what have you are the very last things to spend money on if you own a small cruiser. OK if you are ocean racing, but for us mere mortals, forget them.

Compasses

Compasses are not cheap instruments at the best of times, but it is well worth paying for a good one as the whole business of guiding a well found yacht from A to B is centred on the compass. There are three main types, the grid compass, the dome compass and the edge reading type.

Modern compasses have their cards marked in a simple 360° notation, but older ones may still be found with either points or quadrantal markings. The points and quadrantal compasses are the ones that produce such romantic bearings as (respectively) North ¼ East and North 20 West. They have a 'days of sail' ring about them, but they're very easy to make mistakes with and are best avoided. A compass with degree markings at five degree intervals is quite easy to read and to allow larger figures the last digit is occasionally omitted, thus 030° would be marked 3 and 240° would be 24.

145

The grid compass has a normal card floating in an alcohol/ water mixture and a plain glass top, but it also has a rotatable bezel on top with two parallel wires across it and a 360° notation. In use, the course required (eg 240°) is set by rotating the bezel until the 240° marker lines up with the ship's heading marker (lubberline), then all the helmsman has to do is keep the North pointer on the card between the wires of the grid. The advantages of the grid compass are that it is easier to keep a needle between two marks than it is to align a single mark and a single line (as in dome compasses), and that should the helmsman forget the course set, he has only to look at where the bezel is fixed. The drawback comes when the helmsman cannot lay the set course. He then has to keep on moving the bezel to check his average, but this is not too serious a matter after a little practice.

Dome compasses, as their name implies, have a simple floating card with 360° notation surmounted by a transparent dome. In many of these compasses the card and lubber line are both gimballed within the compass thus avoiding the necessity of any external gimbals – unlike the grid types. The dome acts as a magnifying glass making it easier to read the card.

The third type, the edge reading compass, is more or less back to front. The edge of the card is turned down and marked 180° out from the figures on the surface of the card, ie the edge North mark is just below the South mark of the card's face. Also the lubber line instead of being on the forward side of the compass is on the after side. All of which sounds more complicated than it really is: the helmsman simply reads the markings and uses the lubber line near him rather than the one away from him that he uses on the 'look down on' compasses.

Choice of compass is dictated by where it is to be mounted, and that place must be chosen with regard to two things: it must be where the helmsman can see it, and where it is not going to be close to any ferrous metals. The first point is obvious but not always easy to comply with. Where a boat has wheel steering, the compass can usually be mounted on the steering pedestal and there is then no problem, but few small cruisers have anything but tiller steering and that means mounting the compass at one end of the cockpit. If it is mounted under the tiller at the after end the helmsman is never looking where he is going – either he watches the

79   *Three types of compass card; from top to bottom: points, quadrantal, 360 notation. This last is the commonest today and is by far the easiest to use.*

147

compass and not the ship's head, or vice versa. If it is mounted on a bracket on the after face of the bridgedeck the sheet hand may kick it, and if it is mounted on a board across the companionway it has to be stepped over when going in or out of the cabin. Put it on one bulkhead and the helmsman can't see it properly on one tack. Tricky isn't it? Provided the cockpit is not too long, it can be recessed into the upper surface of the bridgedeck, but the crew mustn't sit on it. Really you have got to look at your own boat and decide on the least objectionable place.

Then of course the compass mustn't be near any ferrous metals or permanent magnets otherwise it will be affected by deviation, which we'll come to later. The helmsman must also be able to look fairly straight at it to avoid parallax. If you look down onto the compass then a grid type is perfectly satisfactory (and somewhat cheaper) but if you cannot, then a dome or edge reading type must be considered. Illumination is another point. Luminous numbers are rarely sufficient and a light must be fitted, but it must not be a bright one which will ruin night vision. All you need is a glow, but a light fitted with a rheostat is the ideal as each helmsman can adjust it to suit himself. The electric wires to the light should be twisted together to avoid any possibility of compass deviation.

Variation

80

Variation is the angular difference between True North and Magnetic North. Unfortunately this angle is not constant, and in some parts of the world it is to the West and in others to the East of North. It must always be applied when converting from Magnetic bearings to True or the other way.

In the middle of a compass rose on the chart you will find a note that says something like 'Variation 8° West (1967) decreasing 6' annually'. That is to say then, in 1977 the variation will be 7° West. Occasionally small scale charts print isogonic lines (lines of equal variation) instead of putting the variation on the compass rose because it changes several times in the area covered by that chart.

Applying variation is really quite simple. Say there is 8° Westerly variation in your area and you read a course off the chart as 095° T (True). The Magnetic course (deg. M) will be 095 + 8 = 103° M. Had it been 8° Easterly variation, then the Magnetic course would have been 095 − 8 = 087° M.

Deviation

81

The close companion of variation is deviation, and together they make up 'compass error'. While variation is the difference between Magnetic North and True North, deviation is the difference between Magnetic North and Compass North. It is caused by ferrous metals close to the compass, such as engines, radio loudspeakers, knives and so on. Steel boats need a lot of careful attention, but with a wooden or grp boat the compass deviation should be very small and almost all

149

of it correctable. Compass correcting is not a simple subject and if you find a large amount of deviation you should call upon expert advice. Of course the best way to reduce deviation is to move the compass away from the inducing object, or vice versa, but most boats carry a degree or two of deviation on some headings.

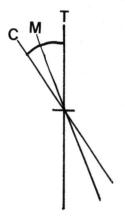

82 *Variation and deviation combine to produce compass error; in this case several degrees westerly error.*

Compass Swinging

The next question, logically, is how do you find out what deviation the compass carries? The answer is to swing the compass. Here the idea is to compare compass bearings of a distant object with the known magnetic bearing while the boat is held on various headings. The difference between the compass reading and the known magnetic bearing is the deviation for that ship's heading. These discrepancies are noted and made up into either a deviation card or a deviation curve, which is used each time you want to convert a True course to Compass or a Compass bearing to a True one.

The procedure is to select a convenient buoy (preferably not a fairway buoy) and a conspicuous landmark about 5–6 miles from it. Read the True bearing of the mark from the buoy off the compass rose on the chart and apply variation to convert it to Magnetic. Next go out to the buoy and get the helmsman to steer first North, then South, East, West, Northeast, Southwest, Northwest, Southeast, while staying very close to the buoy. As he steers each successive heading he should sing out 'On' when actually steering the required

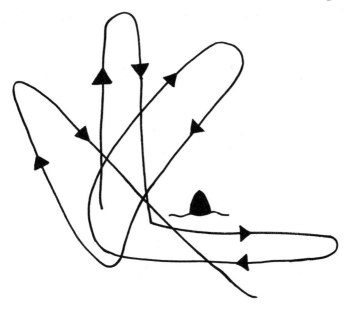

83   Pattern of manoeuvres about a reference buoy when swinging the compass.

course and 'Off' at other times. When he is settled on the course you take bearings of the distant object and note them together with the boat's heading. These bearings are then compared with the known Magnetic bearing and the difference is the deviation on that heading. Thus if the Magnetic bearing is 175° M and the Compass bearing is 173° C on a heading of due East, the deviation on that heading is 2° East. If the bearing is 176° C on a heading of North, the deviation would be 1° West on that heading.

From all these readings a table can be drawn up, for example:

Compass Heading		Deviation
N	0° C	1° E
NE	045° C	0°
E	090° C	3° W
SE	135° C	4° W
S	180° C	3° W
SW	225° C	1° W
W	270° C	1° E
NW	315° C	2° E

This table can also be presented as a deviation curve, thus:

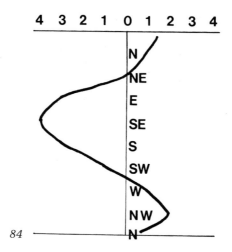

A rough and ready alternative is to trail someone astern in a dinghy with a handbearing compass, and as the ship is put on various headings, the man in the dinghy notes the course on the handbearing compass. This method can be used at sea by holding the handbearing compass clear of all metal objects and sighting along the line of mast and forestay. Here it must be remembered that the deviation so found holds good only for that particular heading, and another check will have to be made again as soon as the course is changed.

The application of variation and deviation is quite simple but must be remembered, whether converting from True courses and bearings to Compass or the other way round. So a few examples:

1 Compass course 135° C, variation 6° W. What is the True course?

Variation	6° W	from compass rose
Deviation	4° W	from deviation card
Error	10° W	
Compass course	135° C	
Error	10° W	
True course	125° T	

2 Compass course 045° C, variation 8° W. What is True course?

Variation	8° W	from compass rose
Deviation	6° E	from deviation card
Error	2° W	
Compass course	045° C	
Error	2° W	
True course	043° T	

3 Compass course 240° C, variation 5° W. What is True course?

Variation	5° W
Deviation	7° E
Error	2° E
Compass course	240° C
Error	2° E
True course	242° T

4 True course 185° T, variation 6° W. What is the Compass course to steer?

Variation	6° W
Deviation	5° E
Error	1° W
True course	185° T
Error	1° W
Compass course	186° C

5 True course 320° T, variation 20° W. What is the Compass course to steer?

True course	320° T
Variation	20° W
Magnetic course	340° M

Here the Magnetic course has been found first because the variation is large and the True and Magnetic courses are therefore rather different. The deviation is found for a Magnetic course of 340°.

Magnetic course	340° M
Deviation	4° E
Compass course	336° C

Buoyage

In UK coastal waters the Lateral buoyage system is used. The principle is that a buoy tells you (by its shape, colour, top-mark or light characteristic) on which side to leave it, rather than the Cardinal system where the buoys tell you on which side of them the danger lies. Provided that you recognise the buoy for what it is, the two systems come to the same thing – they show you how to avoid the danger they mark. The Lateral system is based on the direction of the main flood stream, thus you leave a starboard hand mark to starboard when approaching as it were with the flood, and you leave the same mark to port when going the other way. In general you obey the marks when entering a port from seaward and contradict them when leaving.

Diagram 85 shows the system in operation. Starboard hand marks carry odd numbers (1, 3, 5, etc) and port hand ones carry even numbers (2, 4, 6, etc).

Course Plotting

When we want to get from one port to the pub at the next we need a course to guide us, even if we can check landmarks and buoys on the way. First we need to know where we are starting from (our departure) and second where we want to arrive (or make our landfall). The easiest thing to do is choose a mark of some kind, outside each of the two ports, which is shown on the chart – say a buoy or beacon. The obvious thing then is to join the two points up, transfer that course to the compass rose, read off the True course, apply variation and deviation to give a Compass course, and tell the helmsman to steer it. But if on the way you cross the mouth of a river, won't there be a tide running in or out of it, and won't that tide push you sideways while you cross it? So you'll miss your landfall. All right then, we've got to lay a course allowing for tidal effect.

Tidal streams are anything but constant in strength or direction – they are stronger at springs than neaps; they are stronger at half flood or ebb than close to high or low water. To find out what is happening at any time we have to look at the chartlets in either *Reed's* or the Admiralty Tidal Stream Atlas for our particular area. These show, by means of arrows,

154

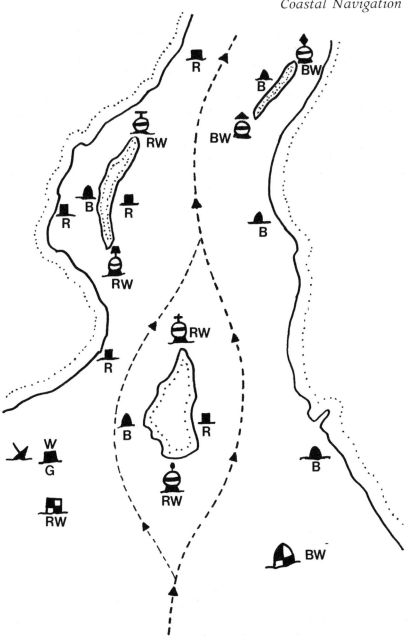

85   *B black, R red, G green, BW black and white, RW red and white. Starboard hand marks B or BW conical, port R or RW can. Middle ground spherical. G buoy with W on marks wreck. Topmarks on middle ground buoys indicate direction of main channel (follow dotted line).*

the direction of streams for each hour, and by means of figures the average rates of neaps and springs, all being related to High Water Dover. A look at the tide tables tells you that it is say 5 hours before HW Dover, then turning to the appropriate stream chart you find there is an arrow across your chart with the figures $\frac{1}{2}$–1 on it. This tells you that on an average neap tide there is a half knot current in the direction of the arrow, and that at springs it is 1 knot. The next hour shows 1–2 kn and the one after $1\frac{1}{2}$–$2\frac{1}{2}$ kn. You now have a three hour period to work with, and as a small boat's speed varies a lot this is a reasonable length of time.

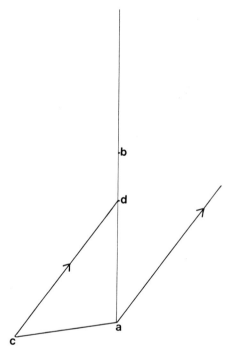

86　*Tidal allowance. Depart A on course parallel CD to arrive point D three hours later.*

Let's say it's springs and your boat is making a steady 3 kn. Then in three hours you can hope to cover 9 miles *through the water.* You may make more or less over the ground depending on whether the tide is helping or hindering you. Now lay off a direct course from your departure point to your desired landfall. Next move over to the margin of the chart with your dividers and open them out to a span of $5\frac{1}{2}$ minutes

156

of latitude. (One minute of latitude equals one nautical mile by definition, so always use the latitude scale nearest to your position to measure distance.) The figure of $5\frac{1}{2}$ was arrived at by adding up the spring tidal rates, ie $1 + 2 + 2\frac{1}{2} = 5\frac{1}{2}$. Set off the $5\frac{1}{2}$ miles down tide from your starting point and that is where you would end up if you drifted for 3 hours (C). But you reckon to be sailing at 3 knots, so now open the dividers to a distance of 9 miles (9 minutes of latitude) and place them with one point on the '$5\frac{1}{2}$ miles of drift' mark (C), swing the other point until it cuts your direct course line (D). Where it does so is where you should be in three hours time if you steer the course from C to the intersection of the direct course line, ie CD.

In light or variable winds when it is much harder to predict the boat's speed with any degree of accuracy it may be necessary to work in hourly periods. The boat will not move in a straight line between two points, and she may in fact take quite a wide sweep away from the direct course, therefore it is essential to be sure there are no shoals, rocks or other navigational hazards that you might be carried onto. If you feel it is possible you will go too near to an obstruction you should shorten the period for which you lay a course, as this will reduce the distance you drift from it.

When undertaking a passage that involves one or two complete tidal cycles it is impossible to predict your time of arrival, and so the navigator can either plot the tides for numerous short periods in the method already described, or else he can simply set the direct course and plot how the boat wanders around that line. This way is often the easier and eventually there will come a time when the navigator can make a prediction and set a course to his destination.

All of this of course assumes a free wind that allows you to sail the desired course – but you pretty soon find this is not always the case. When you are hard on the wind you will almost certainly have to give the helmsman a free hand to steer the best course he can, and then plot all his wanderings. This is called Dead Reckoning (DR) or navigation by Estimated Position (EP), about which more anon.

The other thing to remember when sailing hard on the wind is the principle of 'lee-bowing'. Quite simply you keep the tidal stream hitting your lee bow so that it gives you a lift to windward, which over a period of time can be considerable. If two boats set off together and one lee-bows and the other weather-bows, the one that lee-bows will end up way ahead of her rival.

Tides and Standard Ports

Although local tide tables are published for most areas, if they are not your home waters you probably won't carry them and will rely on our old friend *Reed's*. Again though, *Reed's* publishes complete tide tables for only the 'standard' ports around the UK and adjacent Continental coasts, so you might not find one for where you are. For instance there is no tide table included for Ardrossan. The nearest is for Greenock, which is the standard port for that area, just as Sheerness is the standard port for the Thames Estuary. If you want to know the time of HW at say Ardrossan on a particular day, you look up the table headed 'Tidal differences on Greenock' and against Ardrossan you find − 0h 20 min. This means that the time of HW is 20 minutes before that at Greenock. You then simply look up the time in the Greenock table and subtract 20 minutes.

Reduction to Soundings

Very often we want to know if an anchorage will dry out or if there is sufficient water over a bar when leaving harbour. A straightforward look at the chart will not provide the answer, for the real depth of water is rarely that shown on the chart. These depths are the distance the sea bed lies below chart datum, which on new charts is taken as being the depth of water at the lowest predictable tide (Lowest Astronomical Tide) and on older ones as Mean Low Water Springs (MLWS). Height of tide refers to the *height above chart datum*, so the height at HW is the distance between chart datum and HW mark. Thus a depth charted as 6ft indicates 6ft below chart datum, and a 15ft tide is one that at HW provides a height of 15ft above chart datum. But that tide may not have risen as much as 15ft, it may for instance have risen 12ft from a low water height of 3ft above chart datum. This 15ft tide is then said to have a range of 12ft, and at LW there will in fact be 9ft where the chart shows 6ft.

Now how could we have calculated that there would be 9ft

at LW? First we need to know the Mean Tide Level which is found from *Reed's* on the page showing tidal differences on the nearest standard port. It is the average of MHWS, MHWN, MLWS, MLWN. Then we have (in this case): Height for day 15ft, mean level 9ft. Double the mean level minus height for day equals height of LW above chart datum, thus: $9 \times 2 = 18$. $18 - 15 = 3$ft above chart datum. With a charted depth of 6ft, there will in fact be 9ft at LW.

If we come in to anchor 3 hours after HW, in a depth of 7ft with a boat drawing 3ft, and want to know if we will be afloat at LW, we have to start by finding the tidal range. So, using the above calculation we have: day's Height 15ft, LW 3ft above datum, $15 - 3 = 12$ft tidal range. Now tides don't fall and rise by the same amount each hour, in fact they follow an approximate 'twelfths' rule – in the first hour the tide rises (or falls) 1/12, in the second 2/12, the third 3/12, the fourth 3/12, the fifth 2/12, the sixth 1/12. So when we arrive 3 hours after HW the tide will have fallen 6/12 or half of its range, ie with a 12ft range it will have fallen 6ft. It therefore has another 6ft to fall. We had 7ft when we anchored, so at low water we will have $7 - 6 = 1$ ft, which means we will be well and truly aground and had better move fast.

Occasionally *Reed's* does not give the Mean Level we want, and then we have to approximate, saying: neap range = neap rise for locality $\times 2 -$ spring rise (spring range = spring rise).

I realise the above sounds very complicated, but with careful thought it will make sense, and with practice it will become easy.

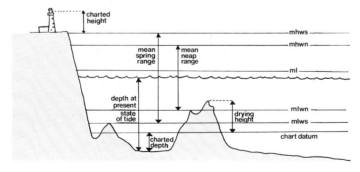

87 *Terms used when dealing with tidal calculations. The abbreviations are thus from the top: mean high water springs, mean high water neaps, mean level, mean low water neaps, mean low water springs.*

159

Bearings and Fixes

When a pilot book, light list or almanac gives the bearing of a light or beacon it generally does so as a True bearing from seaward. That is to say once you have converted your reading of the handbearing compass from Magnetic to True it will (or should) be that given in the pilot – no messing about with reciprocals. The True compass is used as the marks don't move, though a Magnetic bearing would alter the whole time.

Any opportunity you have to check your vessel's position should be welcomed, but there is little point in taking a snap bearing on an unidentified light. Count the light sequence first (preferably using a stopwatch), and then take a bearing and plot your position line. If you take a bearing of a light and lay that bearing off on the chart it follows that you are somewhere on that line. This is called a position line. If at the same time you can get a second and even a third position line you must be where they meet, and this is called a three point fix. However, it is very unusual to find all three position lines crossing at a point; usually they form a triangle called a cocked hat. The size of the cocked hat produced determines the accuracy of the fix.

Any bearings must be taken with great care since even an error of as little as 5 degrees can result in a hell of a big cocked hat, as can be imagined. Best results are obtained by selecting objects that produce position lines more or less at right angles to each other with a third somewhere in between. It makes life very much easier when taking a bearing if your compass is 'dead-beat', which means that the card settles down quickly and stops swinging about. You will also get better fixes if you choose objects that are close to you. Should you get a rather large cocked hat, take all the bearings again (and their new time) and re-plot them. If this is not possible, say, because of poor visibility, assume that you are at whichever corner of the triangle puts you in most danger, and take your next course from there.

Should you have no other marks to take bearings on than a set of buoys, take bearings on as many as you can, because one may be out of position or if you are close to it it may be at the limit of its riding scope. When you are running in on a coastline and getting slightly anxious, by all means take bearings on the looms of lights as a rough guide, but do not rely on them until the light itself dips up over the horizon and you can take a proper bearing of it. Anyway, you rarely need to panic as soon as you think, after all you will probably have to run another few miles before you are anywhere near the coast, and a few miles in a small cruiser means an hour or so, not minutes.

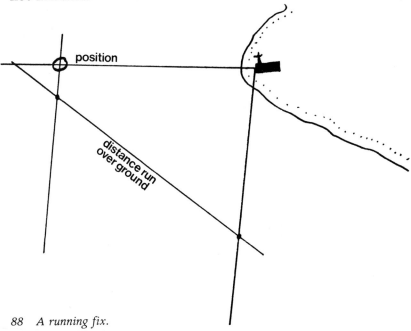

position

distance run over ground

88   *A running fix.*

All opportunities of checking your position should be taken and to this end it is as well to take a bearing on any identified object even if there is nothing to cross it with. By doing this you in fact have half a fix, and if you then run on until the bearing of the object has changed substantially (say 40 degrees), and take a second bearing you are almost there. Plot both bearings, then lay off your course and mark along it how far you have travelled *over the ground*. Move the first position line up until it passes through that point and your fix is where it cuts the second position line. This is called a running fix.

Very similar to the running fix is the method known as doubling-the-angle-on-the-bow. For this you again need but one object. Take a bearing of it when it is say 30° *off the bow*, a second when it is 60° *off the bow*. This you will note is not the same as saying double the bearing. Calculate the distance made good *over the ground* and this is equal to your distance

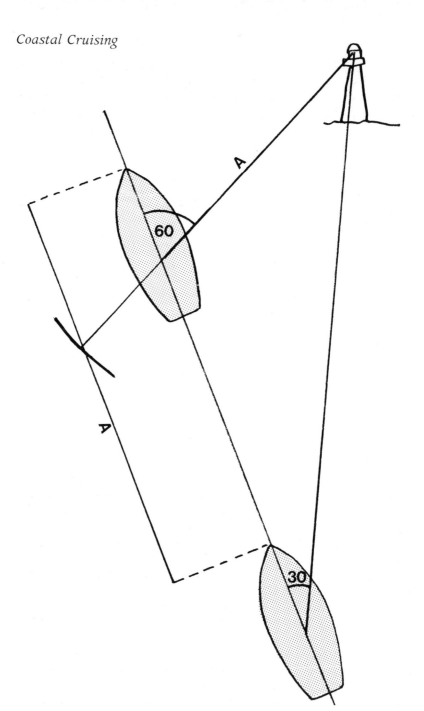

89   *Doubling-angle-on-bow. Distance over ground A equals distance A from lighthouse.*

off the object along the second position line. Thus you have a position and a distance off in one go.

The great stumbling block with both of these methods is that you need to know accurately the distance made good over the ground, and what with varying boat speed and unknown tidal currents this can be a bit of a tall order. It is in fact the essence of Dead Reckoning so I will say more about it later.

Some other points about bearings: it is often helpful when entering a strange harbour to work out 'safe bearings' on certain landmarks beforehand. For example, you may find that if a church is kept between 010° T and 355° T you have a clear passage between two rocks. On leaving harbour it is possible to check your leeway or the effects of a cross current by taking back bearings on some landmark to see how it compares with the reciprocal of your course. Lastly, take bearings on approaching ships. If the bearing stays the same (or nearly

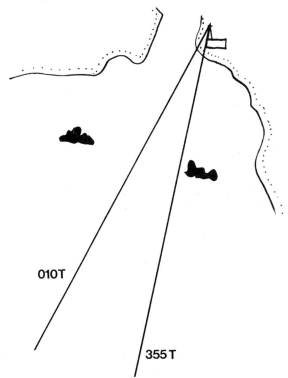

010T

355 T

90 *Safe bearings. Keep church bearing between 010°T and 355°T to avoid rocks.*

163

constant) you are on a collision course and will have to do something. If it changes handsomely you should be clear, but keep checking.

Leeway

This is a much discussed topic as its importance varies from boat to boat. When you are sailing hard on the wind a component of the wind's force pushes you sideways and you make leeway. But how much? In most cases it is not likely to be more than a couple of degrees, and in rough going – when it is likely to be noticeable – the helmsman probably won't be steering to better than $\pm 5°$ anyway, so usually you can get away with ignoring it. A check should be made however by taking a bearing on the wake when sailing a fair course and comparing it to your course. If it is significantly different you will have to make due allowance.

Speed and Distance Made Good

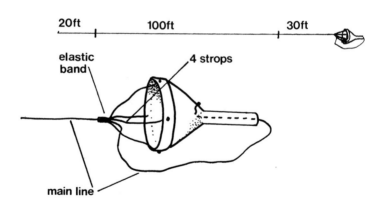

91 Drag log. For recovery main line slips through elastic band round strops and capsizes funnel.

Whether you choose to fit a through-hull log or buy a towing log, some sort of distance recorder is almost essential for serious coastal cruising. You can get away without one if you keep fairly accurate checks on your speed through the water and work out your distance run with that, but as a boat's speed varies the whole time this is no easy matter. However, in case your log should ever pack up on you it is worth going back in history to find out about the drag log.

The term 'knot' (meaning one nautical mile per hour) derives from the time when a weighted piece of wood (the log) was heaved overboard on the end of a line with regularly spaced knots tied in it. The ship's speed was recorded as being so many knots and fathoms run out in the time it took a sand glass to empty. By using exactly the same principle but working in modern materials we can make the arrangement shown in the diagram. The only difference is that we take the time for a hundred feet of line to run out (the length between the two knots) rather than seeing how much runs out in a set time. Here's how to use the drag log: put over the funnel and as the line runs out, watch for the first knot; as it passes through your hand start a stopwatch and keep an eye on the second knot; as the second knot runs out stop the watch and use the table below to find your speed.

1 knot = approximately 100ft per minute, therefore:

$$100\text{ft in 2 mins} = \tfrac{1}{2}\text{ knot}$$
$$100\text{ft in 1 min} = 1\text{ kn}$$
$$100\text{ft in } \tfrac{1}{2}\text{ min} = 2\text{ kn}$$
$$100\text{ft in 20 sec} = 3\text{ kn}$$
$$100\text{ft in 15 sec} = 4\text{ kn}$$
$$100\text{ft in 12 sec} = 5\text{ kn}$$
$$100\text{ft in 10 sec} = 6\text{ kn}$$

If this method is to be at all accurate, the line must be measured out exactly and the time taken carefully. Moreover, the log must be heaved at frequent intervals. Half-hourly would not be too often. On a long passage when people want to eat, sleep, sunbathe or listen to Wagner I have no doubt that they will try to estimate speed by eye or just forget about the whole thing. In the end they will have to get down to some navigation and will probably overestimate their speed – people tend to be optimistic in these things – and spend some time hopping about biting their nails as their DR puts them in pastures green but no land is in sight. So remember the log.

Point to remember: all that a hull log, a towing log, or a drag log can tell you is the speed/distance run *through the water*. This is in no way the same as the distance made good over the ground. If you make 4 kn for three hours you will travel 12 miles through the water, but if there is a 2 kn stream against you, you will only make good 6 miles over the ground. If on the other hand you are being chased by a 2 kn stream then you will make good 18 miles over the ground. Always allow for this when working out how far you still have to run to the next mark.

Log Book and DR

First let me clear up a little bit of terminology: Dead Reckoning is a calculation of the ship's position with regard to course steered and distance run (through the water). Navigation by Estimated Position (EP) is also a computation of the ship's position, but in this case allowance is made for the effects of tidal stream, current and leeway. Generally we are rather lax in our use of DR and EP as definitions and usually talk about Dead Reckoning navigation when we mean EP. A good DR plot (EP) is essential and is the basis of all navigation including celestial navigation, and it is wise to keep up such a plot at all times. In rough weather in a small cruiser this is not always possible, but the DR should be brought up to date as soon as conditions allow.

The process of keeping up a DR is made much simpler if you keep a comprehensive and well planned log book. The best way is to split it into two parts: the front (or one book) is the Deck Log and the back (or a separate book) is the Navigator's Log. The Deck Log must be filled in regularly and accurately by whoever is on watch, while the Navigator's part is the sole responsibility of the navigator. Its format, together with typical entries, made on a cross Channel passage, are shown in the diagrams. The Deck Log is pretty straightforward, except perhaps for the two sections 'course required' and 'course steered'. The first is the course the navigator would like to make and the second is an *honest* account of the course that the helmsman actually manages to make between log entries. I spoke of the importance of this earlier. The Navigator's section is a logical progression through the process of working out a plot, the whole point of it being that trying to think in a small cruiser in rough weather isn't easy, and if the system is laid out step by step you are less likely to make mistakes.

Deck Log

Date Time BST	Log Reading	Course Reg'd	Course Steered Since Last Entry	Wind	Baro.	Boat Speed	Remarks.
1700	65.80	207°c	190°	Nil	991	5½	A/c 215°c Engine On
1800	71.20	215°c	215°	Nil	991	5½	Forecast: Wt. Port N.E. 3-4
1900	76.26	19c°c	215°	Nil	991	5¼	A/c 190°c

Navigator's Log

Date Time B.S.T.	Log Rding	Since Last Plot	Course C°	Dev. E W	Var. E W	T°	Lee Way P S	Wake Course T°	Stream Set c.	Rate Kn	Drift Miles	Plot Position Lat.	Long.
1700	65.80	0.76	190	+10E	-7½w	192½	c	192	080	2	1	50°04'N	01°38'w
1800	71.20	5.40	215	+6E	-7½w	213½	o	213	085	3	3	49°59.5N	01°38'w
1900	76.26	5.06	215	+6E	-7½w	213½	o	213	090	3½	3½	49°55.4N	01°37'w

92

The process for plotting an EP is this. Enter the time in the first column, then take the log reading from the Deck Log and put it in the second. Subtract the previous reading from it and enter that distance in the third column. The course steered is again taken from the Deck Log. Deviation to be applied (±) is found from the deviation curve, and variation is calculated from the error shown in the centre of the nearest compass rose on the chart. These errors are applied to the compass course and the true course (deg. T) is entered in the seventh column. The degree of leeway to port or starboard is entered in the next column and is either added to or subtracted from the true course steered to give the true 'wake course' in column nine, though as I said earlier you may well be able to call leeway zero. Next catch your tidal atlas as it slips off the table and decide what the tide has done to you in the time since the last plot. Enter the average direction (deg. T) in column 10, the rate in the next column and the drift over the last two hours or whatever time since the last plot in column 12. Now you are ready to plot the EP.

From your last EP rule in the wake course (column 9) and mark off the 'since last plot' distance (column 3). From that point rule a line in the direction of the tidal set (column 10) and mark off the drift (column 12), using the latitude scale as usual. (One minute of latitude equals one mile.) Now you have plotted your EP. Believe it or not, this method works, and after a few plots it comes very easily. The final column is just a note of your latitude and longitude in case someone accidentally rubs the plot off the chart or spills coffee on it.

CHAPTER 11

Passage Making

A truly well found boat should be in a fit state to put to sea on a longish passage at any time, but in reality the family cruiser takes some preparation before she can really be called ready for a summer holiday cruise. All of her rigging, both standing and running, should be checked over; her sails looked at and restitched as necessary; fuel, water, food will all have to be taken on; the engine will probably have to be serviced – filters cleaned, oil changed/topped up, spark plugs cleaned and gaps checked, points' gaps checked; some sort of itinerary should be drawn up, no matter how rough, so that the relevant charts and pilots may be obtained and studied.

To decide which charts you need you first have to think about where you propose to go and how far you hope to get. A small cruiser with a young family crew can only really hope to make about 30–40 miles in daylight, and even then if the wind is light or against them they may have to motor sail for a spell. Any passages of more than that distance will involve night sailing, and if the crew is as described then the skipper will probably choose to keep such passages down to a minimum – perhaps no more than two in a 2–3 week cruise. A crew of young, fit, hard-drivers may make several 24 hour passages and will be able to cover twice the ground that the family manages; that is their choice. The whole joy of cruising is that we can do as we please and go where we choose, changing our plans at the merest whim. When thinking about where to make for though it is as well to bear the crew's limitations in mind. You must also consider the half day or so wasted in getting underway at the beginning of the cruise; the two or three days delay with bad weather; the 3–4 days spent in port sight-seeing, shopping, showering; the couple of days at the end 'just to be sure of getting back in time.'

All of which you will notice doesn't leave much time for getting places.

This is perhaps a pessimistic view of things, but it is better to find that you have made better progress than expected and be able to go further, than to set your heart on reaching a particular place and getting nowhere near it. To plan distances with any sense of reality you must have a chart in front of you, a pilot book in one hand and a pair of dividers in the other. The crew will need a day or so to settle down on the boat, but after that it is a good idea to get any long hops (or windward work) over in the early part of the holiday while people are still fresh and eager.

For the purposes of planning a passage, and indeed for much of the actual navigation, a small scale chart showing the whole trip from departure to destination is an asset. You must also have large scale charts of any ports along the way that you can put into if need be, or hope to put into anyway. These, together with relevant pilots and tide tables, should all be studied closely during the planning stages with bearings, marks, lights, possible courses and times to arrive at headlands for a fair tide all being noted and worked out.

Weather, of course, is a deciding factor in the cruising game. Several times I have had to curtail a summer holiday because of an overdose of rain. Gales too have taken their toll of days when we have had to lie up some backwater waiting for it to blow over. If you have young children on board bad weather can be particularly frustrating, but there is nothing you can do about it, you just have to take account of it and alter your plans accordingly. Provided it is fine, when there's a gale blowing out at sea there is no reason why you should not leave the boat safely moored and explore inland for a day; an ancient monument, a museum, or simply a day building sand castles on the beach. After all, sailing may be *your* fun, but it is a family holiday.

On the safety side of things there is an admirable scheme run by HM Coastguard called the Passage Safety Scheme. The idea is for yachtsmen to fill in a form (CG66A) annually, giving details of the boat and her normal cruising grounds, then prior to any cruise a couple of pre-paid postcards (CG66B) are completed giving an itinerary of the voyage. One of these is deposited with the Coastguard and the other is given to a friend or relative. In the event of your being badly overdue at any port that person can send the card to the

Coastguard (or take it to them, or phone them) and a search can be made with a full description of your boat to hand and also a good idea of your likely whereabouts. The whole scheme is free and is, I suggest, a good one to participate in, but in doing so you must play fair and carry out your part of the bargain. That is to say, if you decide to change your plans, or if you are held up by bad weather or mechanical breakdown, and you know that you will be delayed some time, you must contact the Coastguard and your relatives and inform them of the new plans. Otherwise a full scale search may be carried out needlessly.

Departures (Night and Day)

The great thing about departures is to make them. If you're going to go, go. Don't mess about, ditherers are no help at sea. At the same time it is not fair on your crew suddenly to spring a night passage on them when they've been swimming or sightseeing all day and have just come back aboard after a celebratory dinner. Heavy meals, particularly rich ones accompanied by alcohol, are not good stomach liners.

Mostly we make a final decision about a night departure after listening to the 1755 shipping forecast and this allows time (assuming the tide is compliant) for a quick meal, and the necessary preparations for departure before it actually gets dark. Try always to leave in daylight so that the boat is already sailing, the navigator has sorted himself out and the crew is settled down when darkness comes. If you are going to leave at night, try to get some sleep before you go.

Before setting off, either in daylight or at night, go over the whole boat checking all the gear. Show all the crew where flares, fire extinguishers, lifebuoys, etc are and how they work. Lash down any movable objects and point out to everyone how the dinghy is fastened (assuming it to be on deck). The navigator should sort out his charts into the order he is going to need them, and he should make a careful study of the pilots, because the next time he refers to them the boat will be unsteady, he is likely to be tired and probably feeling a bit rough. It will be easier at that time if he is already familiar with the information. He should also make notes of light sequences, buoys and possible courses, besides any available transits and safe bearings (or danger bearings). Each member

Evening departure and the prospect of an easy night passage.

of the crew should dig out his foul weather gear and stow it to hand so that he can get it without disturbing anyone who is asleep. Thermos flasks can be filled with soup, coffee or anything warming. Sandwiches may be prepared, and a box of 'goodies' should be put in an accessible place for hungry helmsmen. A waterproof torch near the helm is a good idea, and all the navigation lights (including the compass light) should be checked.

If you are setting off on a day and night passage, it is necessary to set watches as soon as possible, so that whoever is not on watch can take his rest with a clear conscience. Otherwise, particularly when leaving in the evening, you end up in the potentially dangerous situation of everyone staying on deck getting weary together. I would suggest that if only one person is going to be on watch at a time, two hours is as long as he can really cope with at night. In daylight he should be able to manage a three hour trick. If there are three of you capable of taking watches, then two hours on and four off at night, and three on and six off in the day gives each person a reasonable amount of time to sleep, eat, sunbathe or carry out running repairs.

Where there are two of you, say a man and his wife, things are not quite so easy. It should be no great hardship for a fit man to go without any sleep for one night, but he must be certain of having the chance to catch up on it the next day. Because it is never absolutely certain that he will be able to, it is a great help if his wife can take over for a couple of hours in the middle of the night and allow him to go below for a brew up and a nap. Many wives of course are just as competent to handle the boat as their husbands, and in these cases a two on and two off system can be worked quite well.

Landfalls (Night and Day)

In many ways making a landfall just before dawn is ideal. Lighthouses, light buoys and any other lit navigation marks are still plainly visible, and yet by the time you are getting close inshore it will be daylight. If you are going to have to make your landfall in the dark and make a harbour entrance still in darkness, then great care must be taken. The end of a passage almost certainly means a relaxing of vigilance on the part of the crew, just when concentration is needed to keep clear of 'navigational hazards' – rocks, moored boats, etc.

While it is much easier to pick out lit marks at night than in daylight when perhaps there is a light mist, or the sun is in your eyes, it is difficult to judge distances. Daylight shows clearly that you are still some way offshore, when at night you may think you are about to run up on the beach. This also applies when you get into a harbour. If you are going to anchor, take a good look round before choosing your place, or you may fetch up in the fairway. Don't forget too that you are required to hoist a riding light in the fore rigging. This makes good sense in crowded waters where boats are coming and going all the time. Make sure it burns all night, many small 'hurricane' lamps won't stay alight if you breathe on them, let alone burn through a storm. A proper oil riding light or an electric light run off a roving lead to a battery is the answer.

Choosing a good landfall is important. Some ports have what is called a landfall buoy outside. This is a large, lit buoy some way offshore not marking any hazard, but simply telling you that you are in the right position to line up for the

A simple DF set in use with its own earphones and bearing compass. Having its own compass avoids the difficulties of taking bearings relative to the ship's head.

A simple DF set in use with its own earphones and bearing compass. Having its own compass avoids the difficulties of taking bearings relative to the ship's head.

entrance. Where one of these is not available, then a lighthouse or other mark possibly some little distance up or down the coast from your destination should be chosen. Though this may add time onto your passage it will ensure that you have a good position to navigate from, rather than blinding in hoping to pick out a dim light on a pierhead.

RDF

A lot of people use small radio direction finders on coastal passages. Although they are something of a luxury so far as navigation of a small family cruiser is concerned, they can be very useful and reassuring. Put simply the DF set is a radio with a rotatable aerial. The signal from the transmitting station is picked up and its direction is determined by rotating the aerial until the null or position of least volume is found. Then either from a compass on the set, or by reference to the angle made with the ship's head, the direction of that station can be plotted on the chart. A couple more directions of other stations and you have a three-point fix, just like a handbearing fix.

Radio beacons, as the stations are called, are arranged in

groups for transmitting on the same wavelength. Each beacon goes through the same sequence lasting one minute: first the beacon's two-letter call sign in *slow* morse repeated four times, then a continuous note during which you rotate the aerial and take your bearing, and finally the call sign again, usually repeated a couple of times. The beacon is then silent for five minutes while the other beacons in the group go through their transmissions. Thus in a six minute cycle up to six beacons in a group can be heard.

Ranges of these beacons vary from about 5 miles to 200, though they may be picked up outside their own range. If this is so, be wary of a fix using them. Strange effects can also be found at dusk and dawn, and if there is land between you and the beacon. Frequencies and groupings of beacons around the UK are listed in *Reed's*.

Working the Tides

Anyone who owns a little cruiser with perhaps an outboard engine is pretty soon going to discover that he doesn't make much progress against a foul tide. You won't always be able to go with the tide, but when you can progress is much swifter and on a passage it can give you several free miles. After all, a 3 knot boat and a 2 knot fair tide add up to 5 miles of progress per hour, while a 3 knot boat against a 2 knot tide makes only 1 mile in the hour.

Right back at the planning stage of a passage you must make a careful study of how tides are going to run. Notes should be made of likely arrival times at headlands, races or narrows, and if on looking up the tides you find that you will be bucking the tide at one of these places, you may have to rethink your strategy. Should you in fact split the passage into two parts with a harbour in the middle? Or can you anchor under the lee of a headland and wait out the foul tide and be in a good position to take advantage of the full fair tide round and onward?

Many ports and harbours have bars across their entrances and these must be approached only when the tide serves. So too with drying anchorages. It's all obvious, but you have to think about it beforehand. There is no fun in plunging off any old time and bucking the tide for the first six hours, taking it with you for a couple and then arriving to find you can't make port. The art of working the tides is to keep the effect of foul ones to a minimum.

Night Sailing

The first and most obvious thing about night sailing is that you can't see as much as you can by day. Now that's not quite such a fatuous statement as you may think. Being unable to see properly means that you have got to *know* where each halyard fall is, where each cleat is, where the torch is. While picking out marks is made easier by virtue of their lights, judging your distance from them is difficult. Shipping seems to multiply and approach at horrific speeds. Judgement of your boat speed is tricky, you can't see the sails properly if you are sailing closehauled, and the wind always seems stronger at night. Also, man is not used to being kicked out of his sleep in the middle of the night to be sent outside to sit and get cold for a couple of hours while steering a good course and keeping a sharp lookout.

Night sailing can be a most exhilarating and rewarding experience, certainly some of my happiest memories come from night passages, but the first one should be undertaken only when you are sure of your ability to handle your boat, and when keeping track of your position is second nature. It's dead easy to mix light sequences up as you rise and fall on the waves, and consequently to become confused and panicky.

It is usually cold at night and you can get very wet just from spray and dew, so a few thick sweaters and some oil-skins are in order. A life-harness clipped onto a strong point in the cockpit is sensible, and if working up forward (say changing a headsail), then it should definitely be worn. A hot drink during the watch is a great comfort, and so too is something to munch on. A nice practice is for the man going off watch to make a hot drink for the new man who is straight from his bunk and probably needs waking up. It also means that for this transition period when night vision is being gained and the feel of the boat being acquired, there are two people about.

Steering at night is very much a case of feeling the wind, the helm and the boat. Listening to the sails can also help. A flapping luff makes it pretty clear when you have come up

A light vessel stands out darkly on a moonlit sea, providing a welcome and positive fix during a night passage.

too close on the wind. Naturally a check must be kept on the compass, but staring at it the whole time is not necessary, or a good thing. If you are in an eyes down position the whole time you are not keeping a lookout, and that is a serious and dangerous crime. Usually you can lay the boat on her course, pick a star and steer on that, but remember stars move across the sky and your course must occasionally be checked.

Compasses should be lit only sufficiently to facilitate easy reading, they should not be so bright that they leave the helmsman blind for several minutes after he looks up from it. A red bulb is quite easy on the eyes for this purpose. Remember too if someone goes on deck perhaps to check a lashing, don't look at his torch, and he should take care not to shine it at you.

177

Watchkeeping

The first duty of the man on watch is to keep a good lookout for anything that might affect the safety of the boat and her crew, whether it is the approach of another vessel, flotsam, or a landfall. He is responsible for steering a good course as close as possible to that set. If he is not able to lay it exactly he must note in the log the course actually steered and the times of any alterations. Certainly when you come off watch, but preferably every hour (or even every half hour), you should enter up the log. If a weather forecast comes up during your watch you must be sure not to miss it.

When any situation arises where the watchkeeper is unsure of what to do – a ship coming in close, a rising wind – he should call the skipper. Don't be put off by the fact that he has turned in and fallen asleep after his own watch. It is for such occasions that he *is* the skipper.

On handing over the watch to the new man you must point out and identify all visible lights, if possible showing him your approximate position on the chart. For instance you might say to him, 'That's Port Jovial over there, there's a ship going away from us there, but that light astern seems to be coming up on us.' You must also get him to repeat the course and any alterations that will be needed during his trick. When you first come up on a chilly night your mind is anything but active and if you don't go through this ritual you will find a few minutes later that you are staring at the compass with no idea of the correct course. What makes life easier is to have a slate in the cockpit to write courses and instructions on, such as '020°. Call navigator at 0330'.

Don't look only at the horizon but also watch the sea between you and the horizon. This applies particularly in heavy seas when objects, even big ships, can be completely hidden from view in the trough of a wave. Remember too that a ship's lookout is watching primarily for the lights of other ships, ie high lights out on his horizon level. Your lights are way below this and are arcing across his field of view in a series of flashes as your boat rolls.

Lastly, move quietly at night, the deck always creaks and even hushed voices are loud when you are trying to sleep. If you go foraging in the galley, don't drop the biscuit tin. Shield lights from the eyes of those off watch, and when woken up for your own watch, get up immediately, or you

At the end of a hard watch people tend to fall asleep anywhere, anyhow.

will fall asleep again, then you keep the man at the tiller out beyond his fair time.

Navigation Lights

Under the terms of the International Regulations for Preventing Collisions at Sea – the rule of the road – sailing boats are required to carry a red light showing to port, a green light to starboard and a white light astern. The diagram shows their exact arcs. In addition to these a red light over a green light may be carried at the masthead. On vessels of less than 40ft (which are the ones we are talking about) the port and starboard lights may be combined in one lantern, but there must be an accurate cut-off between them. All of these lights must have a minimum range of 1 mile, and although the rule only requires that they be carried and displayed 'in sufficient time to prevent collision', it is strongly advised that they be permanently fitted and always displayed between the hours of sunset and sunrise when the vessel is at sea. There is one other thing to remember: no matter if the sails are still set, as soon as you start the engine you become a power-driven vessel and must act accordingly. You must also display a

179

white steaming light on the forward side of the mast which shines through an arc of 225°, that is 112½° on either side of dead ahead. The all round white masthead light often fitted is *not* a steaming light and should not be used as such.

93   *Sectors of port, starboard and stern lights.*

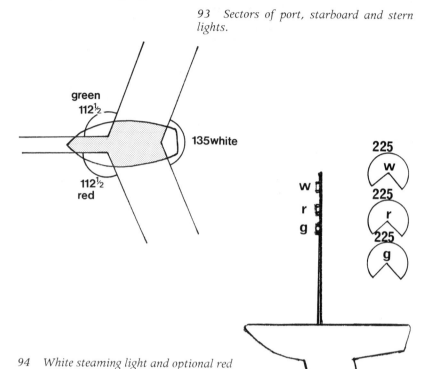

94   *White steaming light and optional red over green.*

Whether you have oil or electric navigation lights, before setting out on a passage which will keep you at sea after sunset, always check that they are working properly, and, in the case of oil lamps, that they are filled and the wicks are trimmed. They should of course be checked at intervals throughout the night. Do also be accurate about sunset and sunrise, don't just wait until it gets dark, or say 'oh well it's light enough now', for this could, in the event of a collision, invalidate your insurance policy.

A thorough study of the regulations must be made (they are reproduced in full in *Reed's*) not only to check up on what lights you are required to carry, but so that you can be fairly sure of recognising another vessel and what she is doing by the lights showing.

Meeting and Avoiding Shipping

Arguably the safest thing to do when sailing at night, particularly in shipping lanes, is to assume that your own boat has not been sighted by the lookout on an approaching vessel. Even in quite deep water, some of today's big tankers have very little room indeed to manoeuvre in, and because of the tight schedules they run to, they are understandably reluctant to alter course on the thin evidence of a lookout saying that he thought he saw a light. I shall say something about radar reflectors when talking about fog, but even though you carry one – and it is very sensible to do so – there is no guarantee that you will be picked out amongst the 'sea clutter' on a ship's radar display. You should still assume that you have not been spotted and act accordingly.

All of this advice assumes that an oncoming ship does not make it plain that she has seen you by altering course to avoid you in good time. Should she alter course appropriately, then you must of course stand on, otherwise you will be creating a confusing and dangerous situation.

At best a yacht's navigation lights will be visible at about a mile, but even this is only so in good visibility and in a calm sea. If the weather is at all thick, or if the boat is bouncing about a bit, this range will be cut drastically, and the lights will show as flashes each time the boat rolls on a wave. When closehauled one light will spend most of its time colouring the sea, while the other flashes messages to the moon. But you must not take the attitude that if a ship cannot see you you need not carry lights. If people did that, how would two yachts see each other? For my part I have had far more scares during a night watch from meeting other yachts with ridiculously small lights than I have from meeting ships looking like Christmas trees.

Obviously the first thing to do on sighting a ship is to determine whether or not you are on a collision course. The simplest way to do this is to sight across the corner of the cabin, or a stanchion, and see if the ship's bearing alters. If it does, she's going clear, but if not you will have to do something. The more sophisticated way is to take a bearing of the ship, with a handbearing compass or by sighting across the steering compass, and seeing how that alters.

Supposing that a ship is coming in at an angle across your bows, then the best avoiding action to take is to head for her

181

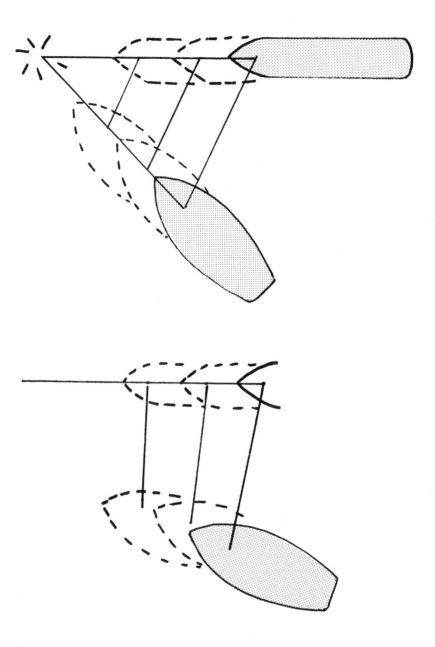

95   Top: *the bearing of the ship remains constant and a collision will result unless avoiding action is taken; lower: the bearings are altering sufficiently to ensure that the ship goes clear.*

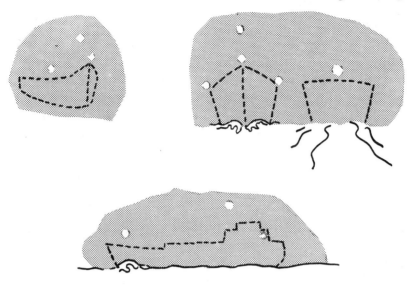

96 *Ships at night indicate their direction of sailing by the lights you can see, particularly the masthead lights and the gap between them.*

stern and follow it round until you are back on course. If she is coming up from astern you must swing well clear of her: in light weather don't be shy of starting the engine to give you greater speed to get clear. Whatever you decide to do, make it a *positive, obvious movement,* and *do it early*. Where the ship's lookout has seen you, there is nothing more confusing for him than to see a set of red and green dots swinging back and forth while you dither about.

Should someone come really close and for some reason you cannot get out of the way, then apart from shining a powerful torch steadily at the ship's bridge and occasionally on your own sails, the best thing to do is light a white flare. Several of these should be carried with your other distress signals, for in a real emergency you may need more than one. A white flare is the recognised signal of a boat's presence not of her distress, so no one will try to 'rescue' you.

At night a ship tells you her direction of travel in the first instance by two white masthead lights, the forward one being lower than the after one, and also by the size of gap between them – the diagrams help to make this clear. How

183

A ship passing as close as this on a bright sunny day is alright, but at night or in poor visibility it can be very alarming.

far off she is poses another problem. The only positive thing is that in good visibility her side lights become visible at 2 miles, but other than that there are very few clues. As she approaches, the masthead lights and the sidelights become more clearly visible, the accommodation lights are seen and finally the dark shape of the hull can be made out and often the sea is lit up. Really, as with so much of sailing, it is practice that tells you. Eventually you will be able to glance at a group of lights and say, 'Oh yes, she's passing clear ahead'. But when you start doing that, you must redouble your vigilance, never get blasé, and always continue to watch a ship that has passed you until she has disappeared over the horizon, for it is only then that she has truly gone clear. Before that she may have to alter course to avoid another ship, and so put the two of you back on a collision course.

One of the most confusing things to meet at night is a fishing fleet. Instantly you may think that the lights are those of a big ship far off; then you realise there are several small boats close to and you've got to avoid them. Those boats are usually quite unable to take any avoiding action themselves

– their gear just won't allow it – and so it is up to you. Tugs and Naval craft should be given the same treatment, and be extra careful if you see another yacht.

Where you have to cross the mouth of a busy commercial port, do so as speedily as you can, even if it means going off course and beating back inshore. Cross as nearly as possible at right angles, since this keeps the danger distance down to a minimum.

Progress Checking

Unless you take great care to *identify* each light you sight, it is horrifyingly easy to get confused about your position at night. One town's lights look just like another, and it may only be by an offlying buoy or a lighthouse near the town that you can distinguish it from its neighbours. In fact all lights – buoys, lighthouses, light vessels, beacons, harbour lights – are identifiable by their characteristics: range, colour and sequence. A list of the characteristics of prominent lights along the coast should have been made before you set off, either from the chart or from the light lists in *Reed's,* and this now comes into its own as a quick reference. The point is that each light must be accurately timed and so identified before you try to take a bearing on it and use it to get a fix. For timing lights there is nothing to beat a stopwatch, though with practice it is possible to become proficient in counting seconds, but this needs care – it's no good saying, 'One, whoops we're off course, two, no three' and so on.

Apart from the fact that you will be bobbing up and down on the waves and will consequently have to wait some time before you can be sure that you have seen the full sequence of a light, there should be no great problems involved with identifying individual lights. The difficult part is looking at the chart, where all the lights are neatly laid out, each one visible in relation to the others, and interpreting this into what is actually seen. You have to allow for the angle at which you are seeing them – there may be a headland obscuring some, or a buoy may appear to be on the wrong side of a shore light, or you may not have noticed a seemingly prominent light has only got a range of a few miles, while another one can show up to 15 miles – it can all get very confusing if you let it. What you have to do is keep calm (an easy piece of advice to give), take each light in turn and determine its colour, group and timing, then find it on the chart. Once you have done that you can take a useful bearing on it.

Actually, taking a bearing on a flashing light is none too easy because it always goes out just as you think you've got it nicely lined up, but with patience it can be done. Remember too that buoys are notoriously hard to find in a seaway even in daylight, so try to use landmarks for making a landfall rather than a buoy. The shore lights will almost certainly have a greater range anyway.

Once more this all sounds a bit daunting, but really it's not that bad if you are careful. In fact night sailing and picking out lights can be very exciting.

Dipping Lights and Looms

One of the more accurate ways of fixing your position is by a bearing of a mark and your distance off it. The bearing is laid off on the chart and your distance off marked along it. The problem at night is to find your distance off a light. As usual *Reed's* comes to the rescue with a table of 'distances off lights just seen or dipping'. These are pre-computed tables that save you a fiddly calculation. First the difference must be understood between the loom of a light and a dipping light. The loom is quite simply the lightening of the sky that is observed while the light itself is still below the observer's horizon. A light is said to be dipping when it stands just clear of the horizon.

When the height of a light is given on the chart the process is dead easy; all you have to do is enter the table with the height of the light and the height of your eye above the water, and read off the dipping distance. This, combined with a bearing of the light provides your fix.

In the case of a light whose height is unknown, but whose range is given, it is slightly more complicated. The range of a light is always given at a height of 15ft, so if your eye is at a height other than 15ft the range will be other than that given. So you have to find the distance from the light to the horizon, and the distance from the observer to the horizon and add the two together. Range of light minus distance to horizon from a height of 15ft equals distance to horizon from light.

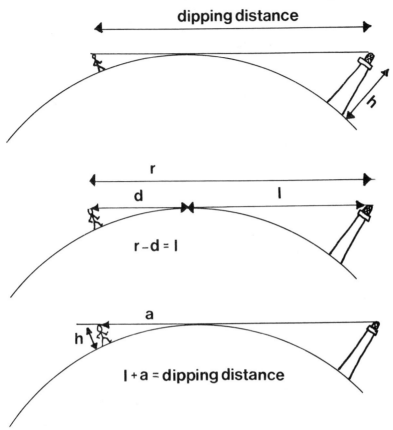

dipping distance

r

d   l

r − d = l

a

h

l + a = dipping distance

97 Top: the height of the lighthouse is known, the height of your eye is known, and all you have to do is look up the dipping distance in the appropriate table. Lower two: the situation is less straightforward − r is the range of the light, d is the distance to horizon at 15 ft, l is the distance to horizon from light, and a is the distance to horizon from observer's eye at height h.

That distance plus distance to horizon from height of observer's eye equals dipping distance from observer.

For example:

Range	20 miles (from chart)
Distance to horizon from 15ft	4.45 miles (*Reed's*)
Distance to horizon from light	15.55 miles
Distance to horizon from observer's eye (eg 8ft)	3.25 miles (*Reed's*)
	18.80 miles

Thus the light should dip at 18.80 miles

187

Something that is worth doing is working out the dipping constant for your own boat and learning it. If for instance your height of eye is 8ft when you are standing in the main hatch, then use this and calculate as follows: distance of horizon at 8ft minus distance of horizon at 15ft (height for charted lights) equals dipping constant. Thus: $3.25 - 4.45 = -1.2$ miles. This applied to the last problem gives dipping distance $20 - 1.2 = 18.80$ miles, which agrees with our previous calculation. It doesn't take long to work out the dipping constant for your own boat, and as can be seen here, it makes calculations much quicker afterwards.

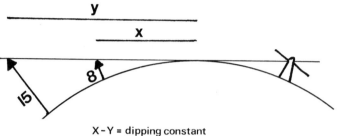

98

X - Y = dipping constant

CHAPTER 12

Engines and Motorsailing

When you buy a secondhand boat you are more or less stuck with whatever motor is already installed, but if you are buying new, then you have a certain freedom of choice. Initially the decision must be between an inboard or an outboard engine. By virtue of the fact that it is a permanent installation, an inboard engine has the advantage of being ready for use at any time, while it is likely that an outboard will have to be heaved up out of a locker and mounted on a bracket on the transom before it can be used. This is all very well in harbour, but at sea it can be the devil of a job. On the other hand, once in position, the outboard takes up no room in the boat, while an inboard completely fills the space under the cockpit sole and may well intrude into the cabin as well. Again because it can be lifted clear of its mountings, an outboard is often easier to work on than an inboard, and certainly clearing a fouled propeller is much simpler.

The propeller of an inboard engine is deeper and further forward than that of an outboard, which makes it much less likely to come out of the water in a seaway, and gives it a better grip on the water. This has to be offset against the fact that because it is always in the water, you suffer immense drag while sailing, which can be avoided by lifting or tilting an outboard out of the water.

An outboard is usually cheaper than an equivalent inboard engine, and you can of course take it ashore to an engineer if anything goes seriously wrong, while someone has to be persuaded to go out to the boat if you have a troublesome inboard. An outboard also bypasses the need for any sort of stern gear or through-hull skin fittings that are required by an inboard engine.

Whichever unit you choose there are bound to be drawbacks, and perhaps the best idea is a compromise: an out-

189

board mounted in a well at the after end of the cockpit. With such an installation you have the best of both worlds, particularly if there is a sliding hatch fitted under the well so that the motor can be tilted up into the boat, and the hatch slid across to produce a smooth underwater hull when sailing.

Diesel or Petrol

If you should decide to install an inboard engine, you are next faced with the problem of whether to have a diesel or petrol engine. By the way, strictly speaking a 'diesel' engine is a compression ignition engine, that is one whose fuel is ignited by heat generated when it is violently compressed. Both these types of engine have their advantages, and you must weigh them all up and see which suits your purposes better.

Starting with money, diesels generally cost more initially than equivalent petrol engines, but their fuel is cheaper and

It is general practice these days to search for a berth in a strange harbour under power, but it is wise to have sails ready for hoisting and the anchor should always be cleared away when making port.

190

tends to go further. Against this, petrol can be bought at any roadside garage while you might have to go looking for one that sells diesel. It should be remembered, however, that petrol is readily combustible and represents a greater fire hazard than does the more docile diesel. It is no good though buying a diesel because it is 'safe' and then stowing a dinghy outboard with petrol dripping out of the carburettor, or keeping a gas bottle with a leaking pressure valve: you have got to be sensible about it. Diesel engines are much more susceptible to stoppage by dirty fuel than are petrol ones, and great care must be taken to keep fuel filters clean.

Possibly the biggest argument in favour of petrol engines is that so many people are familiar with them from servicing their cars. Anyone who can tinker successfully with his car should be able to look after a marine petrol engine without too much difficulty, and this may give him confidence in the motor. On the other hand the workings of a diesel, particularly the fuel injection system, are rather complicated to unfamiliar eyes.

A marine engine of any kind has to work in a damp, corrosive atmosphere, and from this point of view the diesel has the great advantage that it needs no electrics to make it work. You may of course have an electric starter motor, but on the size of engine we are interested in, it is very little trouble to start them by hand – provided decompressors are fitted. These are simple levers that allow the engine to be turned over with little effort until the flywheel is spinning rapidly. The levers are then flipped over and the momentum of the flywheel starts the engine. When choosing a diesel make quite sure that the decompressors are operable by the man who is cranking the motor, because there is not usually enough room round a family cruiser's engine for two people to work, and anyway there may not always be two people available.

A deciding factor in your choice of propulsion may be the weight of the engine. Because of the very high compression forces inside it, a diesel engine is a heavy brute very robustly built to withstand these strains. A petrol engine with its lower compression is a lighter motor altogether and may well take up less space, which is another serious consideration. Finally, diesel engines – at least the very small ones – tend to vibrate more than equivalent petrol engines, though the vibration can be minimised by proper flexible mountings.

Applying the Power

Most small auxiliaries in sailing cruisers drive straight through a gearbox, giving ahead, neutral and astern gears, with the engine final drive and the propeller shaft in more or less a straight line. In fact most gearboxes necessitate the prop shaft being slightly offset – usually lower than the final drive. This is not a bad thing really as it means that the angle of the prop shaft from the horizontal is not too great, so most of the propeller thrust is forwards and very little power is wasted in trying to lift the stern. You can of course do away with a complex gearbox and have a centrifugal or 'sailing' clutch, which allows the propeller to rotate freely when sailing, and only engages when the throttle is opened up, but with this arrangement you cannot have an astern gear. A gearbox usually reduces the engine revs so that the propeller is turned at a much slower speed, usually in the ratio of 2:1.

As we saw earlier, one of the problems with an inboard engine is that it takes up so much space in a small cruiser, and for this reason it is worth considering the possibility of using a transmission other than direct drive. As alternatives you could have a Vee drive, where the final drive from the engine is doubled back on itself through a gearbox; a hydraulic drive, where the engine can be mounted in any convenient place and its power is transmitted to the propeller by pressurised oil flowing in pipes; or a belt drive, which is self-explanatory.

The Vee drive system means mounting the motor back to front, which can produce problems if you want to use hand-starting, but it means that a very small motor could be sited in an after peak locker with only the gearbox under the cockpit. The disadvantage of this is that the engine's weight is right at one end of the boat.

In many ways a hydraulic drive would seem ideal, but problems have been experienced with a loss of efficiency, and as yet no such system has really caught on for small cruisers. The great advantage is that you can mount the engine wherever it suits you. No conventional gearbox is required as the direction of rotation of the propeller is controlled by the flow of hydraulic fluid. I have seen successful installations, and I think it is worth close attention where space is limited.

The other method giving the possibility of an offset mounting is belt drive. It is not very common, but can work per-

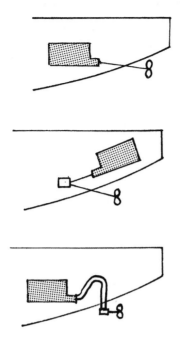

99   *Direct drive, V drive and hydraulic drive engine installations.*

fectly well and could be fitted up easily and cheaply. Of course a direct drive engine can be mounted off-centre, but an offset propeller can make handling tricky under power.

The power output from the engine eventually ends up at the propeller. Much is talked about 'the right propeller for the job', and it is indeed important to have one of the correct design, but finding out just what would be right is very difficult, and most of us throw up our hands in disgust and trust the engine manufacturer to fit the right one. You start off by choosing a two or three-bladed propeller, with the two-bladed type being fixed, folding or feathering. The fixed propeller stays as it is when sailing, the folding one claps its blades together like a butterfly folds its wings, and the feathering one turns its blades so that they line up fore and aft to give the least resistance. A three-bladed propeller is usually fitted on bigger boats with slow-revving diesels.

193

Propellers are described in terms of their diameter and pitch. The diameter is the diameter of a circle through the tips of the blades (see diagram) and the pitch is the distance the propeller would travel in a direction along its axis if it were turned through one revolution (see diagram). This is a difficult one to imagine, but think of a propeller turning and cutting its way through thick mud. It eats its way forward as it turns, and the distance from its starting point to its finishing point after one revolution is its pitch.

Generally a fine pitch propeller (one that doesn't travel far) is used with a high revving engine pushing a heavy boat, while a coarse propeller is used with a slower revving engine. Just to confuse us all there are innumerable ifs and buts with all this, and it is worth making enquiries of engine and propeller manufacturers to find what is suitable for your particular requirements. The biggest confusion comes with the feathering or variable pitch propeller, as this has rotating blades to give ahead, neutral, astern and feathered position with infinite variations in between. Their advantage lies in not requiring a conventional gearbox, and in the ability to vary the pitch according to the load.

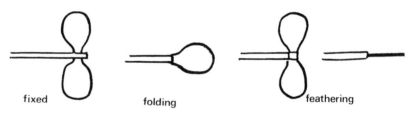

fixed   folding   feathering

100   Types of propeller.

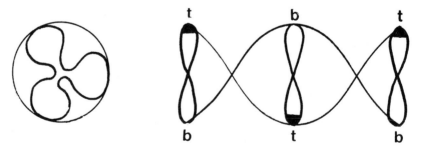

101   Propeller dimensions – left: diameter; right: pitch.

194

Engine Installations

From the point of view of the user, the most important things about an engine installation are that the engine should be completely accessible for working on; it should have its electrics well protected against corrosion; it should have an efficient cooling system, and the engine box should have good acoustic insulation. The actual mechanics of mounting and aligning the engine and arranging the electrics are best left to professionals unless you happen to be particularly good mechanically.

Far too many engines can only be reached, even for routine oil checks, by crawling about on your stomach, contorting yourself round pillars and bulkheads. It should not be too difficult to arrange things so that by removing the companion-way steps and a couple of panels the whole engine is revealed. In many cases you can remove various hatches, but it means unscrewing a couple of dozen bolts – this is no good in a seaway when you are in a hurry. The watertightness of access hatches is important as the engine and its electrics quickly become corroded if saltwater is constantly dripping on them. I remember one boat where we made port after going through some rough weather and found the whole engine coated in salt; it looked like a log in a snowstorm. It also didn't work properly.

Obviously an engine needs an efficient cooling system, whether it is air cooled or water cooled. In the latter case, each of the through-hull skin fittings must have a seacock (a screw-down valve), so that it can be shut off, and the intake must have a strainer on it. All of these seacocks and strainers must of course be within easy reach.

Lastly, it only makes sense that the engine should be made as quiet as possible, and this means covering the inside of the engine box with an acoustic insulating material. Living with a noisy motor is unpleasant and unnecessary as there are some good insulators on the market.

Troubleshooting

The two occasions on which an engine tells you most blatantly that there is something wrong with it are when it refuses to start and when it stops before you intend it to. So let's begin

The birth of a boat: one of the earliest jobs is installing the auxiliary engine, in this case a two-cylinder diesel with direct drive.

with starting troubles, the symptoms of which are pretty obvious. If the engine doesn't even turn over you may have a flat battery, or one whose leads have corroded or come adrift, some other loose electrical connections, or the starter motor may have jammed. First make a visual check of the electrics and if anything is clearly amiss there put it right, otherwise try starting the engine by hand. A jammed starter motor can usually be wound back with a spanner, but check in the owner's handbook. When the engine turns over but still won't start there's a host of things to check: fuel level in tank; blocked fuel lines; flooded carburettor; choked fuel pump; injectors blocked; dirt or water in fuel; dirty filters; damp electrics; oily, dirty, damaged sparking plugs; incorrect ignition timing. The first of these can be remedied quite easily if you carry a spare can of fuel, but with a diesel engine any fiddling about with injectors or fuel systems means that you have to bleed the system when you have finished, and that's not the world's most wonderful job. Blocked fuel lines can usually be cleared all right though it's a messy job. The flooded carburettor will have to be drained and the excess fuel allowed to evaporate. Injectors are surprisingly delicate things and care must be taken not to damage them if they are unscrewed; should they be faulty they will have to be dealt with by an expert and may need replacing. When you suspect contaminated fuel, empty the sludge trap, clear the filters and fuel lines, and hope that does the trick, otherwise you will have to empty and clean the tank before refilling. Dry the electrics and spray them with an aerosol damp retardant. Clean or replace spark plugs, checking gaps at the same time. You will have to follow the owner's handbook to deal with ignition timing.

When an engine that has been running quite happily suddenly cuts out there is an overpowering silence, in which a crew tends to stand still, listening, as if expecting the engine to start up again. It won't. You have got to make it. Almost certainly it will be electrical trouble if an engine cuts out without any sort of warning, so check connections, dry everything and try starting. With luck that should solve the problem, but if not then look at the distributor and see that all is well there – it could be that there is a faulty capacitor.

On most occasions an engine faulters and coughs a bit before giving up the ghost, and in this case there are several possibilities. First and foremost, lack of fuel; fuel lines blocked

197

or broken; fuel pump choked; injectors blocked or damaged; air lock; air vent in outboard motor filler cap closed; contaminated fuel; filters choked; water inlet fouled. Check the level in the fuel tank even if you 'know it's full' – leaks can occur without being noticed. Inspect fuel lines for damage and clear or repair if necessary. Clean fuel pump if blocked. Remember to treat injectors with caution, and preferably leave them alone until all other possibilities have been exhausted. An air lock will mean bleeding the system. Leaving the air vent closed on the outboard's fuel tank is a common failing (it also happens to be very embarrassing), and you might do well to make a surreptitious check that the fuel tap is turned on. Deal with contaminated fuel as before. Clean filters – petrol or diesel are good cleansers – and remember to close the seacock before removing a seawater strainer.

Those are the two basic exigencies with which we are concerned, but close to them comes the discovery that nothing happens when you try to put the engine in gear. The simplest explanation is disconnected gear controls; alternatives are a seized gearbox or a broken prop shaft. After you have fended off whatever you were about to hit (it always seems to happen when coming alongside) follow the control cables or rods and see if anything has come adrift. Failing that put a cautious hand on the gearbox and see how hot it is – lack of oil is the usual cause. With a broken prop shaft you will usually manage to engage gear and hear a graunching noise as you open the throttle – make a visual check of the shaft.

An overheating engine is generally the result of lack of oil or a fault in the cooling system, often occasioned by the water intake valve not being turned on. Alternatively the circulatory pumps could be in trouble and you may have to replace an impeller. The fuel mixture may be wrong in a two-stroke, and the injectors may be faulty in a diesel.

Rough running must be caused by something to do with the electrics, the fuel supply or the air intake, with excess vibration being caused by loose mountings, a damaged propeller blade or a fouled propeller. Go over the electrics as described before and look at the distributor cap to see if it is cracked and therefore shorting. The same applies to the fuel and air supplies. Once you have made port a general overhaul might be a good thing.

Excessive blue exhaust smoke at normal running temperatures indicates a burning of lubricating oil either by its being drawn into the induction manifold from an overfull air filter, or more seriously by its leaking past the pistons due to a mechanical fault there. On the other hand black smoke indicates poor fuel combustion, possibly caused by a faulty choke mechanism or incorrectly adjusted fuel injectors.

Clearly this is only the briefest possible summary of engine troubles, but it is a start. A happy engine is extremely useful, while an unhappy one is a misery to all, so look after your boat's engine and don't curse it; it might decide to sulk just when you need it.

Fuel Consumption

Whereas it is easy enough with a car to talk in terms of miles per gallon this is clearly not possible with boats. For a marine engine we express fuel consumption in terms of gallons used per hour, eg $\frac{1}{2}$ gallon per hour. Occasionally brochures do say that a boat carries so many gallons of fuel to give a range of X miles, but be wary of this figure as it is dependent upon engine revs and sea conditions. Just as a car may not meet its advertised mpg if you sit in several traffic jams, so too a rough head sea will raise a marine engine's fuel consumption. It is, however, wise to carry out trials to determine the approximate fuel consumption at cruising revs for your engine, as you will then have some idea of how long you can motor on a passage.

Maintenance

A well maintained engine is far more likely to work than a neglected one, but many cruiser owners completely ignore the auxiliary until it goes wrong. The owner's handbook will detail the maintenance schedule for the engine and this should be adhered to strictly, but if you are a 'better to leave well alone if it's running' person, the least you should do is to check the oil levels and if you do much motoring on a passage, remember to grease the stern gland regularly. At the same time the water in the batteries should be checked and topped up if low, otherwise they will boil.

Some of the engine manufacturers run maintenance courses

for people who own their make of engine. While they certainly don't promise to turn you into a mechanical genius overnight, such a course will equip you to look after your boat's engine far more efficiently, and give you more confidence in your ability to cope with a breakdown. There are also car maintenance courses run by many evening institutes, and although these are not entirely applicable to marine situations – I'd love to see a boat fitted with disc brakes – they do offer a good grounding in mechanics.

Motor Sailing

The first thing to point out here is that as soon as you begin to motor sail you are immediately bound by the rule of the road for motor vessels, and by day you are required to fly a black cone in the fore rigging, replaced at night by a white steaming light.

There are any number of reasons for motor sailing – punching a foul tide round a headland, making a hard passage to windward easier, trying to beat the tide home. In each case your prime objective is to reach your destination faster, and possibly more comfortably, than you would under sail alone. When you are on a long coastal passage you might decide to motor sail if the boat's speed falls below a certain point in order to save a tide; in other words you are trying to keep the average speed up.

Assuming it is blowing hard, the sea is rough and you want to weather a headland without putting in another tack. You have three options: to motor sail with just the jib set, just the main set or, if conditions allow, with both set. The choice between these is made in the light of your knowledge of the boat and how she handles under a variety of rigs in the conditions prevailing. A boat on which it is usual to reef the mainsail before changing to a smaller headsail will probably drive better under engine and a headsail, whereas one with a small foresail/large mainsail configuration may do better under a well-reefed main (which is more manageable than a headsail) and engine. Of course if you can you will make the best progress with main and jib set. This is something that needs experimentation to discover the best arrangement for your boat. In any case sheets will have to be hardened right in to keep the sails flat and driving, as the apparent wind will be from further forward than when under sail alone.

The effect of apparent wind moving further ahead as the boat goes faster becomes more obvious when on a run or very broad reach, and in such a situation the wind will have to be quite strong before it really fills the sails. When you are motor sailing before a light wind in order to keep up an average speed you will probably not be able to set a jib at all as it will simply backwind the whole time. It is much better to use the main alone with the boom run off and a preventer rigged from the outboard end down to the deck. This is set up hard against the pull of the mainsheet to stop the boom banging about and it helps to keep the sail full. Unless the wind is strong enough to overcome the drawing ahead effect you will never really be on a dead run when motor sailing.

Many people seem to think that if they have got to beat the tide home on a Sunday night, or if the wind is dead down a narrow channel, the thing to do is motor. This may not always be the case – motor sailing may well be the quicker and more comfortable way. If the sea is at all rough – say wind against tide in a narrow channel – then butting straight into it under power means that you will be pitching up and down in the same hole feeling miserable. Surely it is much better to set a bit of mainsail, sheet it in hard and tack out with the engine providing the drive, but the mainsail acting as a strong steadying influence. Under some conditions motoring in a straight line may be just a little faster, but a yacht tends to roll like hell without any sails to steady her, and if you want your crew to come with you again I suggest you don't subject them to too much of that.

CHAPTER 13

Rough Weather

Go into the bar of any yacht club and listen to the conversation. As soon as the beer begins to flow you'll hear somebody starting to swing the lantern a bit. '. . . So there we were, you see, nothing up but a close reefed burgee and still we were surfing along at 10 knots. . .' Don't worry, even if you know it wasn't blowing above Force 6 that day. He's enjoying himself and he may well have been scared stiff at the time. For a small cruiser, particularly one with a couple of youngsters on board, a Force 5 or 6 over a spring tide can seem like a full blown hurricane.

It must also be realised that there is a tremendous difference between sailing in a full gale in the sheltered waters of an estuary and sailing in the same wind several miles offshore. In an estuary with the shores only half a mile or so on either hand the sea gets choppy covered in white horses, but with just a scrap of sail up many boats will still make progress to windward. Take these same boats offshore though and they'll be in a most uncomfortable situation.

When we talk about small boats in gales we are talking about being in a situation that we will have done our utmost to avoid. We *can* fail in our attempts to escape though, and if you are caught out at sea with your pants down and a gale rising, you have not only to prepare the boat for the battering she is going to take, but also the crew.

One point I should make is that the advice in this chapter – and indeed the one on distress – is entirely general. You must think about it all and adapt it to your own boat and circumstances: you just cannot be dogmatic about the sea.

Emergency Reefing and Steering

There will probably be many times during an average season

A rising gale with spume beginning to blow downwind. The sea is still confused and has not settled down into a regular pattern of waves.

When beating to windward in even moderate weather conditions the fitting of a spray hood over the companionway helps enormously to keep the accommodation dry and afford the helmsman some shelter.

203

when you have to reef, but on most occasions it will be a case of changing down the jib and taking three or four rolls in the mainsail – nothing drastic. You may discover that the boom end begins to droop a little when you reef like this, but you don't worry much about it. Fair enough, but what happens when it really comes on to blow and you want to take down six or eight rolls, ten even? If you did, chances are the boom would foul the main hatch or take your head off on a gybe. One of the first things you should do with a new boat is to take a really deep reef in the main and see how it sets, then if it is bad you can do something about altering it before it's too late. A temporary and rather unsatisfactory remedy for a droopy boom is to roll jerseys or trousers into the sail, but a much better solution is to fit tapered battens on the outboard end of the boom.

There are few small cruisers these days not fitted with roller reefing on the main boom, and very good it is too for ease of handling. It has its drawbacks in that it is hard to get a neat reef which won't pull the sail out of shape, and more importantly in foul weather, it can break, jam up, or you can lose all the reefing handles. For this reason alone you should insist on having an alternative reefing system, the obvious one being 'old fashioned' points. Reef points are undeniably fiddly to tie with cold fingers, but there is nothing mechanical to go wrong and a far better reef is possible than you can get with most roller gear. If you won't have anything else, at least have one row of eyes allowing you to reeve a line through them and take in a single, really deep reef – say the equivalent of 8–10 rolls. Then if your roller gear does pack up, or if you have not solved the boom droop problem, you can still get most of the sail off while keeping just enough set to drive.

You will probably be used to changing down the headsail as the wind rises, ending up with a storm or spitfire jib, but if it were blowing a full gale, even this pocket handkerchief might be too much. As you are unlikely to have any smaller sails you have to do something drastic. Before setting the spitfire, lashing can be put round the bunched up head of the sail, and another round the tack (see diagram). Then hank it on as you would normally, and hoist away. I warn you this is not good for the sail, but if it gets you out of trouble then it doesn't really matter.

Just as you need an alternative reefing method, it's as well

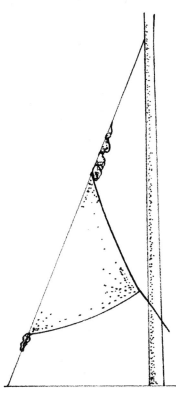

102 In dire emergency when lashings at head and tack cannot be secured, they can instead be knotted, when the sail is said to be Spanish reefed.

to carry a spare tiller, and if you can, to work out how you would devise a simple alternative steering system. The spare tiller is not just for bad weather – I've had one come adrift in a very light breeze, when I had to steer for a while with a Mole wrench clamped on the rudder head. Bigger boats with wheel steering often carry a solid metal tiller that can be fitted directly onto the rudder head if the steering goes wrong – you needn't go to that extent, but it is worth practising changing tillers so you know what tools are needed and how it is done.

Some of the smaller French boats don't bother to fit an engine at all, but simply have a rowlock mounted on the transom and use a long oar to scull in and out of harbour. In an emergency they can also use this oar as a tiller and rudder – not a bad idea. Again though, steering with an oar is not all that easy and it should be practised. It is not unheard of for people to steer only by trimming the sails, but in heavy going this is extremely difficult; nonetheless it is a nice piece of seamanship, and for that reason alone it is good to learn how.

Makeshift Trysail

A trysail is a loosefooted triangular sail set on the mast in place of the mainsail. It can be set when the mainsail cannot be reefed any further, or if by mischance it is torn or otherwise damaged. It is an emergency sail, and as such it is rarely found on small cruisers, and since the advent of lightweight/ high strength synthetic sailcloth it has lost popularity on all sizes of boat. However, sunlight and salt air combine to make synthetic materials brittle, allowing them to split if subjected to unaccustomed strains – such as may be met with in heavy weather. If your mainsail does split, or if the boom were broken and you don't carry a trysail, it is possible to improvise with a small staysail.

A line from the foot of the mast is rove through the tack cringle, the sail is hoisted on the main halyard, and is sheeted to the quarters. If you can do it, the sail will set better if it is bent onto the mast with a line through the hanks. Don't sheet the sail to the boom end (even if it is undamaged), for although you then have the mainsheet as a purchase, it means that the boom will swing about dangerously while setting the sail and while tacking or gybing. A better plan is to lead the sheets through quarter blocks and then forward to sheet winches (assuming some are fitted), but watch for the weather sheet chafing the stowed mainsail, and don't omit to lash the boom down securely – if you can take it off the gooseneck and lash it on deck so much the better.

Jury Rig

While we tend to think of dismasting as being something that happens to some other poor bloke out in the middle of an ocean, a mast can break or bend in only moderate conditions just outside harbour. If you are only two or three miles offshore in reasonable weather, the chances are that you will be able to make port under power, but what if the engine packs up? Obviously you can send up flares and say 'help' loudly, but first of all you must try to help yourself.

The commonest breaking points for an alloy mast are just above, just below and at the crosstrees. Many masts have not only the crosstree roots rivetted on at that point, but also a tang bolted on each side to take the lower shrouds. In other

words this is a region of heavy stress. The other likely breaking point is down at the mast step or at the partners where
the mast passes through the deck. However, as a break there
is likely to be the result of a break higher up, you are most
unlikely to have a mast go by the board in one piece. Wooden
spars have the extra possibility of breaking at a scarf, though
modern glues have lessened the likelihood.

When the whole mast or part of the mast goes it is left
either in a tangled mess alongside in the water, or as a tangled
mess hanging down on deck. Either way you have got to
clear that mess away before it damages the boat or crew. If
you can save the broken part and recover it aboard so much
the better, but if it is trying to puncture the hull and seems
likely to succeed before you can get it on deck, then you will
have to cut it clear and let it go. An axe used to be a standard
piece of equipment on boats, but now you would do better
to carry a hacksaw with a number of spare blades and a large
pair of bolt-croppers or wire cutters.

Once the immediate mess has been cleared you can start
thinking about how best to set up some sort of jury rig. It is
pretty well impossible to give specific advice here as there
are too many parameters, and ingenuity will be the watch-
word, but there are one or two fundamental ideas to consider.
Clearly the idea is to set up a mast on which you can set
sufficient sail to give the boat a chance of making port, even
if it is only downwind. The cartoon raft with two bearded,
shipwrecked figures on board usually has an oar set up as a
mast with a cross piece and a shirt spread on it. We hope to
do a little better than that, but they have obviously impro-
vised with available materials, and that is the best anyone
can do.

If the mast has gone near the crosstrees, but left the lower
part standing, then you are well off. 'All' you have to do is
rig up some shrouds and set a jib whose luff wire acts as a
forestay, and whose halyard will do for a backstay. Three
things that will help in any situation are spare blocks, a
supply of bulldog clips, and perhaps a knowledge of how to
tie a jury or masthead knot. The bulldog clips (see diagram)
are used for holding two pieces of wire together instead of
splicing them, and the jury knot for attaching shrouds to the
masthead.

Apart from the section of mast left standing, you can improvise a mast with the boom, oars from the dinghy in the form of

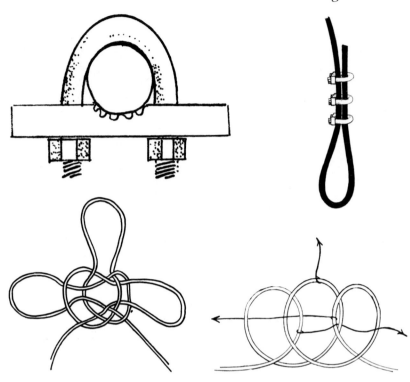

104, 105 *Top: a bulldog clip in use. Above: jury knot and its formation.*
The spar fits in the central space and shrouds attach to the loops. Join ends
for fourth loop.

a bipod, or a piece of the broken mast. In any case you are
not likely to be able to set much sail, but it should allow you
to close the coast. With luck and care – you should check all
rigging and mast fittings at least once during the season –
none of this will happen to you, but it is worth sitting down
and thinking about it on a cold winter evening when there
is not much on television. That thinking could get you out of
a nasty situation.

Seasickness

Most people are attacked at some time or other by seasickness,
though there are a few lucky souls who seem to be immune
to it. Those who are not affected should make a point of not

scoffing or laughing at those who are, because I can assure you they are going through hell, and you never know, it might be your turn one day. For the sufferers, don't be ashamed or embarrassed, good skippers and crew members will be sympathetic and will do what they can for you, but it is mainly up to you, and don't expect anyone to clear up after you. Few people are actually incapacitated by seasickness, and one of the quickest ways of getting over it that I have found is to carry on as normally as possible with your watches and other chores. On many occasions I have arrived on watch grizzly faced, clutching a bucket, and with an icy sweat breaking out all over. In the beginning you think you are going to die; then you hope you are going to die; finally, and worst of all, is the realisation that you are *not* going to die. After that you start to get better.

Individuals have to find their own formula for recovery. There are numerous anti-seasickness drugs available, and it is likely that one of these will prevent you being sick, but watch out for the drowsiness that many of them induce. I have yet to find a drug that really helps me, so I usually let the sickness take its natural course, carrying on as best I can and starting to eat as soon as possible. Some people will say that this is quite wrong and that you should force yourself to eat before you feel like it – let them I say. Again, some people advocate eating dry biscuits and such things – I don't fancy that idea because vomitting hard, undigested items is very painful indeed. Bland things such as bananas, orange juice, well-chewed apples (peeled), Marmite, Bovril; these are the things I start with, but as I said it is very much an individual thing.

When someone takes his trick at the helm and is being sick, insist that he wears a life-harness clipped on to the windward side, so that he can be sick to leeward, but can't go overboard. Down below, give him a bucket, make sure he is kept securely in his bunk or is wedged upright if he is sitting. If he wants to sleep he will. Do call him for his watch and only stop him doing it if he is really bad, but if you are in a shipping lane someone must stick their head outside every so often to make sure all is well. The point here is that a sick man has slow reactions, low concentration and his eyesight may be affected. I scared myself stupid once when I looked up from contemplating the bottom of a bucket and found a ship lying athwart our course about half a mile ahead. I swear she wasn't there a couple of minutes earlier.

Should your wife become sick you must steel yourself not to mollycoddle her as this is the sure way of having her collapse on you completely. Women are far less fragile than they appear. I don't mean that you should drive her on deck with a rope's end, but try to keep her going. Children are often less prone to seasickness than their parents and will often just go to sleep when it's rough – or else laugh at you being sick. However, there are drugs for children, and it may be as well to dose them with one of these before putting to sea and hope that their drowsiness will keep them quiet.

Food

Cooking in a small boat in rough weather is nearly impossible, and it's certainly a brave person with a stronger stomach than mine who tries. However, if you are going to be at sea at the next meal time you must try to be prepared for it, because lack of food, combined with loss of body heat will quickly make you weak, tired and careless. Before the weather gets too bad try to heat up some soup and keep it hot in a Thermos flask, and at the same time make some sandwiches and put out lots of chocolate, raisins, fruit, and anything else which will provide a snack. There is not a lot more than that you can do until you find shelter, but then a good, hot meal is the cure-all.

Clothing

Just as important as food in the battle against cold are good protective clothes. These have to keep you warm without being so cumbersome that your movements are restricted, and most importantly, they must not be tight otherwise they will restrict the blood circulation. Wind and rain can be guarded against with a good suit of oilskins, which should have storm cuffs (to reduce the amount of wind and rain going up the sleeves), and a close-fitting hood with a draw-string to pull it in round the face. A very considerable pro-portion of the total heat lost from the body is lost through the head – so protect it. To help the fight against cold drips running down your neck, wrap a piece of towelling round inside the collar. It is very hard to find a pair of gloves that keep your hands warm and allow you to cleat a rope or winch in a sheet without winding the fingers in too, but any gloves are better than nothing on a cold watch, provided you remember to take them off for fiddly jobs.

Under oilskins it is better to wear several layers of thin jerseys than a couple of thick ones. Seaboot stockings are good, tough and quite cheap, but make sure you are still able to put boots on. There are several types of thermal underwear on the market, but they are not cheap, and I have found the old woollen Long Johns adequate for most occasions, with pyjamas coming a very close second. Remember when going on watch even on a fairly warm night to have oilskins handy, because you can get surprisingly damp just from dew.

Tactics

The obvious way to get prior warning of impending bad weather is to listen to the radio forecasts, in particular the shipping forecasts, which we will look at in detail in Chapter 16. The action you take after hearing a forecast of bad weather is governed by your position and circumstances, together with the imminence or otherwise of the approaching rough and tumble.

In the first place you must bring your dead reckoning plot up to date so that you know fairly accurately where you are. Assuming that the forecast gives you a few hours' grace, you can look around from your plotted position for somewhere that will give you shelter from the coming blow. This may be a harbour or an anchorage in the lee of a headland, but the two requirements are that it should be reachable well within the forecast time limit, and that it should have as simple and clear an approach as possible, taking into consideration the direction from which the wind will be rising. It is possible that there will be two equally sheltered places within reasonable sailing time, one upwind of your position and one downwind. In that case you have to try to picture what the conditions will be like by the time you get there. The downwind harbour or refuge may be reached sooner, but if it is on a lee shore the waves will tend to pile up in the shallowing water, and it does not take much of this to turn an otherwise simple entrance into a very dodgy affair. On the other hand, the upwind harbour may take longer to reach and also means a slog to windward, but the nearer you get the more likely you are to find quieter water, and the longer the entrance will remain passable.

You must also ask yourself if there is any possibility of having to enter in darkness, and if there will be sufficient water at the state of tide you will encounter. Where there are plenty of leading lights or a well marked channel, then the entry after dark should not pose too many problems, but entering an unlit port in a rising wind may be very unwise. In order to make port in reasonable time, or to get round a headland before the tide turns against you, it is worth motor sailing, but don't leave yourself out of fuel when you finally get in.

When the forecast gives warning of a fast approaching blow, the questions to be asked remain the same, but the problem becomes that much more acute. In these circumstances it can be a case of 'any port in a storm'. A forecast blow 'in the next 12 hours' when you are already at sea very often allows you to press on for your planned destination, but an 'imminent' forecast means a drastic re-think. It might mean turning tail and running back whence you came. It will usually mean going into a place that for some reason you would not normally give a second thought to, and now is the time that all the charts you have bought 'just in case' really come into their own. So too does your homework before the trip, which should have included studying all these charts together with the pilots, to find out which harbours would be usable on such occasions. All time so spent will be tremendously valuable, since in an emergency you will be nervous and a bit worried, so familiarity with what you are reading and looking at will make absorbing the detail much simpler.

Clearly the last place you want to be in a high wind is hard by a lee shore. A crack ocean racer may be able to claw her way to windward into the teeth of a gale, but a small, dumpy family cruiser certainly cannot. As soon as it looks like blowing up into an onshore gale you must try to find a safe retreat, and failing that you must gain searoom. This will probably entail motorsailing to windward until you are well offshore and in a position to think again about a harbour, or even about the possibility of heaving to and staying at sea.

213

But it must be done as quickly as possible. Trying to gain an offing by beating into the wind against steep, short, sometimes breaking, shallow-water seas is just not on.

You may of course be too far from a port to be able to get in before it is blowing hard. Then you have two choices: to stay at sea and ride it out (assuming that you have or can gain sufficient searoom), or to make port in rough weather. The former I have already said is notionally romantic but really miserable – it will be uncomfortable and frightening, but it could be safer than trying to get in. A narrow harbour entrance in an onshore gale becomes a place of heavily breaking seas which can easily drive a small boat onto the piers. Entering through such a mess can be far more hairy than staying out. The best hope is to crab across the rising wind and find shelter under a headland if you can, but in any case, think carefully and then act quickly.

CHAPTER 14

Fog

When visibility is reduced to between 2200 yards and 1100 yards we use the term mist, and when it is further reduced to less than 1100 yards we say that it is foggy. Waking up in a nice quiet anchorage and finding the world reduced to a few yards all round the boat and enclosed by cotton wool makes the decision to stay put very easy, but fog is a nasty sneaky thing that will unhesitatingly creep up on you at sea. With its approach come special navigational problems, the obvious ones being how to see and avoid shipping. Leaving aside sound for a minute, the first intimation of the approach of a ship may be a darkening of the fog

'Well, I don't reckon we're going to get far today.'

106   Direction of ship's approach in fog
shown by her bow wave.

in an irregularly shaped patch. This is followed by a defining
of the shape and a whitening of an area low down on the
shape – the bow wave. If this is dead centre the ship is coming straight down on you and you will have to take avoiding
action immediately. When it is at one end of a long dark
shape, then the ship is crossing your line of sight and should
go clear. In between these two extremes you may see a short
side and a long side to the white, showing that the vessel is
crossing at an angle, with the long part on the side nearer
to you and indicating her angle of approach (see diagram).
    Fog produces strange effects with sound: telling from what
direction a sound is coming can be very hard, compounded
by the existence of what are called lanes of silence. These cut
out sound completely, making it impossible to hear an
approaching ship, or the warning fog signal of a lighthouse.
When a ship emerges from the silent lane its siren is heard
with alarming clarity and intensity. For some reason in fog
it is very common only to hear a ship's engines when she is
*down*wind from you, and not to hear anything when she is
upwind. When you try to listen for a faint sound it is a help
if two of you can listen, then there is less chance of imagined

hearings and also a chance of getting the direction of sound right. It looks a bit odd, but to aid concentration you can cup a hand behind each ear and close your eyes – but remember to *tell someone off as lookout*, for you would feel a right fool (apart from anything else) if you hit something when the whole crew had their eyes shut.

Going back again to vision in fog, it is hard to judge distances of visibility, so a frequent check should be made, for instance by dropping a screwed up piece of paper over-board and watching it out of sight. At night a paraffin soaked rag or crumpled paper can be lit and used. Remembering that a ship is moving much faster through the water than you are, even if the paper shows the visibility to be about 400 yards, you are going to have to think and act very fast indeed if a ship does loom up. Some people automatically start the engine when fog is about, but this destroys all chance of hearing a ship. However, if you want to get inshore out of a shipping lane you may well be advised to motorsail.

While you may feel somewhat helpless in fog because there is very little wind and you are perhaps cagey about using the motor, be thankful that we do not normally meet fog and a strong wind together. Such conditions can be very frightening. In any case you must keep as accurate an account of your position as possible, but in fog and wind you need to be doubly careful.

If you are underway in fog vigilance is the keyword, and from a safety point of view, make the crew wear life-jackets not harnesses. Unlikely though the chance may seem, it would be a sad thing if someone were attached to a sinking vessel unable to unclip their harness.

Foghorns

Foghorns come in all shapes and sizes, from steam driven 'Here comes the QE2' types, to embodiments of a Leonardo da Vinci nightmare. There are trumpets that the operator blows through, there are plunger-operated ones, electric ex-car horns, aerosol horns, klaxons and so on. Most small boats carry either a mouth-operated trumpet or an aerosol horn, with car horns found occasionally. I did know one chap who had a plunger-operated horn taken from an old tug; it was about the size of his boat and was a fantastic ship-scarer.

217

Tests carried out by one of the yachting magazines showed that of these commonly used types of foghorn, the aerosol one gave the loudest and most nearly omnidirectional blast, while the trumpet was weaker and very directional. The car horns were weaker still and would of course require the use of a battery or accumulator.

The aerosol horns emit a continuous note for as long as the operating button is depressed, but it is common for the diaphragm to 'freeze'. The gas (usually Freon) freezes droplets of water in the foggy atmosphere and the ice so formed prevents vibration of the diaphragm, so that no sound at all can be obtained until it has melted. Clearly this could prove dangerous, and a standby horn should be carried.

The mouth-operated trumpet, though not as loud as the aerosol horn over short distances, has a better carrying power over longer distances, where the shape of the trumpet projects the sound rather better than the splayed-out aerosol horn. Its advantages are that it emits a continuous note for as long as the operator can blow; it requires no mechanical or electrical aid for operation, and it is robust and reliable. It is also cheap and does not need replacement gas canisters.

Radar Reflectors

While the hoisting of a radar reflector certainly does not make a boat magically immune from being run down by a ship, it does give some comfort to the occupants of a small cruiser by greatly increasing the chances of the boat being picked up on a ship's radar. Its presence in the rigging though must not allow the lookout's vigilance to relax. As its name implies it can only reflect the radar beam of an already operating scanner, and its reflection will only be noted if the operator of the radar set is keeping a close watch. It is also possible for a scanner to miss picking up the reflection of an object that is very close to it if the set is tuned to a long range scale. For instance the echo of a boat about half a mile away may not show on the radar display if the 12 mile range scale is in use.

Without going into details of how they work, the bigger the reflector the better, and it should be hoisted as high as possible to give it a chance of being 'seen' in a rough sea.

Do not waste your time with metal jerrycans or any other substitute, as these are useless. Make sure that the reflector you use is hoisted to display the correct aspect: which way this is can be found quite simply by putting the reflector down on some flat surface and letting go. It will take up the only possible stable position, and that is how it should be displayed.

Hoisting a reflector in the rigging creates problems of chafe on sails and its own halyards, so it must be bowsed down hard and if possible held clear of sails with a lashing. The ideal is arguably to mount a reflector permanently on the masthead, but few people find this aesthetically acceptable, so look for the chance of fixing it up between backstays, or between jumper struts high on the mast.

Fog Signals

The International Regulations for Preventing Collisions at sea lay down precisely the sound signals that vessels shall make in conditions of restricted visibility, and although it is only required of vessels over 40ft to make these signals, it is as well for the owner of a smaller boat to be able to recognise them and use them if necessary.

Power-driven vessels underway and making way through the water blow a prolonged blast at intervals of not more than 2 minutes.
Power-driven vessels underway but not making way sound 2 prolonged blasts with an interval of about 1 second between them.
Sailing vessels on starboard tack sound one blast at intervals of not more than 1 minute.
Sailing vessels on port tack sound 2 blasts in succession.
Sailing vessels with the wind abaft the beam sound 3 blasts in succession.
All anchored vessels ring a bell rapidly for about 5 seconds every minute.

There are further signals for vessels being towed and those that have run aground, but these are the basic ones. A full list can be found in *Reed's* and should be studied.

Look at the chart and you will find that many lighthouses, buoys and light vessels make aural fog signals with various devices, such as: diaphone, siren, tyfon, bell or whistle. Their purpose is to warn people away from danger, and each has its own peculiar sound, thus:

Diaphone – low note ending in a grunt.
Siren – medium powered high or low note (or both together, though it is possible that only one will be heard due to one of fog's many strange effects on sound).
Reed – high note from a horn.
Tyfon – medium pitched note from vibrating diaphragm.
Nautophone – high Reed-like note, electrically operated.
Electric fog horn – several simultaneous frequencies combine to produce medium pitched note.
Gun – self-explanatory.
Explosive – signals explode in mid-air.
Bell – mostly wave-activated fitted to buoys.
Whistle – usually found on isolated buoys.
Gong – self-explanatory.

In conditions of fog always have the foghorn ready to hand and be prepared to make the correct signal describing your boat's movements. Realise also that unless a ship sees you on her radar and is able to avoid you, the onus of collision prevention will be entirely on you, the relatively more manoeuvrable vessel.

Working Inshore

The obvious first course of action on finding yourself in a shipping lane in fog is to get out of it quickly, and the best place to make for – assuming calm conditions – is shallow water. A big ship cannot follow you there, and you can anchor until conditions improve. But navigating towards the coast in poor visibility is rather like inching towards the head of a flight of stairs in the dark – one step too many and you're in trouble.

It is under these conditions that a radio direction finder and an echo-sounder show their worth. If fog closes in quickly and you are not too sure of your position a DF fix can give you a departure for working out your course inshore. Obviously if the DF fix is greatly at variance with your DR plot one or both will have to be reworked, but unreliable bearings may be obtained at dusk, dawn, or when very close to the coast with the signal from the beacon making a small angle to the coastline. Once you have fixed your position you can lay off a course to take you clear of the shipping lane as quickly as possible. The odds are very much against a harbour entrance lying directly along that course, so the coast (or at least shallow water) must be found and then a new course steered to a port (unless you decide to anchor off).

The situation you don't want to be in is the one where you have run your calculated distance, nothing has been sighted, until suddenly land appears looming out of the fog high above you and a rapid about turn has to be executed. To avoid this a chain of soundings is taken on the run in and is compared with the chart. It will be seen that along the course line the seabed rises and falls, or rises slowly with a sharp upward trend close inshore, or shelves steeply the whole way, but whatever it does it follows a recognisable pattern. Thus, if while you sail in you take a series of soundings, correct them for tide, etc, to reduce them to chart datum, plot them on a piece of tracing paper and fit that plot over the chart, an accurate check can be kept on your progress. With a leadline it is probably practical to take soundings only about every $\frac{1}{4}$ mile, but with an echo-sounder a continuous reading can be taken.

The only conceivable advantage of the leadline over the echo-sounder for this sort of navigation is that with a leadline a sample of the seabed can be brought up for examination and comparison with the information given on the chart. This is done by 'arming the lead' with tallow packed in the hollow end, to which shells or shingle or whatever is on the bottom will adhere. It can be a good check on position if, for instance, you are sailing in a generally muddy area and have to cross (or avoid) say a shingle bank.

Once you have got into shallow water out of the danger of shipping you can start thinking about either anchoring or making for a nearby harbour. When choosing an anchorage the normal rules apply with regard to what the bottom is like for holding, whether there is shelter from prevailing or expected winds, if there is a clear escape route, and what depth there will be at low water. Though you are unlikely to persuade any of your crew to keep a full anchor watch, do pop your head out every so often to see that all is well and to make a check on the visibility.

Should you decide to make for port once you are out of

immediate danger from shipping, you must either use the methods discussed in the next section of this chapter, or you may be able to work your way in with a series of DF bearings. Where the harbour itself has a beacon you may be able to home in on that, by checking that it is dead ahead each time it transmits, but great care must still be taken to ensure that you do not run foul of any dangers lying on that direct course. A careful check needs to be kept on distance run, otherwise you stand a chance of being mesmerised by the beacon and of piling up on the shore.

Creek Crawling

Groping along a coast and into a harbour mouth or up a creek consists of a series of buoy-to-buoy hops, interspersed with intervals of worry as to where or when the next mark will appear. Success depends on being able to estimate speed over the ground, and for this we use a ground log. A ground log is just a lead attached to a 150ft (or thereabouts) line with a knot about 40ft from the lead, another 100ft further on, and a tail of 10ft to attach it to the boat. Then, working on the basis that 1 knot = 100ft per minute, you drop the lead over the side, start a stopwatch when the first knot runs out through your fingers and stop it when the second one runs out. Hence the boat's speed over the ground can be determined from the table below:

$$
\begin{array}{ll}
100\text{ft in 2 minutes} & = \tfrac{1}{2}\text{ kn} \\
100\text{ft in 1 minute} & = 1\text{ kn} \\
100\text{ft in } \tfrac{1}{2}\text{ minute} & = 2\text{ kn} \\
100\text{ft in 20 secs} & = 3\text{ kn} \\
100\text{ft in 15 secs} & = 4\text{ kn} \\
100\text{ft in 12 secs} & = 5\text{ kn} \\
100\text{ft in 10 secs} & = 6\text{ kn}
\end{array}
$$

This is the same table used in Chapter 10 for finding boat speed through the water by drag log. It is repeated here as we will refer to it several times.

To determine the strength of current, the boat is anchored and the lead is replaced with a bucket or the funnel drag log.

The bucket is thrown over on the end of the same line and its time and direction of running out are noted, then the table given above is used to find the rate of current flowing. Incidentally, don't try to run this line out from a coil, it will foul up. Rather flake the whole lot down in a plastic washing up bowl, or push it higgledy-piggledy into a bucket. It is then contained but should run freely.

Now we have the current rate and direction and with our speed over the ground we can calculate the course between two buoys allowing for tidal set, and work out the time it should take to make the passage. From the point of view of keeping up a constant speed, you might consider it worthwhile using the motor, otherwise frequent speed checks will have to be made. Fine then, we run our distance (time) and no buoy appears, what now? The immediate reaction is to 'play a hunch' and shoot off to where we think the buoy might be. This is fatal. If the buoy is not there, then you are truly lost. The only thing to do is work out and follow a search pattern. How would you conduct such a search?

First it is important to determine the visibility in the thickest patches of fog. This can be achieved by throwing overboard a balled up piece of newspaper and timing it out of sight. Then by reference to the table given before and knowing the current rate, the visibility can be found.

Secondly, an effort must be made to determine in which direction the buoy lies. If the tide is foul it is reasonable to assume that you have under-shot on the distance run, and if it is fair that you have over-shot. The other possibility is lateral error caused by a poor compass course or a cross-setting current. Assuming that you have under-shot and headed to one side of the buoy, but don't know to which side, a search pattern must be set up and followed. With say 50 yards visibility you can already scan a band 100 yards wide athwart your track, so that in fact you are not likely to have to go far to either side of your course to find the buoy. The following search pattern seems to work quite well. Put on a 90° turn to one side for about half a minute, followed by a 180° turn and an equal period of time to bring you back onto your track. This search can be repeated on the opposite side of the track and back again as many times as needed. (See diagram.)

Following a depth contour with the echo-sounder is a perfectly good way of keeping track of your progress, but

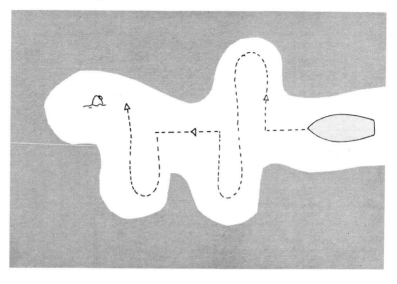

107   *Pattern of search for buoy in fog. White space shows area of visibility.*

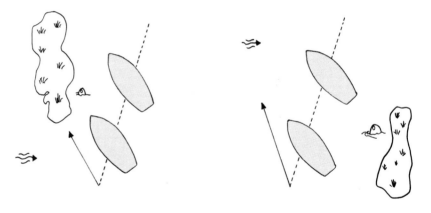

108   *Left: deliberate underestimation of tide; right: deliberate over-estimation.*

is not as easy as it sounds. Unless the edge of a bank is well defined it is hard to tell exactly when you are sailing along it. A gradually shelving bottom may take a hundred yards to rise a significant amount, and even a rapidly changing contour is hard to find if approached at a narrow angle. If you do want a position check, approach the allotted contour as nearly at right angles as possible.

224

Sometimes it is necessary to be certain that you are going to leave a buoy marking some danger on one particular side. In such situations you need to introduce a known error. Where the buoy lies on the downtide side of a danger (see diagram) the tidal allowances must be worked out accurately and deliberately *under*estimated. In that way you will be sure that the tide is pushing you away from the buoy and so keeping you clear of the danger. On the other hand, if the buoy lies on the uptide side of the danger the allowance for tide must be deliberately *over*estimated. It is likely of course that by doing this you will miss seeing the buoy at all, but you can be fairly sure of its being clear on the safe hand.

Throughout your dealings with navigation in fog, keep up a very careful plot of your position, and when an expected mark does not appear on time, don't go off following a hunch, but organise a search pattern and follow it, plotting it as you go. Even when all seems lost, keep plotting as it is likely that a depth reading or the chance sight of a landmark will suddenly make everything fit like a jigsaw and you will be sure of yourself again. The following table of speed against distance is useful when buoy-hopping.

Speed in

Knots	1	2	3	4	5	6	7	8	9
1	6	3	2	$1\frac{1}{2}$	$1\frac{1}{4}$	1	$\frac{3}{4}$	$\frac{3}{4}$	$\frac{3}{4}$
2	12	6	4	3	$2\frac{1}{2}$	2	$1\frac{3}{4}$	$1\frac{1}{2}$	$1\frac{1}{4}$
3	18	9	6	$4\frac{1}{2}$	$3\frac{1}{2}$	3	$2\frac{1}{2}$	$2\frac{1}{4}$	2
4	24	12	8	6	$4\frac{3}{4}$	4	$3\frac{1}{2}$	3	$2\frac{3}{4}$
5	30	15	10	$7\frac{1}{2}$	6	5	$4\frac{1}{4}$	$3\frac{3}{4}$	$3\frac{1}{4}$
6	36	18	12	9	$7\frac{1}{4}$	6	$5\frac{1}{4}$	$4\frac{1}{2}$	4
7	42	21	14	$10\frac{1}{2}$	$8\frac{1}{2}$	7	6	$5\frac{1}{4}$	$4\frac{3}{4}$
8	48	24	16	12	$9\frac{1}{2}$	8	$6\frac{3}{4}$	6	$5\frac{1}{4}$
9	54	27	18	$13\frac{1}{2}$	$10\frac{3}{4}$	9	$7\frac{3}{4}$	$6\frac{3}{4}$	6
10	60	30	20	15	12	10	$8\frac{1}{2}$	$7\frac{1}{2}$	$6\frac{3}{4}$

Distance in Cables

CHAPTER 15

Distress (Gloom and Doom)

When you go to sea you take on the responsibility not only for the safety of your vessel, but also for the lives of your crew. In Britain there is a volunteer Life-boat service (financed by public contribution) that undertakes hundreds of rescue operations each year, many of them involving small boats. Other countries such as the United States have government sponsored organisations to deal with rescue operations. The presence of any such service is a great comfort, but if you stop to think about it, there is no reason at all why the Life-boat crews should put their own lives at risk to help complete strangers who have got themselves into trouble. Your intention should always be to avoid trouble, but equally importantly you must cultivate the ability to get yourself out of a mess.

Whether it is a matter of a fouled anchor or a broken mast, the onus is on you and the key is usually improvisation. Good seamanship naturally plays a big part, and indeed on many occasions it is poor seamanship that gets you into trouble in the first place. Some people are gifted with the ability to make something out of nothing and others have to carry as much in the way of spare parts, tools and bits of wood as they can.

In all this I am certainly not suggesting that if help is forthcoming it should be turned down on principle. If there is something wrong with your engine and the man on the next boat is an engineer you would be foolish to say no to an offer of a helping hand. What you must do is realise your responsibility, face up to it, and try to carry it through.

Flares

The time you need flares (pyrotechnics, distress signals, call them what you will) is when you have done your utmost to get out of a disaster situation and failed. They are your last resort and should therefore be reserved for true emergency situations. Running out of petrol on a nice day with a light breeze blowing is no time to call out the Life-boat, but being aground on an exposed lee shore with a rising gale may well be. Don't leave calling for help too late; dithering about saying 'shall I, or shan't I' could cost a life.

Four main types of distress signals are available which are suitable for use by yachtsmen: rockets (often called parachute flares) propelling a red star to a height of more than 1000ft, where it is ejected and then falls over a period of about 40 seconds suspended from a small parachute. These are designed for use when out of sight of land or immediate assistance and are visible up to 35 miles on a clear night or some 6–7 miles in daylight. With help in sight a red star flare is recommended, and the most common form of this is a two-star signal which projects a star to a height of 150–200ft, followed after a few seconds by a second one. The stars have a burning time of 6–7 seconds. When you have been sighted and help is on its way a red hand flare should be used at night, or an orange smoke flare by day, to guide rescuers to your exact location. Five-star signals are also available which work in similar fashion to the two-star ones, and there are still some Very lights around, though their modern counterpart, the Miniflare, is more common. White flares should also be carried to warn ships of your presence, but it must be remembered that these are not signals of distress.

It is essential that every member of the crew knows where flares are kept – they must be in a very easily accessible place – and they must know how to use them without having first to read the instructions. Each flare is marked with an expiry date and you are advised not to rely on the signal after that date. It is easy to advise renewal at the expiry date, but they are not cheap items and many people hang onto them longer than they should. The danger in this is that should you have to use them in a crisis they may have been damaged in some way and will fail to operate correctly or at full strength. Always check the condition of flares at the beginning of each season and *several times during the season*. Flares that show any signs of having been wetted or of cracking along the casing must be treated with suspicion. Small dents in metal casings or caps may not be important, but if they are badly damaged they could be dangerous to the user. Despite being

227

encased in polythene it is still possible for damp to affect flares and a bag of silica gel or some other drying agent should be included to absorb some of the moisture. Once lit, a flare will continue to burn even though soused in water, and in fact one of the standard tests for flares is that they should still work immediately after being soaked for a minute with the caps off.

For the kind of cruising we are interested in it should be sufficient to carry a couple of parachute flares, four hand flares, two smoke flares and some white ship scarers. Manufacturers do produce packs of flares for various types of small craft and one of these is usually suitable with the addition of say the white flares.

Fire Extinguishers

Whether it is as the result of fuel spilled when topping up tanks, or a leaky gas bottle, or a lighted match dropped in a rubbish bin, a fire on a boat is devastating unless tackled instantly with adequate extinguishers. Many people placate their consciences by hanging a solitary aerosol extinguisher on the bulkhead, but this is hardly enough for even the smallest of fires. I know it is always easy to tell someone else to spend money, but with fire extinguishers you really do get what you pay for and economy is not achieved by buying small, cheap appliances. Look for a maker's date stamp when buying and make sure that the extinguisher is still well within the guaranteed life.

Care must be taken not to damage the extinguisher as any loss of stored pressure will result in a loss of efficiency, and even possibly failure to operate at all. Always store an extinguisher in proper mounting brackets to ensure that the firing pin cannot be knocked, thus partially releasing the pressure. Denting indicates a loss of stored pressure, and excess corrosion also warns of possible damage, but in any case you are advised to have appliances serviced about every three years.

Do make quite sure that you learn how to operate all the fire extinguishers you carry, and make sure that your crew understands how to use them as well, because in a real situation there will be no time to fiddle about trying to read faded wording. Remember too that total discharge takes only a few seconds, so a good aim is essential. Fight the fire from the point nearest to you as you will then be able to get in closer to the real seat of the fire. Use a sweeping motion from side to side, low down and as close as you can safely get to the flames.

It is recommended that boats up to 30ft (9m) carry at least two 3 lb (1.4 kilos) extinguishers of either the dry powder or foam type. Ensure that they are readily accessible at all times. It is absolutely useless if you have to hunt in lockers for them, wasting precious seconds. A fire blanket is very useful for smothering galley fires and makes much less mess than an extinguisher does.

First Aid

Unless you are prepared to complete a course in first aid you must buy and read a simple book on the subject such as that produced by the St John Ambulance Brigade. There is also a section on the subject in *Reed's,* should you need a quick reference.

You cannot expect to be able to deal with very serious injuries, but a basic first aid kit should be carried including the following: assorted dressings, bandages, adhesive tape, cotton wool, sterilised lint, scissors (sharp), safety pins, anti-septic cream, splinter forceps, indigestion pills, anti-sea-sickness pills, aspirin or similar, sunburn ointment or calamine lotion, thermometer.

With a kit like this you will be able to treat minor ailments, but must be prepared to seek proper medical aid for serious injuries or illnesses. It must also be realised that first aid is only what its name implies, that is a preliminary treatment, enough to suffice until qualified aid can be sought.

Hull Damage

While holing is, thankfully, a rare occurrence, some thought should be given to the possibility of hull damage – and under-water damage in particular. The convex shape of a boat's hull gives immense impact resistance, and this strength in combination with the inherent toughness of modern materials means that a very severe blow will be needed to puncture the hull. What can happen though (especially with wooden boats) is the opening up of a seam, which can soon let in more water than you can happily keep pumping out.

With a glassfibre boat the best course is to plug a hole or crack with softwood plugs. These must be tapered and wrapped in rag before being driven in and secured with shores to strong points. Once the main leak is under control it may be necessary to fill hairline cracks with a stopping compound. On a wooden boat it is feasible to tack well-greased canvas over small leaks (if possible both inside and outside the hull), and a copper tingle can then be tacked over the canvas.

Should you get a hole underwater, either by pounding on rocks or hitting a baulk of timber or a piece of wreckage, obviously you must immediately try to raise the hole above the waterline. This will require the boat to be laid on the tack which keeps the damage to windward. You may have to heave to, and in rough weather you should shorten sail to reduce the strain on the hull and stop it opening up further. Where such serious damage has occurred the crew must be prepared to abandon the boat, either by taking to the dinghy, or if it is reasonably safe, by beaching the boat and wading ashore, though this could clearly be a highly risky move.

Cushions, mattresses, oilskins, towels, clothing, anything like that can be used to stuff into a hole, but it will be more effective if an oilskin or a sail is wrapped around the clothing first. Once something has been pushed into the hole it must be wedged there as tightly as possible with shores to strength members. Lashing a sail or an oilskin over the outside of the damage will also help, but is difficult, as ropes will have to be passed under the hull and hove bar taut.

Unless a boat is very badly holed it should be possible to control the inflow of water sufficiently to allow her to reach port, even if the pumps have to be manned frequently. Permanent repairs can then be effected in safety, and to this end a glassfibre repair kit is a good thing to carry on boats built of that material. A wooden boat is likely to need professional attention unless you have proper working facilities and are a dab hand at carpentry.

Salvage

Yachtsmen have always done their level best to help each

other out of difficulty with no thought of reward, and long may they continue to do so, but it is possible that you may find yourself in a salvageable situation and it is then that you will need to know how to keep a salvage claim down to a minimum, or better, how to avoid one altogether. Salvage, let me make clear, is the act of saving or helping to save a vessel or cargo of any sort when in danger. Salvage is not claimable by the vessel's crew or by a pilot, and is not payable when life only is saved.

Do not accept a tow until agreement has been reached about price and destination, then, if you can avoid it, don't allow anyone from the towing vessel to come aboard your boat. Also if possible, always pass your own rope for the tow rather than accept one from the rescuer. If the would-be rescuer starts demanding salvage before doing anything to help you, try to reach a witnessed (and preferably written) agreement. If a mutually agreeable price cannot be found try to get your helpers to agree to the reward being decided according to the provisions of Lloyd's Salvage Contract. This will at least ensure a fair deal. Remember that, for a salvage claim to hold good, danger must be proved to have existed and the rescue attempts must have been successful. When a claim is made you will have to provide a chart showing your vessel's position, and your log book will help to establish the prevailing weather conditions. A friendly offer of a pluck off a mudbank when you have grounded on a falling tide should not be turned down out of hand, but be sure to point out that you are in no danger and can easily lay out a kedge and await the flood. Finally, never disclose the value of your boat or whether or not you are insured.

Insurance

Considering the high market value of boats it is well worth the premium asked to insure them, and in particular it is essential to get a large third party cover. Damage to another vessel can be very expensive to repair and damage to a person will certainly cost a great deal of money. It is worthwhile shopping around the insurance companies to see which one will give you a policy best suited to your needs, and when you are considering a policy make sure you read it closely before committing yourself. You will usually do better to go to a firm specialising in marine insurance as they have a good idea of what the risks of sailing are and will be better informed about the whole matter than a general insurance company.

Some insurance companies ask different rates for the months when the boat is in commission and the time during which she is laid up. It is usual also to have to specify your cruising limits, which for the first couple of seasons may be quite modest. Having stated such limits be sure to inform your insurers if you intend at any time to sail outside the area. If you think of doing any racing you will have to get a policy that covers you for damage happening during the course of a race as most policies specifically exclude it. The other point to remember is that you may have to make special arrangements with the insurance company if you are going to do any singlehanded sailing, as the boat is not then considered to be properly manned.

Code Flags

While it is most unlikely that the small family cruiser will carry a complete set of International Code Flags I suggested back in Chapter 4 that it was 'highly desirable' to carry the flags U, G, H, N, C. According to the International Code of Signals all the letters of the alphabet, bar letter R, have individual meanings, thus U means 'You are running into danger', G means 'I require a pilot' and is replaced with H (meaning 'I have a pilot on board') as soon as that gentleman comes aboard. The letters NC hoisted together mean: 'I am in distress and require immediate assistance.' These four signals can therefore cover most situations and should be learnt so that recognition is immediate.

CHAPTER 16

Weather Forecasts

Of prime importance to the yachtsman is the question of what wind strength he may expect during a proposed passage. Given a fair wind of moderate force he can sail in rain, hail or shine, but with either no wind at all or far too much he isn't going to get anywhere. When talking about wind we speak in terms of the *direction from which it comes* and its strength as indicated by the Beaufort Scale. I have emphasised the direction from which it comes as we talk of tides and currents in terms of the direction in which they are going or setting, thus an east-going current and an easterly wind will be in opposition to each other.

The Beaufort Scale is normally used from Force 0 (calm) to Force 12 (hurricane), each Force being defined by lower and upper wind speeds measured in knots. In open waters the wind strength can be judged by sea conditions, but in inshore waters this is more difficult. Electronic wind instruments refer only to wind speed and may be in either knots or miles per hour.

Beaufort Wind Scale

BEAUFORT NO.	LIMITS OF WIND SPEED IN KNOTS	DESCRIPTIVE TERM	SEA CRITERION
0	Less than 1	Calm	Sea like a mirror
1	1–3	Light air	Ripples like scales
2	4–6	Light breeze	Pronounced wavelets, glassy tops

BEAUFORT NO.	LIMITS OF WIND SPEED IN KNOTS	DESCRIPTIVE TERM	SEA CRITERION
3	7–10	Gentle breeze	Large wavelets, crests begin to foam
4	11–16	Moderate breeze	Small waves, lengthening; whitehorses
5	17–21	Fresh breeze	Moderate waves, pronounced long form; many whitehorses, possibly some spray
6	22–27	Strong breeze	Large waves; extensive foaming crests, probably some spray
7	28–33	Near gale	Heaped seas, foam begins to blow in streaks downwind
8	34–40	Gale	Moderately high waves of greater length; pronounced streaks of spindrift

Don't bother too much about the higher Forces (9 upwards), it gets too nasty, but if you want to frighten yourself, they are listed up to 12 in *Reed's*. The wind speeds are measured at a height of 33ft (10m) above sea level and will be somewhat less close to the surface of the water. The sea criteria listed for each force refer to open sea well away from land effects, but they will be similar inshore, though the seas will be shorter and steeper.

It is not easy to say, 'We won't put to sea if a Force so-and-so is forecast' because much depends upon the duration of the proposed passage and whether it is to be a beat the whole way or mainly sailing free. We can all take a certain amount of spray and slog to windward, but we sail primarily for pleasure and while our boats may be able to batter their way into a 5 or 6, why should we have to endure the associated discomfort? On the other hand, if there is a Force 4–5 forecast which will be from abaft the beam we may well have a fast and exhilarating sail. Once more it is a case of knowing the boat's and the crew's capabilities and judging accordingly whether to put to sea or stay in port.

Sea Areas

The shipping forecasts, which are the ones most relevant to our interests, are broadcast for a number of individual sea areas round the British Isles and adjacent waters. The exact areas together with their names are shown in the illustration on p. 238. In several of the sea areas there are weather reporting stations which provide information about conditions existing at specified times, and these reports are included at the end of the shipping forecasts.

Obtaining and Interpreting Forecasts

Where does the yachtsman get a weather forecast from? First and foremost he listens to the shipping forecasts broadcast by the BBC on 1500 m (200 kHz) Radio 2. These reports, which we will look at in detail later are broadcast daily at 0033 hrs, 0633 hrs, 1155 hrs (Sunday only), 1355 hrs (except Sunday), 1755 hrs.

In addition to these shipping forecasts, the BBC broadcasts numerous land forecasts which are of less usefulness to the yachtsman, and they will also break into programmes to give gale warnings for sea areas when they are received, and will repeat them at the next half hour following. A number of local radio stations also broadcast weather reports for their own area, and the yachtsman can obtain reports from his local Coastguard station or by telephoning a local meteorological office. So with all these services readily available, the yachtsman has little excuse for being caught completely unawares by the weather.

Diagram 109 shows the sea areas covered by the shipping forecasts, together with a list of weather stations from which reports are received of current weather conditions. Each of the shipping forecasts starts off with a summary of gale warnings in force. This is followed by the general synopsis, the area forecasts for the next 24 hours and at the end any reports from coastal stations. To make all this a bit clearer, the following is a rather nasty report broadcast at 0033 hrs one night:

'And now on 1500 metres the shipping forecast issued by the Met Office at two three three oh on the 28th September.

There are warnings of gales in Viking, Forties, Cromarty, Forth, Tyne, Dogger, Fisher, German Bight, Humber, Lundy, Fastnet, Irish Sea, Shannon, Rockall, Malin, Hebrides, Bailey, Fair Isle, Faeroes, and South East Iceland.

The general synopsis at one nine double oh: Low 976 just west of Shetlands now filling slowly and soon moving north east 15 knots to west Norwegian coast with secondary low 994 forming in Skaggerak by midnight. Anticyclone 1029 Azores stationary with ridge to Denmark Straits moving steadily east.

Now the area forecasts for the next 24 hours.
Viking, Forties, Cromarty. SW to W 7 to severe gale 9 veering NW and becoming cyclonic 5 near Norwegian coast later. Showers, good.
Forth, Tyne, Dogger. SW slowly veering west to NW 6 to gale 8. Squally showers, good.
Fisher. SW veering NW 7 to severe gale 9. Becoming cyclonic 6 in East later. Showers, good.
German Bight, Humber. SW veering W to NW 6 to gale 8. Occasional showers, good.
Thames, Dover, Wight, Portland, Plymouth. W to NW 5 to 7. Scattered showers, good.
Biscay, Finisterre. NW 5 to 6 in N, 3 in S. Scattered showers, good.
Sole. NW 5–7 moderating slowly later. Showers, good.
Lundy, Fastnet, Irish Sea, Shannon. W becoming NW 5–7 locally gale 8 moderating later. Occasional showers, good.
Rockall, Malin, Hebrides, Minches, Bailey. NW 6 to gale 8 locally severe gale 9, moderating slowly from W later. Squally showers, good.
Fair Isle. Cyclonic becoming N 7 to severe gale 9. Rain at first, moderate or good.
Faeroes, South East Iceland. NE to N 7 to severe gale 9. Squally showers, good. Icing nil.

Now the reports from coastal stations for 2300 BST on Friday.
Wick. SW by W 5, slight rain shower, 8 miles, 980 falling slowly.
Dowsing. WSW 7, lightning, 5 miles 999.
Galloper. W 7, 11 miles, 1004, falling slowly.
Royal Sovereign. WSW 6, rain showers in the past hour,

11 miles, 1006 falling slowly.
Portland Bill. W 6, 13 miles, 1006, falling slowly.
Scilly. W by N 5, 13 miles, 1008, falling slowly.
Valentia. W by N 4, rain showers in past hour, 13 miles, 1007, steady.
Ronaldsway. WSW 4, 27 miles, 999 steady.
Prestwick. W 4, 12 miles, 995 rising slowly.
Tiree. W by N 6, rain showers in past hour, 19 miles, 992 steady.

And a report at 2200 BST from Bell Rock. WSW 6, 16 miles, 989 falling more slowly. And for the same time, 2200, Varne, W 5, 11 miles, 1005.

And that's the end of our service for shipping at this time.'

The above is a complete shipping forecast, lasting in this case some $5\frac{1}{2}$ minutes. I have quoted it in full here so that an idea of the sequence of events can be obtained, but what does it all mean? Why do they make such seemingly silly comments as 'showers, good'?

The general synopsis is pretty well self-explanatory, but it is useful to know the terms used to describe the expected movement of highs and lows across the forecast areas. A system is said to be moving slowly if it is progressing at less than 15 knots, steadily from 15–25 knots, rather quickly between 25 and 35 knots, rapidly at 35–45 knots, and very rapidly when it is making more than 45 knots. The importance of knowing how fast a weather system is moving lies in the fact that it is the highs, lows, ridges and troughs that determine our winds and weather, thus if we know where a particular system will be at a particular time, we can make a reasonable forecast of the conditions that will then prevail.

Next the sea area forecasts 'for the next 24 hours'. Because of the limited air time allowed for shipping forecasts, sea areas are often grouped together and an average wind strength given, but usually this is quite acceptable for the weekend yachtsman. For each area or group of areas the information is given in a set sequence, and that is: wind direction and strength followed by any alterations to either; whether or not there will be rain, snow, thunder, hail, fog, etc; visibility; an icing report for SE Iceland.

In these forecasts, visibility is described as being good (more than 5 miles), moderate (2–5 miles), poor (1100 yards to

2 miles), and fog (less than 1100 yards). In the coastal station reports a further term, mist or haze, is used when visibility is between 1100 and 2200 yards. So then, when you hear 'showers, good', the announcer is not pleased, he is saying that there will be showers but visibility will be more than 5 miles.

109 Coastal stations supplying weather reports broadcast at the end of shipping forecasts: 1 Wick, 2 Bell Rock, 3 Dowsing, 4 Galloper, 5 Varne, 6 Royal Sovereign, 7 Portland Bill, 8 Scilly, 9 Valentia, 10 Ronaldsway, 11 Prestwick, 12 Tiree.

The reports from coastal stations, normally timed much later than the general synopsis, give a good indication of what is happening at the moment and of how far the weather system has moved since the synopsis time. They too stick to a pattern of information with wind direction and strength first, then a report of any rain, fog, etc, and visibility, the barometric pressure in millibars, and finally a comment on whether the barometer is steady, rising or falling, and how fast it is doing so. By the way, they often speak of 'precipitation in sight', which simply means that they can see rain, sleet, hail, etc.

Using Forecasts

It is not sufficient just to listen to a forecast for your particular sea area, you must at the very least listen to those for the areas either side of you and to the weather reports from the nearest coastal stations. The experienced yachtsman listens to the whole forecast and builds up a picture of the current and expected weather patterns, thus enabling him to hazard a pretty good guess as to what will happen in his particular locale. Since individual sea areas are so large, and as they are often grouped together, it is quite likely that the weather just a few miles offshore will be quite different from that forecast for the general area, although that forecast may still be accurate as an overall picture. To decide exactly what is going to happen locally needs an understanding of pressure systems and their effects but it is made easier by the construction of a weather map from the forecasts. Pads of charts are readily available and with practice it is possible to draw a map by using the synopsis given at the beginning of the forecast, individual area forecasts and the reports from coastal stations, though it must be remembered that these are given at a different time from the synopsis.

Taking down a forecast is not always easy as the announcers have to rush to fit the whole forecast into the allotted time, so a system of shorthand must be used. Alternatively, and much better for 'delayed use', is a battery-operated tape recorder of the cassette type, as you can then refer back to it at any time. Whatever happens do not rely on memory alone – few people remember accurately after breakfast what they heard sleepily at 0633.

Before setting off even for a weekend afloat it is well worth studying the weather maps printed in some of the daily newspapers for several days in advance, particularly the Atlantic maps. By doing so you build up a continuous picture of how the pressure systems are moving, deepening, filling or whatever, and you can then make a surer judgement of current forecasts. A regular study of these weather maps helps to familiarise the newcomer with conditions associated with various pressure patterns. This knowledge will be invaluable at sea in predicting windshifts and changes in strength, particularly the speed with which these things will happen.

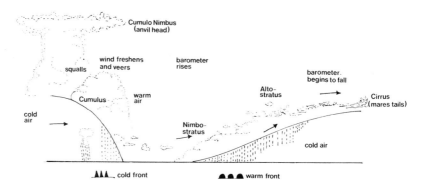

110 *The ideal frontal system. Unfortunately, things are seldom as simple as this, but it is the basic state on which the weather usually elaborates.*

DIY Forecasting

Apart from weather maps and forecasts, an idea of approaching weather changes can be obtained from watching the sky, a barometer and the sea. Meteorology is far from being a simple subject and the following notes are necessarily rather broad generalisations, but they serve to show how useful a closer study of the subject can be for the yachtsman.

Cirrus clouds, the rather fibrous clouds often referred to as mares' tails, very often precede a period of bad weather. If they are seen moving in from the N or NW and thickening into a sheet of cirrostratus, through which the sun shows surrounded by a halo, then a backing and freshening wind can be expected, especially if the barometer falls sharply. The development of altostratus (a level sheet of grey cloud) following cirrostratus produced what is commonly called a watery

240

sky, and does indeed herald rain and general deterioration.

Small happy-type cumulus clouds like bits of cotton wool are signs of fair weather, while larger, towering cumulus with dark patches in them indicate showers and squalls.

Rapidly moving clouds in the upper layers are signs of unstable conditions, but do not give a defnite indication of approaching bad weather, although you should be wary of squalls and showers. Cumulo-nimbus often produces severe squalls from quite unexpected directions. Alto-cumulus, thin middle cloud formed in regular layers and waves, with castellated edges indicates widespread thunderstorms.

Should the wind veer to the NW after the passage of a cold front, then a short spell of fair weather can be expected, but if the barometer subsequently starts to fall and the wind backs to the SW, then bad weather is fast approaching. Generally speaking, whenever clouds get lower you should be on the lookout for bad weather.

A couple of relevant rhymes to be accepted with caution:

> If clouds are gathering thick and fast,
> Keep sharp lookout for sail and mast,
> But if they slowly onward crawl,
> Shoot your lines, nets and trawl.
>
> When rain comes before the wind
> Halyards, sheets and braces mind,
> But when the wind comes before rain,
> Soon you may make sail again.

The barometer too gives an indication of weather trends, but it is often rather ambiguous. For example, a gale can be heralded by a falling barometer and backing wind as well as it can by a rising glass and veering wind, but both barometer and wind usually give significant indications if anything serious is going to happen. Gales blowing with a falling barometer are generally less squally than those with a rising barometer.

A steady rise in pressure during the summer usually indicates a period of fairly settled weather. During a period of unsettled weather a rapid rise is often followed by a fall, but a general improvement of conditions can be expected if the rise reaches a reasonably high level.

Aftermath of a storm.

Another couple of relevant rhymes also to be accepted with caution:

> When the glass falls low
> Prepare for a blow;
> When it slowly rises high,
> Lofty canvas you may fly.

> Long foretold, long last,
> Short notice, soon past,
> Quick rise after low,
> Sure sign of stronger blow.

Sea state changes with the strength of the prevailing wind, and in fact there is a description of the sea for each of the Beaufort Forces, as we saw earlier. This is fine for judging the strength of present wind, though it is not so easy in coastal waters as it is well offshore, but the descriptions in no way forecast coming winds. About the only indication one can get is when a swell builds up. This unfortunately is also an ambiguous sign as it can either be the result of a dying gale far out to sea, or it can presage a rising wind from the direction of the swell. The sea is altogether a mysterious thing.

CHAPTER 17

Trailing

The facility for transporting a small boat from place to place by loading her onto a trailer and hitching up to the family car is a great boon for anyone contemplating winter storage in the back yard or extending his cruising grounds beyond normal limits. However it is necessary to comply with the legal requirements governing trailers and trailing combinations before setting off on the highway. It is fairly safe to assume that a trailer produced by a reputable manufacturer will conform to these requirements, but this may not be the case with an amateur-built one. The law can be split into five broad categories: brakes, towing speed, trailer dimensions, lighting and construction.

Brakes

Surprisingly there is no legal requirement for a trailer to be fitted with brakes if its unladen weight does not exceed 2 cwt, but as you are then totally reliant on the brakes of the towing vehicle, it is sensible to insist on having some form of trailer braking system even on ones of less than 2 cwt. Heavier trailers must have some form of braking, plus a parking brake operable when the trailer is detached from the towing vehicle, though this too is sensible for all trailers.

While mechanical over-ride brakes are almost universal in the UK, I believe they are banned in many parts of the USA. The alternative to over-ride brakes is a costly independent system allowing the trailer to be braked and controlled quite separately from the towing vehicle. This is an excellent idea, but it would add far more onto the cost of a trailer than most people can afford to pay.

The straightforward over-ride brakes on a trailer should

be fitted with a compensator to equalise the pull, since cables running directly to each wheel can stretch, resulting in uneven braking – a potentially dangerous situation.

Towing Speed

In derestricted areas the maximum towing speed is 40 mph unless the towing combination complies with the following regulations, in which case the maximum is raised to 50 mph.
(i) A trailer fitted with brakes must not exceed the kerbside weight of the towing vehicle when the trailer is laden.
(ii) Trailers without brakes must not exceed 60 per cent of the kerbside weight of the towing vehicle when the trailer is laden.

If these requirements are met with, then a number 50 must be displayed either on the trailer lighting board or in an equally prominent place. It is an offence to display such a sign if the combination does not comply with the weight ratio restrictions.

Kerbside weight of a vehicle is defined as being the weight of that vehicle with a full fuel tank, no passengers, no load, and only carrying the normal equipment, ie tool kit, jack etc. Probably the best way of checking whether or not a towing combination does comply with the weight ratio restrictions is to drive it onto a public weighbridge.

These regulations apply to all passenger carrying vehicles and light vans of less than 30 cwt unladen and to dual purpose vehicles such as Land-Rovers which do not exceed 2 tons. In the case of dual purpose vehicles it is also a requirement that they be capable of four-wheel drive or satisfy certain conditions of construction.

Where a vehicle is over 30 cwt it can tow a two-wheeled or four-wheeled close-coupled trailer at 50 mph without satisfying these conditions. Vehicles towing four-wheeled trailers which are not close-coupled are outside these restrictions and can trail at up to 70 mph.

A trailer is described as having close-coupled wheels when 'the wheels on the same side of the trailer are so fitted that at all times while it is in motion they remain parallel to the longitudinal axis of the trailer and that the distance between the centres of the respective areas of contact with the road surface does not exceed 33in'.

244

Trailer Dimensions

The maximum allowable width of a trailer is 7ft 6in although an overhang of 1ft is permissible without extra lighting. In terms of length, the maximum allowable is 23ft (7m), and a 3ft 6in overhang is alright. Vehicles of 2 tons or more can tow trailers up to 39ft (12m) long. At least one wing mirror, on the off-side, giving a clear view back past the boat must be fitted.

The maximum weight that can be carried on a two-wheeled trailer is 9 tons, while for a four-wheeled trailer it is 14 tons. Maximum permitted laden weight of vehicle and trailer is 24 tons.

Lighting

Trailer lighting has more or less to duplicate that of the towing vehicle. The lighting board should be fitted to the trailer, but if it would then be obscured by the overhang of the boat, it is acceptable to attach the board to the boat. This board must carry brake lights, flashing indicators, reflectors and triangular reflectors besides a lit number plate. This plate must be of the reflective type if the car is so fitted, and can be reflective even though the car has non-reflective plates. All of the car's rear lights must continue to function when the trailer is connected up. The lights and triangular reflectors must be no less than 15in above the ground, and no more than 3ft 6in, though the flashing indicators can go up to 7ft 6in. Triangular reflectors have to have sides of 150–200mm, the rear lights must have an area at least equal to that of a $1\frac{1}{2}$in diameter circle, and both must be within 16in of the extremities of the trailer (or boat).

Construction

All trailers have to be sprung. This is a legal requirement, but it is common sense as well; if there aren't any springs, then all the bumps and batterings of the road will be transmitted to the hull, straining and possibly damaging it. For the same reason inflatable tyres are insisted on. The suspension must not be too hard, or the boat will be hurt almost as much as if there were no suspension.

Mudguards also have to be fitted under UK law, but again this is only sensible to protect the bottom of the boat from flying stones. Regulations regarding size of mudguard vary greatly from country to country, some requiring much fuller ones than Britain where the most minute guards will do.

Insurance

If you are planning to trail your boat at any time you must make a very careful check that you are insured to do so. It is quite possible that you will have to ask either the car or boat insurance company (or indeed both) for special cover while the combination is on the road. This should not be an expensive item, but do give plenty of notice to the insurers and be specific about dates and details of the towing combination.

Trailers

First and foremost when looking for a trailer is that it must be suitably designed for the type and size of boat you want to put on it. There must be proper channels to take bilge keels if the boat is a twin keeler, or there must be adequate side supports if she is a fin keeled boat. For trailers with a capacity of less than about 1000 lb a simple T bar arrangement is adopted, where the upright of the letter is the drawbar and the cross piece the axle. In larger trailers an A frame is used or even a T form with big box-section girders forming a chassis framework.

Trailers are destined when built for a rough and tough life as they will almost certainly be left out of doors the whole time, and will often be subjected if not to total immersion, then to a corrosive salt atmosphere. Under such conditions it is impossible for even the very best paintwork to last long and it is well worth the extra cost of having a new trailer galvanised to prolong its life.

The other parts of the trailer most likely to give trouble are the wheels and hubs. So-called sealed bearings on trailer wheels are recognised as being (in most cases) only resistant to the entry of salt or sand, and once either of these does manage to get into them it quickly destroys the water seal. The problem is eased and the life expectancy of the bearings is increased by pumping plenty of medium heavy grease into them before and after immersion, but don't use underwater grease as this is unsuitable for road running temperatures. Remember that it is best when possible to let the hubs cool right down before immersing them, as quenching a hot hub in cold water creates an internal vacuum which will tend to suck water in.

It is possible in some cases to avoid immersing the trailer by using one with a tilting frame – a broken backed trailer. These are usually only suitable for quite small, light displacement cruisers.

A jockey wheel is very useful on a trailer as it can then be manoeuvred separately from the car and can stand level. It is also useful to be able to level up the trailer, back the car up to it and only have to lift slightly to hitch up. You must remember after hitching up to lift and secure the jockey wheel well clear of the ground.

A heavy duty winch mounted on the trailer is a great help when recovering a boat, and can sometimes make recovery a one-man operation. In an emergency the winch can be reversed and the trailer plus boat winched up a softish slope to the towing vehicle parked on hard standing.

While it is adequate to grease keel channels well and slide a boat on or off her trailer relying on brute force and the slipperyness of the grease, it is much better to fit keel rollers in the channels. These are usually made of very heavy duty rubber with spindles that should be greased frequently. Most amateur-built trailers do without rollers, but it is worth paying the extra on a manufactured trailer if you expect to be doing a lot of trailing.

Bilge keeled boats are in the happy position of being able to stand on their own two feet, but for single keeled boats it is necessary to provide adequate side chocks on the trailer. Unless the trailer is tailor-made for the boat the chocks should be adjustable, and they must always be well padded against damage to the hull.

Ball type towing hitches have been standardised at 50mm, but the older 2in variety is still to be found. Do not try to mix ball and socket parts of differing sizes.

One thing not required under UK law, but still a good safety idea, is a chain between trailer and car. This chain (or chains) prevents the trailer nose from hitting the ground in the thankfully rare event of a towing coupling failure. The chain must still be long enough to let the combination corner tightly.

Loading and Securing

Getting a small cruiser of about 17 or 18ft onto a trailer does not present too much of a problem especially if she is trailed stern first and has twin keels. All you need are a couple of strong backs and a third person to move the trailer. Third Person lines the trailer up, while Strong Backs place themselves under the quarters and lift the stern off the ground or chocks. The trailer can then be run in as far as the keels, and with a bit of juggling the whole boat can be tipped and slid onto the trailer. Lots of grease in the keel channels or on the rollers helps.

The same principle can be applied to a boat being trailed in the more conventional bows-first attitude, but in this case the boat needs to be raised up onto chocks first in order that she may be tipped aft without damaging the rudder by bashing it on the ground. Again it's not too difficult to work her up onto progressively higher chocks by putting your shoulders under the bows or stern while someone slides in the new set. Incidentally if you can get hold of any old wooden railway sleepers they make excellent chocks.

111 Loading bilge keeler onto trailer by lifting stern and running trailer underneath keels.

248

In the case of even a fairly small fin keel boat you are pretty well lumbered with hiring a mobile crane and having her lifted onto the trailer. A system of jacks working on a frame that holds the boat level can be used, but is tricky. Once the boat is down at the water it is of course feasible to launch and recover her from a slipway or hard by submerging the trailer, but more of that later.

Before you start climbing on board to stow gear – and the boat does make a good carrying place if the weight has been allowed for when choosing the trailer – it is advisable to secure her on the trailer. The lashings need not be the final ones, but just something to restrain her.

When you choose a trailer, you have to decide on an all-up weight for the boat, that is with all the gear on board. Do remember this figure, and do not exceed it otherwise you put an unfair strain on the trailer, and you would be breaking the law if your trailer then exceeded the weight of your car and you still towed at 50 mph. Keep all of the heavy items as low down in the boat as is reasonable to avoid raising the centre of gravity unduly, and try to keep them out of the ends of the boat, remembering that she is not as evenly supported by a trailer as she is by water and heavy weights at the extremities of the hull could strain it. Lash everything down securely; where crockery, pots and pans and such like have been put in lockers, push a couple of cushions or a suit of oilskins in after them to hold everything still. Just before you fix everything down finally, check the loading on the trailer coupling. Generally speaking the trailer and car hitch should have about 10 per cent of the weight on it, though front wheel drive cars may need slightly less. If the trailer is 'heavy on' it affects steering and could cause front wheel skids, while if it is 'light on' it can cause snaking. If the load is not quite balanced you will have to juggle gear about inside, or in an extreme case move the whole axle (which on many trailers is adjustable along the drawbar) until the correct loading is achieved. Unfortunately this means off-loading the boat.

Once the weight is distributed correctly you are ready to lash the boat down properly. The first problem here is that any knot in any rope is going to settle and the lashing is going to slacken, so regular checks will have to be made en route. An alternative to rope is synthetic fibre webbing of the type used in car seat belts, with special clips or buckles on the ends. Natural fibre webbing could of course be used, but it is not proof against rot and is not as strong for the same dimensions as the synthetic stuff.

When securing a boat on her trailer you are trying to stop her jumping up and down, sliding forwards when you brake or backwards when going up hills. Starting at the keel then, hammer wooden wedges between it and the sides of the channel on both sides to stop any lateral movement there. If the trailer is not a proper boat trailer, but one with a flat overall back (say a low-loader lorry), you will probably have to hammer wedges under the keel again to stop sideways wandering. Apart from the normal securings, bilge keel boats are often held down by bolts through the keels and steel straps rising from one side (usually the inside) of the keel channels. These straps not only help to secure the boat, but also ensure that she is in exactly the same position each time.

A block should be placed under the bow of the boat so that when a lashing is put over the deck and bowsed down onto the trailer there is no likelihood of hogging. The same applies at the stern for a boat with either a transom hung

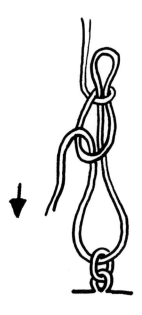

112 *Lorry driver's or waggoner's hitch provides 2:1 purchase by hauling on fall in direction of arrow.*

rudder or one with no skeg, since in both cases it is essential to avoid damaging the rudder stock.

Strong and tight lashings over the bow and stern will hold the boat down, and 'springs' from the bow diagonally to the after end of the trailer, and from each quarter forward to a point on the trailer under the bows will prevent her moving fore and aft. It's easy enough to put a rope over the bow, haul on it and make fast, but to get a lashing really tight is another matter. One way of helping things is to run a line horizontally between the bow and stern lashings and try to heave them together. The same can be done athwartship. A particularly useful hitch is the lorry driver's or waggoner's hitch, which gives a 2:1 purchase and is illustrated in diagram 112.

If you carry the mast on deck, make sure that it too is supported evenly along its length to stop bending and that it is tightly secured. Pads of foam rubber between the spar and its supports will help to prevent chafing, just as they will between lashings and the hull.

Lastly check the tyre pressures on the car and trailer. The owner's handbook for the car should give an indication of the correct pressures and the trailer manufacturer should do the same for the trailer. Generally the rear tyres of the car should be pumped up another 2–4 lb over the normal pressures, but for the trailer so much depends on the type of tyres fitted that advice will have to be sought from the manufacturer. These pressures are most important since low pressures will cause overheating, and possibly a blow-out.

Route Planning

A few evenings spent with an Ordnance Survey map planning out your route can save a lot of embarrassment. Finding yourself stuck halfway over a narrow humpback bridge is only funny for onlookers. Obviously you must try to avoid very steep gradients and very narrow or twisty lanes, but try also to keep out of big towns when everybody is doing their shopping. A few fuel stations and cafés are handy to note as well. Otherwise look carefully for any marked obstructions or hazards and make out a route card giving the road numbers and towns, with alternatives if possible.

Trailing

Immediately you get underway you will discover how different driving with a trailer is from driving without. Acceleration appears to be zero and so too does your stopping power. Get used to using each gear to its maximum torque, and don't be afraid to change down. Accelerate gently and brake gently; it is better when approaching traffic lights to slow down well before them and keep crawling than to zoom up and try to stop at the last moment.

When passing an obstruction don't be too hasty in pulling in – remember the trailer. Also allow yourself very much more time to overtake, as again you cannot accelerate or brake sharply.

After you have been on the road a short while, pull over and check all the lashings as they may well have slackened off. Pulling off the road every so often is also courteous to other road users as it allows them to get past you without the dangers inherent in overtaking a long trailer and car combination.

When going down hill always use a low gear and never ride on the foot brake as it will overheat and fade. If you have to stop on a hill, either going up or down, set the handbrake and put chocks under the trailer wheels, especially if going up hill as the over-ride brakes do not then work.

Trailer snaking is a danger to be watched for. It is usually indicated by a sudden lightening of the steering and is caused by bumps in the road, gusts of wind, unbalanced wheels, or incorrectly inflated tyres. If you do find the trailer is snaking, *do not brake,* but ease off on the accelerator until it is controlled again.

Manoeuvring and particularly backing a trailer for the first time is a tricky game. Going forwards presents few problems apart from those of knowing how wide a berth to give either obstructions in the road or curbstones when going round corners, but backing a trailer is a sport on its own. Practise with an empty trailer and remember that you must turn the steering wheel the way you want the hitch to move; you must also correct as soon as it starts to swing or the trailer will jack-knife. In such a situation you must either draw forward again or unhitch and manhandle the trailer – which with a light boat may be the better way in the first place.

Launching and Recovery

Though launching and recovering a boat with a trailer need not be a difficult job, it is not always straightforward. Any softness of the 'hard' and the car sinks into it; any chop on the water and the boat surges about damaging herself on the trailer. In fact the initial consideration must be to select a hard or slipway that has a firm bottom extending well off below the water's edge, and if possible, select a site sheltered from the prevailing wind.

Take care not to run the car so far into the water that the exhaust goes under, and to help in this it is not a bad idea to fit a vertical extension. If there is any doubt about the hardness of the launching site, set the car on firm ground and run a tackle between the towing hitch and the trailer, using that to ease the trailer down or haul it up – here a winch on the trailer would help. Should the trailer get bogged down, it is often possible to make fast the fall of the tackle and move the car forward, thus drawing the trailer out of its 'stick in the mud' situation.

When launching from the trailer you can either slide the boat off and wait for the tide to rise, which on softish ground is perfectly all right, or else immerse the trailer and float the boat off. Choosing the former method, make sure that the car and trailer are removed to a place above high water mark, and that you are on board when the boat floats. With the total immersion method make fast a painter before the boat floats off the trailer.

Come time to recover the boat, you are faced with the same tidal/submersion choice. For boats with a fin keel it is easier to float them on. Mark the position of the trailer under water by attaching bamboo canes to the wheels and mark the draught on one of them. Fitted with a good winch and rollers on the keel channels, it is not difficult to draw even a fairly large boat onto her trailer, but lining her up and keeping her in place with a strong cross wind or tide is not so easy.

Centring the boat on her trailer is helped by running crossed lines under the hull with marks at deck level, so that if one mark is way below the sheerline then the boat is over that side, and by hauling on that line she can be moved back towards the centre. Where there is a cross wind or tide, a kedge laid out to windward or uptide from the boat can be used to help stop her swinging away.

113   Lines attached to the trailer and crossed under the boat help in centring her.

Once the boat is correctly positioned over the trailer, lash down bow or stern (depending on which is forward on the trailer) and draw the trailer into shallower water either manually or by a line to the car hitch and driving up the slope. If you have only put the trailer in deep enough to bring the forefoot onto it, then winch the boat at least most of the way on before trying to hold the trailer flat and pull it out of the water, or you could damage the boat. When the boat, trailer and car are safely reunited and clear of the water, pump some grease into the hub bearings before starting home.

CHAPTER 18

Fitting Out

Fitting out is rather like spring cleaning, it's the time when we take a very close look at all the gear and equipment on our boats; we scrape and paint; we make and mend. As most people try to get it all done in the couple of months leading up to Easter the yards and sailmakers are working flat out, so it is as well to put any major work in hand well before this, even as far ahead as the end of the current season. The weather is often unsettled so early in the year and it is as well to have two work schedules prepared, one for dry days and the other for wet. Preparations of these lists is made easier if you keep notes during the season of 'jobs to be done', then when you sit down with a blank piece of paper you are less likely to miss some small but important job.

The Hull

Although it is a nasty, messy job which everyone likes to put off, using the slightest excuse, scraping weed and barnacles off the bottom is definitely a job to be tackled immediately the boat comes out of the water. While the hull is still wet it is comparatively easy to scrape off the marine hitchhikers, but wait until it has dried and you have a devil of a job. Fouling also acts as a water trap close to the hull and can induce rot in a wooden boat. When you have taken the worst of the mess off wash the whole of the bottom thoroughly with detergent (non-abrasive) and water before starting to rub down and prepare the surface for application of new anti-fouling. Use wet-and-dry sandpaper to produce a fair surface which the paint will key into.

Once the bottom is clean, inspect it closely. With a *wooden hull*, prod around and see if there are any soft spots that may

indicate rot. Pay particular attention to the garboards, water-line, around the chain plates, stem scarph, sheerstrake and skin fittings. If you do suspect rot have a word with the boat-yard or call in a surveyor before trying to tackle the repair yourself. Take a careful look at all caulked seams and see if any of it needs replacing – did you find any leaks during the season?

Any scrapes, chips or other minor damage to a *glassfibre hull* can be filled fairly easily with the aid of a repair kit. If the hull is coloured, the appropriate colour pigment must be added to the resin; this may be obtainable from the boat's builder, but as colour fades with time, a perfect match will be very hard to achieve. If the hull has been seriously damaged you may need to seek advice from a glassfibre specialist, but even quite major repairs can be made success-fully, though the hull may have to be painted afterwards to hide the work.

Though modern research has vastly improved the protec-tion of *steel hulls,* certainly on older ones even the slightest chip or scratch will rust very quickly indeed when exposed to a salt atmosphere, making it abundantly clear which areas must be rubbed down and painted immediately. Apart from general scrubbing and painting there should not be a lot of work to be done on a steel hull unless you have really knocked into something during the season.

Replace any sacrificial anodes – anti-electrolysis devices – that are badly wasted and go round all the skin fittings check-ing for corrosion. Each seacock should be stripped down and repacked and greased. Chip or brush rust off the keel if it is cast iron, and grease the rudder hangings using an under-water grease.

While looking at the hull we can raise our sights and cover the decks. Any leaks you noticed during the season should be tackled now. Opened seams round the cabin top can be cut right back and refilled with stopper – time spent on this is worth it in terms of a dry bunk. Any deck covering should be looked at carefully for signs of lifting where water may be trapped, and again if you have to replace any covering material cut it well back from the obviously poor area and make a thorough job of it.

Check stanchion roots for any looseness and also the pulpit and pushpit. Sheet tracks should have their holding screws tightened, locker lids may need a new hinge or fastening.

Dried out for a scrub and a paint. Do be sure that any jobs you plan to carry out below the waterline can be completed between tides. 257

Cockpit drains must be cleared out and also the scuppers, for a boat that has been laid up ashore is almost certain to have collected twigs and leaves to clog these. Make sure all deck hardware is secure and not corroded.

The Interior

As this is where you live, it tends to collect a lot of dust and dirt, no matter how careful you are, so first thing to do is give the place a good clean. Worst offenders are the bilges, home of dirty water, lost teaspoons and one or two less savoury items. A close second comes the chain locker with its mud and decaying seaweed. Once you have stripped all movable items out of the boat you can give it a good wash down with detergent and water, then it must be allowed to dry out. Leave the floorboards up, lockers and hatches open, and if necessary use a heater (not an oil heater as this causes condensation).

While the boat is drying out you can either clean and paint the internal ballast if your boat has any, or make a search for rot behind panelling, along deck beams, ribs, knees, hog, engine bearers and around the centreboard case.

Spars and Rigging

All of the running and standing rigging should be taken off and examined carefully for signs of wear. Label everything as it is removed and when unreeving internal halyards you would be well advised to pass a messenger through in their place, that is to say replace each halyard with a piece of cord that can be used to pull the halyard back down inside the mast. The useful life of all-rope halyards can be increased by turning them end for end. Replace worn or bent shackles and rigging screws, otherwise soak them in, say, petrol to clean them and then coat with grease. Stainless steel rigging does not give much warning of weakening; replace if there is a single broken strand. Galvanised wire should be soaked in a petrol/linseed oil mixture, and the serving on the splices should be renewed as necessary. When purchasing new stainless steel rigging check the terminals very carefully to see that the swage has not cut any strands.

Alloy spars really only need to be checked for bends and dents. Where these are found consult the manufacturer about the remedy. If the spars are not anodised you can smooth out the luff and foot tracks with a wire wool Brillo pad. Look for transverse (compression) cracks in wooden spars and any signs of rot at heel, hounds, where it passes through the deck, and around any cleats and fittings.

Oil and grease roller reefing gear and make sure you still have a spare reefing handle.

Sails

Unless you are confident of your sewing ability, major sail repairs are best done by a sailmaker – but send the sails to him in plenty of time for the season, they are busy people. Minor repairs such as loose stitching on seams, a split batten pocket, replacing a hank, can be done by yourself without much trouble and make weekday evening jobs. Proper needles and a palm make the job easier, as does following the old stitch pattern.

Engine

Whether your boat is powered by an inboard or an outboard engine the best thing to do when overhauling it is to follow the makers' instructions. That sounds like the easy way out for an author who's not very good with engines, but each make of engine has its own peculiarities and only the makers can tell you the right way to deal with them. However, there are some things to be done which are common to all engines, like checking all the fuel lines for wear or cracking, and draining and cleaning the sludge trap on the fuel tank.

Go over all the electrics for corroded terminals, and do the boat's general circuitry at the same time. Clean and preferably replace spark plugs on petrol engines, or test (have tested if you don't have the facilities) the injectors on diesels. Actually, unless you are really capable at mechanics it is probably best to let a service agent deal with injectors as they are tricky toys.

Batteries should be looked after throughout the winter lay-up. Top them up with distilled water to $\frac{1}{4}$in over the plates and recharge them as necessary; it is a good thing to charge and partially discharge them occasionally.

Examine the whole water cooling system, dismantling the circulating pump and renewing the impeller if it is worn. If it is a raw water system flush through with fresh water. Drain and clean the carburettor and fuel lines, making sure the fuel filters are clean.

Start the engine and run it till warm, then drain off the sump oil and replace it with a flushing oil recommended by the engine manufacturer. Run the motor briefly with the flushing oil in then drain it off and refill with ordinary oil. Fit new oil filters when necessary and clean out their covers.

If your engine is fitted with hand start, check the sprocket chain for wear and replace it if it's bad. Check adjustment of the tappets in accordance with the instruction book, and before you replace the rocker box cover fit a new cork gasket making sure that the lid and top of the box are free of grease. Check the contact breaker points for adjustment and replace if worn.

Retighten the engine bearer bolts. Draw the prop shaft and if it's worn, either have it machined and built up again, or replace it completely. Marvellous how easy it all sounds, isn't it? If the stuffing box was leaking much during the season, repack it rather than over-tightening the stern gland, as this causes drag on the shaft. A badly chipped or bent propeller will have to be renewed, but lesser damage can be repaired.

When removing a recoil start for cleaning and checking, have a care that the spring doesn't decide to take a closer look at your face.

Navigational

One of the few fitting out jobs that should in theory be left till the last possible moment is that of having the charts corrected. Unfortunately chart correctors can only cope with a limited number in a given time, so don't leave it literally until the last minute. Do have them done – if you don't want to do them yourself – as an out-of-date chart can be worse than no chart at all.

Electronic navigation aids either don't go wrong or have to be returned to their makers for repair. For routine maintenance follow the makers' instructions implicitly or you may invalidate any guarantee. Have any bubbles removed from the compass and check that its light is working. Clean and oil the log and its rotator.

Loose Ends

Secure or whip them as appropriate.

Go round with an oil can and grease tin to inspect all the oddments like winches, shackle pins, stopcocks and so on. Clean up the stove, bunk cushions, navigation lights, life-jackets, oilskins and life-harnesses.

Take a very careful look at all gas lines and check all the washers and seals. Check too the expiry date on flares and fire extinguishers, replacing as necessary.

When the mast is stepped and the bottlescrews tightened, make sure the locking nuts are tight, or else wire the bottle-screws to stop them undoing.

Mouse the shackle between cable and anchor with wire to stop that working loose. (Mousing means passing a few turns round the arm of the shackle and through the eye in the pin.)

Dinghies

Inflatables must be cleaned and the seams all checked for any lifting. If repairs are needed you may have to take it to a service agent. Watch out for chafed material on the tubes, particularly by the rowlocks.

Rigid dinghies should be treated in the same way as the parent boat; cleaned, repaired, painted and varnished. Glass-fibre dinghies can be repaired with a simple glassfibre repair kit, but for major jobs you will probably require extra resin, hardener and mat. Make sure that buoyancy compartments are properly sealed and that air bags are not punctured. Check the securings for the bags as well.

Painting

The basis of good painting seems to be preparation of the surface to be painted, whether this involves a lot of sandpaper and elbow grease, a heavy duty orbital sander, or burning layers of old paint off to get down to the bare wood. Whichever way you go about it, it is hard work.

The essential is to produce a clean surface to which the paint will key in and adhere well. A lot of people treat the old paint too gently and tend to polish it rather than break it by using too fine a sandpaper. What you want to do instead is to break the surface with good coarse paper and then smooth over with fine stuff to take out irregularities. Sanding a flat surface is made easier and more effective if the sandpaper is wrapped around a block of cork.

Whatever kind of painting you are doing, be it varnishing, enamelling, or antifouling, always use good quality brushes. They are not cheap initially, but looked after properly they will last a long time, and an old brush is often better to paint with than a new one. Fewer hairs drop out.

When choosing a brush, go for a fairly large one, as it will cover a bigger area in one go and will produce a more even finish than a narrow one. Store brushes in a jar of cleanser; don't let them rest on their bristles, drill a hole through the metal part and push a piece of wire through, long enough to reach across the neck of the jar. By the time you have finished all the paintwork there are likely to be some odd bristles sticking out at crazy angles, but don't trim them off. When you have cleaned the brush thoroughly, wrap the bristles in cloth; this will straighten the bent bristles and keep the brush in good shape for next winter.

Dip only about a third or a half of the length of the bristles in the paint, and don't wipe excess paint off too vigorously on the side of the tin as you will pick up bits of paint 'skin' which will mar the finish. Also, don't slap the paint on any old how, work it in with strokes parallel to the grain, at right angles to it, and finally parallel again. By doing this you should be able to finish off nicely with no brush marks showing.

Choice of paint for a job is often dictated by 'same as I've always used', or by what the yard sells. In general there is little difference between top brands, and it *is* a matter of personal choice. With antifoulings it is a case of choosing one most suitable for the waters in which the boat will be moored. Depending upon local fouling types, one paint will have no apparent effect, while another keeps the hull perfectly clean. Other factors are whether or not the mooring dries out, and

There are jobs for all the family at fitting-out time, but when several people are working on the same boat a work plan is essential to avoid them getting in each other's way.

the availability of scrubbing facilities. Either the yard or a manufacturer should be able to advise you on the best type for your purpose.

Most of us get soft fingers during the winter and breed a lovely family of blisters when painting, but one way of reducing them is to wrap adhesive tape round fingers wherever they are going to be rubbed. Alternatively, wearing an old pair of gloves can help.

When a wooden boat is being painted for the first time, the wood must first be sealed with a coat of thinned primer. This should then be sanded down and a coat of full strength primer put on. When dry sand down again and fill any imperfections with a hard stopper. After this has been rubbed down a final coat of primer is applied. Rub down the primer and apply a coat of undercoat. When dry this is sanded down and a second coat applied, then sand down and apply the top coat(s) – the number being ordered by the standard of finish required, the more coats (up to a point) the better the finish. Rub down carefully in between each layer.

If you are simply repainting the boat, rub down the enamel carefully and apply one coat of undercoat. Sand that down and apply the top coat(s). If the paintwork is in a really bad state it should be burned off and the hull treated as if it were being painted for the first time.

Iron keels or ballast should be brushed free of rust and painted with several coats of metallic primer before being antifouled (in the case of the keels).

Wood that is to be varnished for the first time needs to be sealed with a coat of thinned varnish. Then apply several coats of full strength varnish, rubbing down between each coat sufficiently to ensure that the next coat keys in properly. If you are just renewing varnish, rub it down sufficiently to break the surface and apply a couple of coats. Don't be mean with the final coat of varnish, flow it on to obtain a flat, mirror-smooth finish.

Starting a steel boat from scratch, apply one coat of bare plate primer, rub down and apply a second coat. Then use a stopper and apply a third coat of primer. After it has dried, sand down and apply a coat of undercoat, then sand and apply a second coat. Allow to dry, sand, and apply as many top coats of enamel as you require.

Doing a plain repaint job, just apply two undercoats, and then top coats.

264

Be a bit careful about antifoulings as you must not set up an electrolytic action between the dissimilar metals of hull and skin fittings.

A glassfibre boat will only require cleaning and polishing for many years, but when eventually she is looking rather too dowdy, then is the time to paint her. Until recently it has been a case of using special grp primers to soften the gel coat and allow paint to adhere, but recently a special paint has been developed that is said to produce a finish as tough and glossy as the original gel coat. This should of course be applied according to the manufacturers' instructions, and it would be best to consult them about the whole project.

To antifoul a bare hull you must first take *all* the residual releasing agent off that is left from the mould. A coat of grp primer is then applied followed by the antifouling. If repainting, treat the hull as you would any other.

CHAPTER 19

Pipe Dreams

After a couple of seasons spent getting to know your boat and your own capabilities it's quite likely that one bright day you'll be sitting at the helm and instead of watching the passing coastline your attention will be drawn seaward to the horizon. An unspoken desire to sail off to distant places will implant itself in your mind and from then on you won't rest easy till you've done it. Many of us have found this desire for distant horizons almost as malignant a disease as boats themselves.

Initially of course you would be wise to limit your ambitions to a short passage to foreign waters entailing only a few hours out of sight of land, because I can assure you that those hours will be long ones however few they may be. It is possible also that you may have to think about the purchase of a larger boat for such trips, but even if this is the case, provided you have learnt and practised the arts of coastal cruising you should have few problems with 'going foreign' for the first time.

RYA

If you do have some worries about your experience and whether you are really qualified to take a boat out of coastal waters, the Yachtmasters' Certificates provide a controlled and worthwhile means of gaining that experience. The Yachtmasters' (Offshore) Certificate falls into four parts: (a) the shore based course; (b) the practical course; (c) seatime; (d) the final examination.

The shore based course can be completed by attending a series of evening classes at any one of a large number of further education establishments, or it can be done by

A towing log records the miles passing under the keel.

correspondence course, though this is not perhaps such a good way of doing it.

The practical course requires you to attend a total of six days practical instruction at a recognised sailing school.

Seatime is recorded as you build it up. A special Log Book is used for this and must be signed by the skipper of any boat you sail on (yourself if you are the skipper). Seatime must include at least 20 days as an active member of the crew of a cruising yacht with at least 12 hours at sea at night, and a total distance of at least 500 miles must be recorded. Clearly this is likely to be achieved without much trouble over two or three seasons cruising with the family.

When you have done all that you reach the final examination in which you face an oral test given by an RYA examiner. After that you receive your Certificate – and you will have earned it.

The fact that you hold a Yachtmasters' Ticket does not mean that you know everything and can do anything, but it does without doubt set you on the right course and give you a good start. Details of courses can be obtained from the Royal Yachting Association, Victoria Way, Woking, Surrey.

Papers and Regulations

When cruising in foreign waters or returning from abroad there are certain rules and regulations to comply with. In general, cruising yachts are subject to very few restrictions and are left pretty much alone by the authorities, and this is exactly why you must be quite sure to comply with what regulations there are, otherwise some government is going to clamp down and spoil our fun and freedom.

The basic papers you need to carry are: ship's papers, log book, and passports for each member of the crew. The ship's papers are intended to prove ownership of the boat and are usually either a Certificate of Registry or a Certificat d'Identité. The former is the certificate to show that the boat is registered as a British vessel, and the latter is a certificate for non-registered vessels issued by the Royal Yachting Association which is generally accepted by foreign Customs Officials as being sufficient proof of ownership.

Besides these papers you will need to carry currency or traveller's cheques, a Q flag, and the appropriate courtesy flags. The Q flag (a yellow flag) is flown from the crosstrees to show that the vessel is clean and the crew healthy and that free pratique is requested. The courtesy flag for the country in whose waters you are sailing is flown throughout the period you are in those waters. It is a small version of that country's maritime ensign. Before leaving your home port for a foreign cruise it is as well to notify the Customs of your departure and to ask for a Bill of Health, since this will make entry to the foreign country simpler.

On approaching a foreign port the courtesy ensign is hoisted (plus of course the Red Ensign) and also the Q flag, then once in port you wait until the Customs Officials arrive to clear your vessel. In some small ports it may be necessary to notify the officials by telephone, but this is not usual, and anyway you should make for a recognised port of entry. When returning to home waters you must again fly the Q flag and go through the same clearance procedure.

One last word of warning – don't try to smuggle. You probably won't get away with it, and any such attempt will spoil the yachtsman's current good relationship with the Customs and Excise men. If you play fair with them, they'll play fair with you. Let's keep it that way.

Sextants and Coastal Navigation

The sextant, far from the mystical beast it is usually portrayed as being, is really a very simple instrument. All it does is measure angles. So far as coastal navigation is concerned it can be used vertically or horizontally to measure the angular height of an object or the angular distance between two objects.

If you measure the angular height of a charted object and refer to a table in *Reed's* it is very simple to determine how far you are away from the object, ie your distance off. This distance, combined with a careful bearing will give a good position fix.

Where there are three charted objects available a horizontal sextant angle fix may be made, and that is one of the most accurate fixes possible.

Knowing your distance off an object can be vitally important, if, for instance, you need to be outside an off-lying shoal that is unmarked, or the other way round if you want to pass inshore of a submerged rock. In practise all that you do is measure the angular height of the object above sea level (or more accurately high water mark), note its charted height and refer to a table of distances off. When using a lighthouse as the object it should be remembered that you use the centre of the lantern not the actual top of the lighthouse, as the charted height is that of the light, not the tower.

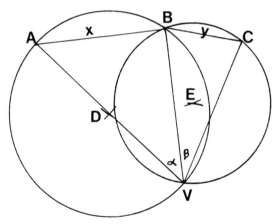

114

A horizontal angle fix is more complicated. Diagram 114 shows the set up with A, B and C as the charted objects with x and y as the distances between them. Angles alpha (α) and beta (β) are measured with the sextant, then they are used in conjunction with their associated distances x and y to find (from a table again in *Reed's*) the radii of the two circles.

269

With compasses centred alternately on A and B (then B and C with the second radius) small arcs are drawn to intersect at D and E. Where these circles intersect – in this case at V – is the vessel's position. As I said, it is complicated, but it can be extremely accurate.

A simpler, though possibly less accurate, method is to construct the angles alpha and beta on a piece of tracing paper with a protractor and move this around on the chart until the lines pass through the objects marked on the chart.

In my opinion the ability to find distance off quickly and accurately is reason enough for carrying a sextant aboard the family coastal cruiser. Add to that the precision possible with a horizontal angle fix and no one can deny its usefulness.

CHAPTER 20

Further Reading

It is impossible in a book trying to cover such a variety of topics as this one to do more than partial justice to many of them. Some of the chapters could be expanded into books in their own right and there are many subjects worthy of further study. The list of books I am going to give here is in itself far from complete, but they are representative of what is available, and are ones that I have found useful myself.

Seamanship and Cruising

Cruising Under Sail, Eric Hiscock. Oxford University Press.
   A compendium of more advanced cruising practice.
Seawife's Handbook, Joyce Sleightholme. Angus and Robertson.
   A manual for sailing wives.

Navigation

Practical Yacht Navigator, Kenneth Wilkes. Nautical.
   Just what the title says.
Navigation for Yachtsmen, Mary Blewitt. Stanford Maritime.
   An excellent tutor by a highly experienced navigator.
Coastwise Navigation, G. G. Watkins. Kandy Paperback.
   A clear, simple guide.
Exercises in Coastal Navigation, G. W. White. Kandy.
   Worthwhile dry land practice.

Engines

Marine Engines and Boating Mechanics, Dermot Wright. David and Charles.
As title explains; very clearly written.

Rough Weather

Heavy Weather Sailing, K. Adlard Coles. Adlard Coles.
Good and interesting, if scary reading, by a father of ocean racing.

Weather

Interpreting the Weather, Ingrid Holford. David and Charles.
Clear explanations of meteorology.
Instant Weather Forecasting, Alan Watts. Adlard Coles.
Do-it-yourself predictions from the sky.
Weather for Yachtsmen, Capt. Watts. Adlard Coles.
Handy pocketbook of forecasting.

Maintenance and Repairs

Fitting Out, J. D. Sleightholme. Adlard Coles.
Practical information.
The Boat Owner's Maintenance Manual, Jeff Toghill. David and Charles.
A full reference book.

Reference

A Dictionary of Sailing, F. H. Burgess. Penguin Reference Books.
Nautical terms.

General Interest

There are many, many books of sea stories, accounts of cruises to distant waters and general books to dream over. The ones I list here are simply ones picked off my own shelves that I read over and over again with equal pleasure. I could have chosen a hundred others but this is supposed to be a brief list.

All Season's Yachtsman, Peter Haward. Adlard Coles.
    The early days of top yacht delivery skipper.
The Magic of the Swatchways, Maurice Griffiths. Conway Maritime Press.
    Has delighted generations of readers.
Shoal Water and Fairway, H. Alker Tripp. Conway Maritime Press.
    Cruising yarns to entrance.
Two and a Half Ton Dream, Ray Whitaker. Herbert Jenkins.
    Husband and wife beginning cruising.
World Wanderer, Des Kearns. Angus and Robertson.
    Truly the stuff dreams are made of.

Brought up for the night.

INDEX